MARIE
UGUAY

JOURNAL

MARIE
UGUAY

JOURNAL

TRANSLATED BY
JENNIFER MOXLEY

Cormorant Books

 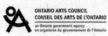 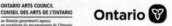

We acknowledge financial support for our publishing activities: the
Government of Canada, through the Canada Book Fund and The Canada
Council for the Arts; the Government of Ontario, through the Ontario Arts
Council, Ontario Creates, and the Ontario Book Publishing Tax Credit.

LIBRARY AND ARCHIVES CANADA CATALOGUING IN PUBLICATION

Title: Journal / Marie Uguay ; translated by Jennifer Moxley.
Other titles: Journal. English
Names: Uguay, Marie, 1955-1981, author. | Moxley, Jennifer, 1964- translator.
Description: Translation of: Journal.
Identifiers: Canadiana (print) 20230563856 | Canadiana (ebook) 20230563864 |
ISBN 9781770867260 (softcover) | ISBN 9781770867277 (EPUB)
Subjects: LCSH: Uguay, Marie, 1955-1981. | LCSH: Poets, French-Canadian—
Québec (Province)—Diaries. | CSH: Poets, Canadian (French)—Québec
(Province)—Diaries. | LCGFT: Autobiographies. | LCGFT: Diaries. | LCGFT: Poetry.
Classification: LCC PS8591.G82 Z5313 2024 | DDC C848/.5403—dc23

United States Library of Congress Control Number: 2023949908

Cover and interior text design: Marijke Friesen
Manufactured by Friesens in Altona, Manitoba in November 2023.

CORMORANT BOOKS INC.
260 ISHPADINAA (SPADINA) AVENUE, SUITE 502,
TKARONTO (TORONTO), ON M5T 2E4

SUITE 110, 7068 PORTAL WAY, FERNDALE, WA 98248, USA

www.cormorantbooks.com

CONTENTS

Introduction

I first met Marie Uguay in September of 1975. We were both students in the same college at the Université de Québec à Montréal. Very soon after, I moved into her little apartment in the working-class Montréal neighbourhood of Ville-Émard, where we lived together until the end of her life in October 1981. Our rapport was immediate and unconditional. This powerful affinity created a strong bond between us and our artistic endeavours. Though writing had long been central to Marie's life, she hadn't yet published. She decided to send a manuscript of poems to a new publishing house called Noroît. They responded enthusiastically and planned to publish her book the following year. During the entirety of our first year together, therefore, Marie was buoyed by the excitement of having completed and placed her first book of poems, *Sign and Rumour*. Other projects were defined and took shape, including a long stay on the Magdalen Islands in spring of 1976, made possible by a photography grant I had received. It was here that Marie, inspired by the maritime landscape, began working on new poems.

As guarantor to the future, our life in the present made anything seem possible. We had no way of knowing that an unthinkable tragedy would, almost overnight, compel one of us, at so young an age, to face their finitude. In September of 1977, Marie learned that she had developed bone cancer in her right leg. After two months of anxiety, struggle, and waiting in the hospital, Marie's doctors had to resign themselves to amputating her leg. Through this measure, and a round of preventative treatments, they hoped that the disease could be completely eradicated. Marie was only twenty-two years old when she went through this terrible trauma. It was a break with who she had been, shattering her sense of self and creating a new reality that she had no choice but to accept. For a young woman who wanted so much to live her life with intensity and to realize herself through her art, through her poetry, the loss of her body's wholeness, the constant threat of the disease, and the sudden need to count every minute, was a difficult and heroic struggle.

In putting together her second book, *The Life Beyond*, Marie combined poems she had written during her hospital stay and just after with poems composed right before these traumatic events. *The Life Beyond* came out in 1979. The year before, Marie and I had spent the fall together in Paris, realizing a long-held dream of Marie's. Yet, when we returned to Montréal, Marie's life became more difficult, her reality suddenly more oppressive and unsatisfying. As a result, her writing became increasingly speculative, her questions more urgent. This contributed to the confident new poetic voice that became central to her third book, *Self-portraits*. Then Marie had a recurrence of her cancer at the beginning of 1980. This setback, along with the treatments she would have to repeatedly undergo from that point forward, hobbled her resolve and amplified the fatalism against which she had struggled. On October 26, 1981, Marie Uguay died at the age of twenty-six. Less than a year later, *Self-portraits* was published.

I will now attempt to outline Marie Uguay's story, and a bit of my own as well, without trying to fill in every contour, development, or nuance. Since my main goal is to establish a chronology of her brief artistic career, I have chosen to skip over her life before we met. Sometimes one life contains another, a more complex and intense life of inner conflict; a life that is searching for meaning, and a deeper understanding of things. This is the drama that Uguay's *Journal* gives witness to. Though it's not part of the "official story," the total upheaval she underwent during the fall of 1977 had a profound impact on her life and work.

———

First and foremost, Marie Uguay was a poet. And even if, from time to time, she tried her hand at other genres, she always came back to poetry. It was the form that answered best to her way of being and understanding the world: poetry's freedom, its connection to lived experience, and its ability to help her live even more intensely, to expand her life, was irresistible. Her three published books share a common goal: all are self-contained projects that explore new poetic forms in an attempt to create a poetry driven by desire that, while remaining accessible, goes beyond mere biography. Marie had felt the need to keep a journal when younger, but had done so only sporadically, and without a clearly defined framework. She wrote only when she felt a tension between her personal life and her circumstances. This is how most private journals function. They tend to express conflict and pain, while leaving out all other parts of a life. They paint but a partial portrait of their authors. It is important to keep this in mind when reading Uguay's *Journal*.

The upset that Marie Uguay's illness caused in her life made her return to the journal form almost inevitable. It was quickly made clear that the private journal would be one of the few textual spaces that would allow her to recover her sense of identity and put her fragmented self back together. It was at this point that she began to keep her journal more regularly and fully. Yet her approach remained distinct, insofar as her journal was never separate from her poetry. It functioned as an integrated part of it, and of her writing as a whole. She composed the final poems of her second book *The*

Life Beyond in it, and, notably, all the poems that went into her last book, *Self-portraits*. These poems were, almost by definition, at the very core of her journal. Covering the last four years of her life, she wrote her journal in twelve separate notebooks of differing formats. Each notebook contained diverse literary forms, representing the breadth of Marie's writing: her poetry, her autobiographical jottings and writing about writing, her desires, and her thoughts. The *Journal* is a unique space, a record of both her oeuvre and her life.

From the moment she was admitted to the hospital and discovered that she had cancer, Marie Uguay began keeping her journal. Once her body was threatened, two opposing poles began their pull on her: the one, against her will, toward death; the other, her inclination, toward poetry, desire, and life (three things that were synonymous for Uguay). In her solitude and distress, her first impulse, extreme in its drive, was toward love. This is because, for Uguay, the fight to survive was an act of love. Little by little, her impulse toward love began to focus on a single desire, a comforting, yet inaccessible idea that would drag her through a lucid, if shattering, reappraisal of the way she conducted her desires and the motives behind her creativity. This desire, her secret and impossible love, turned into an enigma she was determined to unpuzzle, the incarnation of both her life and death, an obstinate quest that fed the whole of her creative work.

The lion's share of Marie Uguay's *Journal* is driven by this reigning passion. It was, as a refuge, almost as destructive as her illness: a self-annihilating crisis of love inextricably linked to her physical crisis, which she perpetuated in total solitude. A passion which, nevertheless, gave her the energy to plumb the very depths of herself, to explore the power and intensity of her eloquence, and the range of her contradictions; to tirelessly seek meaning in life, in her own life, though it might never manifest.

———

After I decided to publish Marie Uguay's *Journal*, I realized that, because her autobiographical prose was so intertwined with her poetry, I had underestimated the difficulty of my editorial task. I felt it was important to preserve this aspect of her writing, the sort of echo between the two genres. I wanted to account for both parts of her work, at once distinct, and yet so tightly linked together in the *Journal*. I had to figure out the various sections of the many poems included, given that the manuscript not only contained published poems, but a large number of unpublished ones as well. They all needed to be inventoried and evaluated in order to determine whether to include them in her body of work.

The period during which Marie Uguay composed the *Journal*, though overlapping with her writing of the final poems that went into *The Life Beyond*, was mainly focused on the work of her last book, *Self-portraits*. As circumstances would have it, she did not have the time to complete this manuscript before she died. She made a provisional gathering of some poems, but left several others unaccounted for. I carefully examined all of the poems she wrote during this period, as well as those published in *Self-portraits*. I retained a certain number of poems, which I reordered chronologically under two distinct titles, and which now have been added to her complete *Poems* (published jointly along with the *Journal* by Boréal in 2005). These are *Prose Poems* and *Poems at the Margin*. *Prose Poems* served as a transition between *The Life Beyond* and *Self-portraits*. These poems are intimately connected to her everyday life, and mostly written in a single go; those in *Poems at the Margin*, on the other hand, are stylistically complementary to the poems in *Self-portraits*, though they were not included in Uguay's original conception of the book.

Drafting poems was central to Uguay's *Journal*. She included multiple drafts, with a lot of overlap, as well as unrealized plans or projects. It was necessary to cut out much of these sections. That said, all of the poems written during this period that now make up part of Uguay's complete work are either noted or reproduced in full in the *Journal*. Because it wasn't possible to reproduce all the working drafts, I chose to include those that were directly connected to her autobiographical prose. As these were often spread out over long time periods and intercut with other texts, it took some care to establish their place in the *Journal*. I also reproduced, throughout the entire *Journal*, certain isolated lines, which are not, strictly speaking, part of Uguay's oeuvre, but are more like "draft clusters," mental sparks functioning like little detonators in the larger field of poetic action.

Marie Uguay never edited or rewrote her journal. She wrote at different times and according to her moods, with no concern for publication, and with complete freedom as to what she wrote. I respected, so far as it was possible, her way of proceeding, but in spite of everything I had to cut or correct certain things in the autobiographical prose writings in order to maintain cohesion and give a sense to the whole. Passages that were fragmentary, out of context, or which seemed not quite up to snuff, were removed. I also removed several quotations, either because they were too long or I couldn't verify their accuracy. Marie Uguay had a habit of appropriation, sometimes going so far as to alter a quotation with her own words. Out of consideration for people still living, certain first names were changed, and on occasion, passages were removed if they indicated someone too directly or permitted a person be identified. In addition, I didn't think it was appropriate to begin the *Journal* while she was going through that first crisis in the hospital and still confused about the state of her health and her feelings. To this end I cut the first half of the first notebook, and began instead once she was on the eve of returning home, where, when settled, she cast a calmer retrospective glance on what had befallen her.

Rather than organize the *Journal* by year, I kept its original division into notebooks. This made sense given that most of the notebooks had titles that corresponded to an ongoing writing project, such that a new notebook often marks a new tone in the continuity of her writing. Yet there are times when the poetic work she was engaged in would provoke a change to a notebook's title. This is why, in addition to the titles that Uguay finally settled on, I also made note of those that had been crossed out. The evolution of her titles is important to the development of both the *Journal* and *Self-portraits*. There are times when an isolated title appears in the middle of one of the notebooks. I left these as such, because they generally signal a nascent writing project, named before coming to fruition. In addition, I've added two elements not in Uguay's original notebooks — indications of which manuscripts the poems belong to, and a short text written at the end of her life — both are noted in the body of the *Journal*.

Marie Uguay did not keep her journal daily. Sometimes long periods elapsed between entries, and she was not systematic about recording dates. In light of this fact, I took the liberty of inserting a horizontal line between entries written at different times. In preparing the manuscript for publication, I felt that the contents of the original, an amalgam of various kinds of writing and poem drafts, needed these dividers to balance the layout of page. I have not noted all of my edits or corrections, for such numerous interruptions would have hindered reading; however, the notes mark places where important sections, for one reason or another, have been cut. Finally, in the interest of presenting the *Journal* chronologically, it was my idea to number the notebooks. All other additions have been indicated with brackets.

———

It's been many years since Marie Uguay died; a span of time doubtless necessary to accept, with more objectivity, this occult part of her life, this intimate tragedy. Uguay's remarkable journey in the face of death, whether translated into poetry or prose, remains, and will remain relevant because of her intense and authentic humanity. The circumstances and the outcome notwithstanding, we are here in the presence of a love song of undeniable power. Out from under the shadow of her life there at times shine passages so luminous as to justify the publication of Uguay's *Journal*, for it casts an exceptional light on her final years, and on the workings of her poetic art.

— Stéphan Kovacs, June 2004

The Life Beyond[1]

It snowed this morning. The first snow since my body was muti-
lated. Silent little flakes of death. I feel like I'm lying on sheets of
ice. Snow makes me feel both calm and endlessly sad. There is only
this snow, relentless, divine, permeating my soul, everything else
has vanished. I close my eyes and refuse to open them so I can con-
centrate on this expressionless music, this blankness: snow. When
I rejoin the world, it will have been chilled by your gaze. Like a
ghastly shadow, you frighten me even in daylight. Each of your
precise and devastating steps is filled with death, while from the
utmost heights of this wooziness I'm doing my best to find my life,
looking for summer's sustenance and sun, its water and wind, the
clarion call of the city. I'm trying to find the thousand heartbeats
of a dream that will awaken every inch of my aching body. Despite
all this snow, the birds will return; despite the walls of this room,
my eyes will take flight. How have I managed to survive for so long
attached to this bed, like a drowning victim, alone, so alone, with
my legs in death's clutches? Will I see you again, my little love? And
where will I go? Paris? Will I see Paris, if only for a day?

I can't go on. My nerves feel stretched so tight, as if my entire being
is being menaced by some strange affliction. I feel a deep urgency
to write poetry.

———

I carry you inside of me like a dead dawn

———

November 20 [1977]

LET'S TALK ABOUT THE LIFE BEYOND
ALLIANCES

A breathless two years. At home in bed, I look through photos. That first November, a mix of death and joy. After burning with grief for two years following Grandpapa's death, I met Stéphan, and then he moved in with me. My place was half empty, the bare wood floors gleamed in the November cold. Stéphan brought his rugs with him, his colours, his photos, his wooden furniture. My plants grew miraculously large, the windows woke up. My hours took on a ritual quality, early mornings were honey coloured and in the blue satin of the long winter the twilight was orange. Then summer, winter, and summer again; this pearl necklace.

Like a single pillar, life can't be steadied. It becomes opaque. Nothing. Empty. A life shrunken, restrained, there isn't enough time to let a single moment, pregnant with potential like a terrible, marvellous fruit, slip away.

I'm not trying to make my thinking cohesive. So many hours of physical pain have totally discombobulated my usual way of thinking.

I note: a gentle, cold rain hitting the skylights in a uniform rhythm. The fragile little cry of a faraway sparrow. In the distance, behind the apartment, the muffled cadence of cars gliding over wet asphalt. I feel an unparalleled delight hearing these everyday, common, and old sounds. The whole house breathes: the noise of the furnace, of the fridge; my breath keeps time with the rain hitting the window; I feel still and cold.

Stéphan's breathing. My heart swells, my life expands. No one should read these lines, maybe at some later date they'll go into a novel. For the time being, they'll stay live weapons, and then there's my sudden burst of love. I'm still amazed by it, and skeptical. I look at Stéphan. For two years, we've been like two kids, stable and happy. I look at him. Connection, desire, astonishment, his immense arms, generous, comforting, vast like a beautiful summer afternoon; always ready to hold me. I want him to take me in them again and again. Connection, emotion, I read so much into him; he is transparent, pure and profound like a secret, primordial natural spring.

His kindness moves me, his intelligence seduces me, but more importantly, the beauty of his face, which isn't just the way his features are arranged, but goes further than that, I don't know where. Unnameable.

Louis, a puzzle, endlessly incendiary. So many uncertainties, contradictions, yet so many flights. An elusive face, though his hands are extraordinary open rivers. I love him in spite of him. No one can understand these two intersecting trajectories, even me. But they are real, they ring true like metal. Unalloyed. Pure.

I love them both passionately with a life force that overpowers me (both of them? maybe even all three). What matters is the force. Right now, I can see each of them in freeze-frame. My focused attention on them overflows. They'll change places, I'm sure of it. I have this fierce longing to dive into them. To give? To receive? My feelings transcend such terms. It's a kind of journey, an astonishment. A magnetic current, inviolable, inexhaustible, which no single face could possibly satisfy. Where nothing is refused and there's no meanness: Love! But at what cost? Solitude. My love is like an outpouring, a wellspring. Will it turn into a tower? Insurmountable? No, that would be impossible.

My life is enriched by having multiple passions at once. I won't name all the other faces in case this starts to sound like some crazy story I've just made up. I can't describe it all in one go, it's too vast.

———

December 8 or 9, 1977

A perfect blue powder outside the window.

   Nice and cozy inside, the hail's interfering music sounds to me like a sequence of love poems dedicated to different households, all customized, each word typed forcefully.

The powder creates a cinematic play of light: blues and whites moving about.

Don't say anything, just believe that poetry is more astute and true, more alive than prose. It's efficient, says a lot with little, and so serendipitously that even the writer stands in wonder. The poem waiting to be written is always a discovery, a new continent.

———

I attempt, in this new mutilated body, to move about the way I used to. Physically disoriented in this conquered country that used to be my body. Tears.

———

December 13, 1977

In the apartment, alone, evening, feeling nostalgic already. I have changed so little it's almost a disappointment. My body is changed, mutilated, turned into an other, well, almost an other. A different environment, which moves differently, but my heart is still its old self. An anvil, an anchor, as heavy and indefatigable as ever. I think about those two months I spent chained to a bed, eyes glued to the blue wall of that sad hospital room. I remember the pain, my frequent howling over that attached leg, and my fear, which stood by the door and kept watch; it imprisoned me at the bottom of a well, crushed me with those tombstone nights. It steered me toward your dear eyes and your hands, which held my hands, clenched and desperate, and kept them safe. I'd never known faces such as yours, they were completely new to me, but I only needed two months. My pattern is always the same. And now we no longer talk. I fear that our paths are diverging, separating, moving apart, as so often happens. But I've got my dreams and my city back, its soft clouds and tired skies, my Montréal freshly tensed with frost. I inhale this glowing room, the trees in the distance, the faceless passersby, all my daydreams. Yet your faces and the things we talked about keep insisting. Louis, with his turbulence, his pointless promises, his sadness, always looking so wiped-out; the way he takes off his glasses, wipes his hand across his forehead and over his eyes, just to the bridge of his nose, right between his eyebrows. Paul, with his silent entrances, that impenetrable way he had of looking at me like I was an enigma. His attention and curiosity made me so self-conscious I'd talk even more than usual. Calm, reassuring. His interest made me feel special.

I barely knew either of them. But because I was undergoing such a terrible trauma, I took their affection and generosity for real outbursts of love. At the centre of this traumatic chapter, their actions took on an inflated importance. One was the first to discover my cancer, the other my only lifeline, that is, if the treatments had been effective. Then maybe I would still have my leg. But there was a dark prediction of my next undoing.

It's all still so confusing.

I'm jotting down these notes quickly, so as not to forget anything. I'm not sure why, but I now feel I need to make a record of this story, even though it's fast becoming unreal to me. But what is the source of this unreality? Perhaps its sharpness. Yesterday I felt calm, I did nothing, Stéphan and I were good together and talked in hushed and dreamy tones about taking a trip. Then it came out of nowhere, the cut-off. That reality so vast my mind can't process it: death. And all these other men suddenly in my life. Men from worlds so unlike my own, who think so differently. Two men connected to my death, not because they wanted to be, but just like me, victims of chance. "Chance kills," says Brel.[3] And despite our different ways of talking, a dialogue developed, a double dialogue. Louis, always in a hurry, never listening, always talking. Paul, slow, silent, standing before me, letting me go on too long. One's a comedian, the other a spectator.

Right now, I feel good. The nightmare is letting me be. I make up a dream that conforms to my desires and slowly exhaust its possibilities, just for myself. I love them both tenderly, each differently and in secret, as if I was fifteen years old. I tell myself the story of the novel that I will never write. About this person who leaves for the hospital on the night of September 15, heading into the unknown, the sudden horror. Now, daily life has been restored and everything is almost the same as it was before. It's a question of balance. Learning how to balance on one leg. Learning that my leg is no longer there, that it will never again be there, never. Just to get used to this idea. To recognize that I'm still alive, but for how long? I have no idea, nor how to take advantage of each moment. On the other hand, there's Stéphan, with his bottomless eyes, eyes like giant luminous towers ... our friendship, our tender bond, whispers and then laughter. We share so many dreams, so many of the same urgencies, the same hopes, the same worries, the same tastes. With him, I can breathe easy. But love doesn't issue from just one spring, there are other tributaries, farther away but very real, as clear as stories made up by a child.

I think about life. I imagine other places. At night, I travel through landscapes by great leaps. An airport, another American city, angular, shiny, with greenish nights, or a villa under the palms of Provence, the sea, and then Paris. My own room in Paris. The measureless intoxication of one day being able to say when opening a window or walking down the street: "Paris is mine." I'm in Paris, every one of its *arrondissements* feeds my reveries such that living poems spring from the stones, pavements, porticos, skies, and trees of Paris. To live life to the fullest, not waiting for anyone, collecting memories, loving. And if tomorrow I never see them again, or see past their words, grown stern once at a distance from me and my trauma (the crisis over, they bolt), if I never see them again, I will continue to love them. I will always remember those days, those hours they stayed by my side. Perhaps I love them without knowing them; it doesn't matter. I have my way of knowing them.

And now, how should I go about starting over, and what exactly am I starting over? What do I have left? Already I had nothing, except for the freedom to come and go. An afternoon in a café, meetings, dreams, work, as well as walks through Montréal, the cold, dry, brutal winter, a thin strip of countryside in the distance. Now I must wait. I can no longer do much of anything without help. When Stéphan is not at home, I am useless. There's too much silence in this apartment. It's making me write these stupid things. Because I'm being stalked by these floods of silence, the poems I'm not writing, this internal standstill, this waiting, impenetrable, unchanging, wild. Your voices trail off. I love you. It's written, as if carved in stone. This hard reality inside of me, laughable, sickly, heartbreaking. I keep it inside, no one can measure the impact of what has happened to me, not even me, really. My entire future keeps slipping through my hands.

And my body, which I barely recognize in the mirror. My face looks the same, but when I look at this body, I waver between affection and fear. This body, my body, inside of which I feel ill at ease.

My head turns like a bird, or the sun, still the same, still pursuing its crazy romantic escapades. The little body at its centre with its two frail arms also rolls, like a ball. Since the leg can no longer hold it up, it rolls toward the right, sways, in need of an airlift. My other leg is a thread, with all of my body's weight pressing down on it. And in my dreams, I can't see who I've become; I try, that's it! Without my leg, with crutches ... or with this artificial leg. I don't have the strength to imagine this any more than I do my death.

Had I known sooner, would they have been able to save my leg? In June, those beautiful fragrant and lazy days, I was happy. I had a slight limp. I thought it was due to the cold. I felt a little pain in my leg. Would they have been able to save it if I had known then and not in the fall? September 15, trembling with terror and in tears; rain then greyness ...

I try and return to my old routine, take up my old ways of doing things, but it isn't the same. I've completely changed physically, and there are the bruises left behind by those interminable days of pain that carved up both my body and spirit. And my love. Falling in love during such a heavy time was like summoning a light in the middle of the darkness, a gentle oblivion, a way to forget my banal and dry reality, if only temporarily. This wellspring of emotion ... but now I'm hit by the ever-growing silence, hard. Start over, forget this hurricane. I throw out these little words in haste to keep myself from completely dying inside. At this moment, it's difficult. What will I do tomorrow? Write like this, without purpose, order, or calm? Not even bothering to form sentences. What kind of poem is this? What sort of text even? And these days when I can't even go outside weigh heavily on my shoulders. The snow, the ice, get it? Dragging these rotten crutches, which drag me down. And time, which slowly sucks me in. All that's left for me to do is to write down in these sparse little sentences the few memories of my experience I can still recall, though they're somewhat blurry, made dim by the drugs and the pain, and by the monotony of my days.

I know I'm writing it down so it's not all lost. I went to the edge of death, into an endless night, bumping into people and things. Exhausted, completely wiped out by an almost sleepless night, interrupted by faint, neurotic dreams trying to pull me back up to the surface.

———

December 23 [1977]

I spent the entire afternoon at the hospital with Louis. Glimpses of connection. Moments of welcome, then waiting. Outside the window of the little hospital room, the city was shining. I got the full report on my operation.

On the pink hospital buildings, on the closed faces in the tightly pulled sheets, the impassive and monotonous moon of last September.

———

Note

Sometimes, he said, I would wake up the mountain with a single stone.

———

THE LIFE BEYOND

What is *The Life Beyond*?
What kind of book does it want to be?
Some poems are connected to the seasons, others to "femitude,"

others to pain (the hospital), all deal with love, more or less.
Tenuous connection: the manifold nature of indefatigable desire.
Each poem, like in *Sign and Rumour*, should represent a moment,
whether special or not.
Following my brief descent into hell, I want to climb back up
toward the fruit.
Fruit: body, earth, fullness.
Life beyond: journey through life; alienation, pain or absence,
well-being, encounter, desire, pleasure.
Multiple themes: I must conserve, maintain, and transmit the voice.
Invent a universe, name things, as if for first time? (Poetry is
always defined this way.)

> *I am an avid omnivore of feelings, of living beings, of*
> *events and battles. I could eat the earth entire. I could drink*
> *the whole ocean.*

> *Poetry must walk in the darkness and rediscover the heart*
> *of man, the eyes of woman, the nameless people of the*
> *streets, those who at a certain hour of dusk or in the middle*
> *of a starry night have need of it, even if it's only a matter of*
> *a single line.*
> —Pablo Neruda, *I Confess that I Have Lived*

> *The poem is the love that's accomplished when desire*
> *remains desire.*

> *The poet answers each failure of evidence with a salvo to*
> *the future.*

> *You will be a part of the fruit's savour.*

*It's the hour where the windows escape the houses to light
up the end of the world where our world will dawn.*
— René Char [*The Formal Part* and *Leaves of Hypnos*]

Stable landscapes for a while.

———

December 31 [1977]
I look out at the city and feel a growing desire to describe it. I
am fascinated by the way it's lit up in winter, the illuminations
of nighttime, the many pedestrians, each with their own halo of
mystery: even the beat of their lives. But I'm seeing it all through
tired, inexact words, ardent carriers of little hollow lies. I'm going
too fast. I can't capture anything. I let myself go, dragged along by
the stranger driving this car. I'm passive. I see life unspool before
me, my many loves revealing their handsome faces: the talkers, the
keepers of secrets, the gorgeous furtive hands of the one and the
affectionate maritime eyes of the other, and then the arms and then
the whole joyful body of my love.

———

"Real life" isn't elsewhere, but inside of us. By which I mean, our
interiority. But you won't necessarily find the source of your life,
the foundation of your breath, by turning inward. You must allow
your life to spring forth, to shine through; to manifest in the arts.
Not to conflate life with existence. Existence, social rituals, gestures,
meaningless acts that stay on the surface. You must push past the
surface, deep into the core of existence, either that or really see and
feel the whole of the exterior, existence itself, so as to decipher life,
its fertile fruit.

We are more connected to sounds, light, atmosphere, than we realize; just as the elements affect trees and plants, they affect us. They create us. Poetry is nothing but the opening of intelligence onto life. A vital source not subjugated to or created by reason.

Important: develop, going forward, a great deal of tenderness toward my own body.

What I took from having cancer: learn by experience, let life spring forth (in other words, the love that called to me was just my life's innate drive), a more intimate knowledge of life (the refusal of death, of giving in). My movements were reduced to the bare minimum. Attached to a bed, unable to see anything outside, what haven't I lived through yet? This entire trauma has deepened my search, my journey through the quotidian. My questioning of everything has intensified. (My mind has grafted this meaning onto my illness. It wasn't there before.) Thus, the entire episode, and what I wrote while hospitalized, becomes completely integrated with my pre-hospitalization poems. Continuity.

At first, I thought that woman, her condition, was a repository of life, the way that the city I live in is a repository of life, in all its teeming majesty, seemingly disordered on the surface, but perfectly ordered underneath in a way we just can't see.

Love was always connected to life for me, so much that I cannot distinguish the one from the other. Love, which shines in me unexpectedly when I stand before a tree. The love of my parents, who gave me life. Fighting for survival is for me an act of love, and my childhood, which was filled with love, continues to be the first intuition of my poetry.

Beneath the appearances of the real, seek out the vital breath.

All art is nothing more than this, man's date with life, a relationship that makes him reject death.

Poems are the incorruptible ends of existence which we
throw into the repugnant maw of death ...

— René Char

THE DESPAIR AND SERENITY OF MAKING ART

All art participates in these two extremes. Man feels despair because
it is impossible for him to become completely in tune, to become
one, with life, that force that sometimes fills him with a mysterious
serenity. When I sit before a poplar tree, I am filled with a tremen-
dous sense of wonder, transported by a feeling of love, a hunger for
life, a fruitful and transparent enthusiasm that creates an imperish-
able, ineluctable sun inside of me. I can keep this feeling with me for
a while, but cannot sustain it. I retrieve it through writing. Making
art is a rediscovery of the mind, is witness to the despair born of the
futility of ever totally accessing that powerful serenity that comes
of being one with the earth. The futility of maintaining that mys-
terious peacefulness that wells up in me when I look at a tree, or
am filled with love, and which feels so true. The serenity brought
on by the finished work: from having achieved, having created this
happy feeling I'm talking about. Also, listening to Bach, looking at
a Cezanne, reading René Char: donors of this same light, beyond
all understanding, that nourishes me like the sun nourishes a plant.

Man's painful distance from this calm at-homeness in the world
gives birth to song. Therefore, his song tends to be about alienation
(especially in Québec) and terror, and maybe even hope, or despair
(a form of giving in to sleep, or to death, which is another kind of
serenity, but mute). The poem is man's impulse to live in the world,
yet also gives voice to the futility of this waking dream. In certain
poems of Neruda, of Miron, of Nelligan.

At other times, the poem gives voice to those happy moments
when we feel at home in the world, often due to love. Like Miron's

"The Walk toward Love" [*La Marche à l'amour*], which conflates the feeling of a loving women with finally having a country, with Miron's love of that country. Song of despair: a monologue of delirious alienation. Songs of tranquility: "The Walk toward Love," Neruda's *Residence on Earth*; also the love poems at the end of his *Black Island Memorial*, the light in Éluard's love poems.

Before the unbearable reality of sickness and torture all these thoughts become idiotic. Even love is trampled, as though it no longer has any place to be, as if feeling good in the face of so much bloodletting in the world, so many intolerable screams, can only make you feel bad about yourself ...

———

January 3, 1978

Oh, my little blank notebook, you are all I have left. My solitude is vast, infinite, indefatigable, and I am worn out by it, right down to the flood of tears I'm still choking back. I reproach Stéphan for no reason when I know that I am the one who should be reproached. If I haven't made any progress for two years, it's not Stéphan's fault. I have only myself to blame for allowing this terrible anxiety to flatten me. Ever since I've been with Stéphan, I've used him as a refuge, which has allowed me to hide from the outside world, to take cover in an unrealistic harmony. I still haven't let go of my childhood. And if, as many people say, anxiety causes cancer, how can I rid myself of it to survive, how can I get rid of this terrible anxiety? "People who think they alone carry the weight of the world." How presumptuous of me. The weight of the world. There are those who support it far better than I, fighters.

I dream of Paul constantly. Why? Why do I sometimes dream of no longer being with Stéphan? And yet he is so wonderful. He's got all the things I want. We are so bonded, such friends, sharing the same tastes, the same pleasures. Is it because Paul conforms to my image of the father? With his assured way of talking, his attentive ear, his furrowed brow. He is the image of maturity, of certainty and calm, like a sun-drenched harbour. A person with whom you can relax and be guided, who will shelter you. The image of security, and of ease. What's more, he embodies my desire to run away from it all. He embodies logic, reason, experience, everything I lack. He is my opposite, he is "manly." I am alienated, like all women, by social "patterns." I get it.

I haven't had any money for the last five years. Years during which, though I dream of Paris, I have been unable to give myself that gift. Five years of writing, but all without creating, really, a music that is entirely personal, my own. I'm only twenty-two years old, but already I'm being killed by anxiety, my future feels like a dead end, and now the fact that I've become handicapped has pushed me into an even deeper well. Years of feeling like I'm ugly, and I'm afraid that I'll end up without a man, or love. Not making love makes me just as nuts as not writing. I'm afraid, hideously afraid, of finding myself alone. I will make so many compromises in order not to be alone. I am not the strong, liberated, sane person that I aspire to be. I must, for once, be honest with myself. And if I must die, let me die knowing who I am, in the calm of that self-knowledge, of having seen myself.

Stéphan kept me awake all night with his cold. I took refuge in obsessive reveries. I thought about Paul. Memories came back, reshaped by my imagination: brief moments filtered through calmness and light ... I couldn't add anything. I am empty, completely. I attempt to stretch out my hand to Stéphan, but a weakling in both spirit and heart, I can't do it. And yet all I want is to be in love, to live again. I think about Louis, always distraught and sad, terribly alone. He wants me to give him something, to listen to him, but I can't do it. I feel so guilty. I think about all I owe to Stéphan. Those times when I was so difficult to love he stayed so close, so tender, so loving, and of all those times that Louis spent by my side, helping me, loving me, talking to me. I feel bad that I am so deficient, but it's irrefutable. If I am improving physically, morally I'm stagnant. I want to face each day without worry, without thoughts of sadness or remorse.

God, a little rest, happiness, lightness, and affection before I die. On this cold morning, I admire the sun, the window is frosted over in such a way that I can't see the world outside, yet I can still detect a sweet, peach-coloured light spinning with the entire city. I imagine the outside trees, the bustling crowds. People in love, going to work, leaving home and then returning. I love thinking of all the lives heading out into the street, of the places in the city where people live.

God, sometimes life seems so easy and love so free and sweet, it's easy to bestir myself, without a trace of heartbreak, though such moments of clear vision disappear fast, provoked as they are by certain bodily movements, or the sound of a piece of music drifting through the room, but most of all by certain colours, a particular way that the sun can appear, and sometimes also by a scent. The grey-pink softness of a sky filled with heavy snow. A gorgeous velvet sky filled with refreshing breezes perfumed by all the savours of the city. I dream of a lost garden. A garden of stone waiting for me. It's there I will go to find my older sister,[4] whom I never knew, and who I'm sure, had she lived, would have helped me, and next to her the most important man in my life: my grandfather.[5] On the island of my childhood[6] I could sleep in peace, surrounded by imaginary apple trees, in every detail a mirror of the tree under which

my languorous summer self found cover, a happy dream of my shel-
tered youth spent travelling in books. To sleep, to disappear, no
longer exist; nothing of me remaining but a small book of poems, a
few pages here and there, and those too will soon enough disappear
into total oblivion ...

The time of the woman artist has not yet arrived. A two-thousand-
year-old alienation doesn't retract its morbid, horrifying claws over-
night. Québecois alienation is three hundred years old, and it is still
a big drama. In general, women do not make much noise, they are
like tireless ants working for the promise of tomorrow and, far too
often, it is they who carry the heaviest burden in this already dif-
ficult life. Though there are many thousands of women, people
whine when a few feminists raise their voices. Given the magnitude
of our alienation, their numbers are miniscule. Over two thousand
years. This all dates back to the origins of religion, and all the
books, the Bible most of all. Back to our collective story ...

Paul ... stupidly I keep on dreaming about men. You can't just
pull such a deep alienation up by the roots. I will always love them
because of the way they seem so strong and mature. I will always
be searching for my father, a man so like my grandfather when
it comes to self-confidence, certainty, and work ethic. My father's
clear-headed thinking is superior to my own. I get bogged down in
a riot of ideas and can't organize my thoughts.

But what is a woman, actually? Most likely, even now, she's a
purely masculine creation. Who is she, when will her time come?

Springtime one day and nothing else ...

———

When I dream of happiness I see a sand-coloured house drenched
in sun, Venetian sun, a summer home, not like the houses around
here. It's strange, this house, which I must have seen long ago in

a children's book. The facade changes, but the feeling it gives off, the ambience, doesn't. The sweetness remains the same, as does its weathered grandeur. The grandeur is more about the feel of the surrounding air, or the colour, than the structural details.

Lucidity is the wound that gets closest to the sun.
— René Char [*Leaves of Hypnos*]

———

My dear Marie-Claude[7]
If I've taken a long time to respond, it's partly due to the fact that I haven't had much time, because recently I've been writing a lot for myself. But your letter profoundly moved me. Your words were like sisterly music, and so you, who are always so touchingly solicitous and attentive. At present, my health is better. My relentless appetite has returned. If my long stay at the hospital was something like a descent into hell, there were also many luminous days, because I could feel life stirring inside of me, blindly fighting, obstinate, but most of all lovingly. Faces approached me, made beautiful by being full of love. Each moment we are alive is neither really good, nor entirely bad, it depends on how we look at it, it's up to us to make the moment viable or not. Truthfully, I still haven't fully processed what happened to me. I think of the child you will have; I don't know if this world is worth knowing, but I do know that childhood is so fertile a place, so warm, so wonderfully full of dreams and sweet clarity ... And a happy childhood is the best tool for learning how to be human. Thinking of you, sending hugs.

———

January 4, 1978

Yesterday morning I felt low, but today an imaginary springtime leaps through my head; I hear the sparrows in the alleyway, the sun streams into the kitchen, timid and gracious. I can feel the sweetness of April's breezes. I feel overwhelmed by a kind of mad joy. The accumulated sensations of twenty-two springs settle in my hair. I laugh without reason ... Last night I had a detailed dream about summer ... All my senses twirl about as if I was completely lost in love. I dream to the point of losing my breath. Now I know I will love you forever. This love is light and full of aromas, maintained by nothing so much as silence. This love has no consistency or reason, not a single declaration. It will end in the same way it began. It's kept alive by a single image, a kind of makeshift springtime, not real or tangible, which is mine alone. It's the hum of life. My pale secret, my old passion, which I had thought lost.

———

Got my whole mind back. Returned to lucidity, back-to-earth, reasonable, quiet, composed. Was able to write a poem again, diligently, passionately. In a marvellous setting, with roseate sunshine under a beachfront awning. The window defrosts just a bit and I think it's spring. How can I make the words recreate my mind's experience of suddenly being suffused, haunted, by this bizarre spring out of time? The baroque oaks fan their leaves and the street changes into a gilded and perfumed tributary. I'm obsessed and annoyed by this pointless illusion. For a second, this January, in spite of the bitter cold, seems easy and gracious. I want to get a grip on how I'm haunted, why sometimes I become so happy after being in the terrible vice grip of my anxieties. I'm constantly moving between one state and the other. The first is the work of my spirit and heart, a place forged by my entire being, and certain words I can't quite capture. The second is slippery, a black bog I can't escape from. It arises from my deepest distress and, for no real reason, presses in on me. It's partly my fear of death and of suffering, of being abandoned, but also my thoughts about the months that led up to everything, all mixed up together. Summer, the wheat-shimmering countryside. Little faded images, old photographs, ordinary places.

The music of straw and footsteps flooding into your sightline.

———

Brief agreements and my dream
Your impassive furrowed brow
I see you from so far back
you and your soft circling silences,
Let the streets be dissolved by my desire
It will be an insignificant day that turns to dust
You will listen to me without impatience or shaking

[*The Life Beyond*]

———

January 8, 1978

EXILE

A story about alienation. In a large hospital, the story of a young woman who becomes disabled, Helen, and her relationship with two doctors. A battle with cancer.

All three protagonists are on a life quest. The woman is an artist, she writes. The woman is oppressed by myths about love, her relationship to a domineering father image, representations of women's bodies in a masculine world. How many failed love affairs and attachments must this woman go through in order to be able to express her love fully?

———

> *To see the frozen river*
> *Wanting to be springtime*
> [...]
> *To see the grey of suburbs*
> *Wanting to be a Renoir*
> [Brel]

Live, surpass myself, live to the nth degree, push my passion as far as it can go, but not like I've got all the time in the world, this time get it right. If I can't have experiences, I will write a novel. If I can live what I feel, I will write poems. But I would prefer to write poems, I prefer my words to come more from lived experience than from the imagination. I want my words to be anchored in the very depths of existence.

Since I'm so inert, I use my senses to imagine and anticipate situations. But when I write, I start from a situation (a story) and try to locate its subtle flavour, the meaning it records. Poetry of a love lived. Prose of a love felt, but never lived.

I never want to stop pushing myself. For me, genuine creation always originates in life. All of my words must be rooted in my lived experience in order for me to feel right about them. (What bullshit, I sound like a philosophy professor.)

———

It's odd how the men in my life have always showed up in pairs. Either I'm alone, or I meet two at the same time. And you can't go through something with two people at the same time. Bummer.

———

I read a little gossip, pseudo-literary stuff, I keep avoiding what's important. These days, I don't do anything. I wait. I wish I could completely sever my emotional dependence on Paul, because, with this affair, I know all too well the risk I'm taking. To be in a one-sided love, and no longer be able to live without that person. Or worse, to *feel*, or believe that you can no longer live without them. I think about his face, about the joy I felt when he visited. I worry over how stupid I seem, the powerful and overwhelming desire I still feel for him. I can feel my old mania creeping back. My whole body trembles with such an incredible force. Of course, I'm afraid. Afraid of undergoing this desire all alone, of becoming it. But I must delve into the very depths of myself, down deep without shame or guilt. I'm not going to write a novel; I'm never going to retreat from life. My poetry is the only viable weapon. I am going to live my life without barriers. I'm not going to be a passive object.

At the start, I was treated like an object by the health care system. They wanted to dictate my care. But I said no, I wanted to go another way, and with a doctor's help I fought to be treated like a subject, to have a say over my care. That's when he and I established a real dialogue. I must continue to take this tack, in everything. Paul wasn't there to make me feel safe, but to support me through my struggle. I should continue to think of him this way. Absolutely. I should expect nothing from him but a dialogue. I shouldn't act like I did with Pierre,[8] all silent, passive, and falling all over myself with admiration. That would put my recovery back in his hands, and I must fight this battle on my own. I've always wanted to discover things on my own, to be in control. I discovered pleasure on my own so that I could one day experience it with a man, but I wanted to understand myself, not be figured out by someone else. I knew I wanted to write from a very young age, no man gave me that. I was my own creator and must continue to be so. Pierre was my first true unrequited love. My love for him did not depend on his returning it. I should continue along this vein, a sleepless woman. No Sleeping Beauty in need of a man's kiss to bring her to life, but a woman who goes out to meet herself, keeping only her desire in view.

When I was sick, I didn't want the health care system to turn me into an object. I didn't want to be anesthetized, even on the operating table, since that would have meant becoming an object in their hands once again. I fought long and hard for this. It's what matters and I shouldn't give up on it, no matter the cost. This isn't the time to be complaisant. I want to be in charge of everything that happens to me, and if my will is forced to submit because of my body, all will be recovered through clarity and creativity. Live life to the fullest, don't be a silent gulf into which all disappears. Don't feel shame about emotions: fear, excitement, dizziness, love. Learn how to stop being the one who waits. I lived my cancer, even though the entire hospital system is set up to turn the patient into a passive being, to infantilize them (just as society is set up to turn women into passive, infantile beings). I want to break this relation-ship, to completely know my case, dispute it, so far as I understand it, be informed, have ownership over my body. I don't want to be turned into a mere thing in the hands of "knowledgeable men." But there's the trap of wanting to seduce my mentor. If I love Paul, I must love him in a clear-sighted and detached way. As I feel it, only as needed. This experience could help me to become more creative. Subject: what established mechanisms wanted to turn me into a passive patient? None, except the mentality of the doctor, the nurse, and as a result, my own. I had to struggle against the easy way out, against resignation. Besides, I am incapable of letting some stranger take charge of me, even here, because every bit of my lived experience must belong to me, it's my creativity that is at stake.

———

DESIRE ENVIRONMENTS

What arouses this burning feeling, and why am I so tortured by it? I can't forget about you. Your confession stays with me, and haunts me constantly. It's intolerable. After Pierre, I told myself that I would never again live through such a crushing obsession, but here it comes, just like before, in my stomach, in my hands. It's both light and dark. I feel elated and gripped by a madness I can't name; I can't think straight for thinking about you. But we are worlds apart, there's a thousand faces separating me from you, light years. *We are separated by story mazes, maybe roses ...*[9] My love has no other name. O, if only this burden could be love's last and then turn into the lightest thing in the world. The only light thing. If only there was a way I could stop caring about you, just love you while you're here, then breezily forget you. And laugh at each moment, existence is so brief, so precious. So small.

———

EXILE

Rooms that are going to drown themselves in our dim mirrors
These rotting flowers watching us with compassion

———

THE EXHAUSTED ROMANCE

The love that makes our hands gush
can no longer be enacted or spoken of

———

Alienation: fear of no longer being able to seduce men because my leg is missing. Extreme embarrassment and reserve. Yet I'm pretty sure that my fear of failure won't stop me from pursuing men, just like I did before. I'll probably go a little slower. When I feel that I want a man, I should let it be known. Not wait around.

The built-in severity of taking breaths

———

I have a fanatic springtime
that watches you with passionate eyes

———

I have become a barometer, affected by the slightest change in atmosphere. I'm continually being reborn, floored by a ray of sun, a sparrow's cry. I walk with astonishment, my shoes prune the dry sidewalk.

———

Yesterday there were heavy floods of rain
and over the drowned parks even more water fell
reminding us of spring

our dreams at odds we were together
in apartments levied with soft breaths
yesterday was about you and the blue chains articulating the city
and tomorrow it's you again at the confessions of sites and the
instant

My desire to be in love came back at the palace
along with my capitulation to pleasure
the balancing of restricted days
nothing but a slippage in the smiles
yesterday from a lone reframed conversation
and now more of the same seasonal fever
the same tranquil waters inside the same lips

You here illustrating my patience
you are the exact severity of our breaths
just these copious and joyous waters
rebelling over the entire earth
the rains exploring our bedtimes
hidden fountains pulled from our bodies
just these residential affections

                                                  [*The Life Beyond*]

———

Note
The writing should be more rigorously modern.

———

THE EXHAUSTED ROMANCE

Words describing the first moments of falling in love, and especially about desire, are tired. I must talk about the old, eternal desire from my perspective, as a woman, what women seldom speak of, given the many ways they are culturally and socially alienated. Woman's desire has to overcome prohibitions and stereotypes, and yet it still manages to be born. Despite everything, woman's desire awakens her most intimate vitality, her perpetual regeneration, like the freest of human acts.

———

Of this man I would say that he is both my day's beginning and end, following which he sinks into all the forgotten arteries of the city, into all of the wounding or calming shadows of the walls and stones, he fades into the incurable whiteness of the concrete just like he fades into my hopes. He borders on indescribable, absorbed into the earth I shovel in my sleep. From his absence, fairytales are born.

[*Prose poems*]

———

March 4, 1978

It's been five months since I met you. Now I think I can see a sweeter season up ahead, a new world, radiant and free, a season so sweet it fends off death ...[10] I imagine fields of wheat and oat, sunlit fields swaying beneath the wind in front of cozy homes, beautiful revelatory rainfall, tireless seas that go on forever, mirroring the movement of the blowing wheat. The past will have become the future, everything bound together in a single sigh. Yes, a present possessed of the delicate and tinted texture of memories. Just like my childhood, intoxicated by light alone, never hurried, but free and without worry.

———

Behold an unusual form of time
that moves forward in rose and gold
a necessity of my well-worn dreams
an irregular and baroque time
filled with deep breaths
close to the rain
on lethargic July nights

There was so much redeeming sweetness
the wounds became easy
now we no longer hunt down
atmospheric outpourings
before the threshold haloed by our silences

My desire for you doesn't come from some place
or a decisive word
but from an invisible plea
where all exalted feelings converge

O how useless when everything breaks and is full of feeling
when certain words become tarnished by insecurity and love
and you become as remote as the distant blue downpour

I have begun to slow down
as everything opens out
toward an incredible ocean

as your eyes turn to grey
and let it be that you should soften
yet be indescribable
such a slowdown
of this handout from time
of this apprehension of the heart

I look at you I dare nothing
for this vision which leaves and undoes me
nor for these daily masks
heavy like plate armour

I stay still

An iris sways its light purple petals
where the sun drowns
and all the sadness from day's beginning to end
takes up residence in my body
I am shut down
with no more understanding or memory
but this diminishing light
I have no sense of time
amped-up but inert
There's nothing left but this sunlit shard
this blank impulse where life unfolds
this sense of the light
where everything secretly takes note of you

The grand metamorphosed city sets forth
in the stiff white of winter
or in its magical glass skyscrapers
(Behind a window a back relaxed

against a straw chair
evokes the happy braiding
of any sunlit vacation)

Against the darkness the birch is a sign of love
a divisible river and the waiting
its whiteness seems to cleave the clear night
Out of all these days and nights of illness
I have only the torment of my love
that and the sky's monotonous destruction
that and the slow suffocation of my senses
I no longer recognize my body
I have come into a clumsy universe
filled with nothing but dreaded streets

[*The Life Beyond*]

———

THE LIFE BEYOND

Life beyond: elsewhere. A journey though the quotidian, the habitual. Desire and death. Desire in every poem. Whiteness, precious silence, the ideal place, intense light, the return of physical desire, "the other side of the mirror."

A white in which all the colours are present, primordial desire. The photographs[11] bring this whiteness into relief, this fatal silence, the unsaid, this multiple life, this slowdown, this desire.

The erasure of space. The return of time.

The Exhausted Romance[1]

The air is so sweet it fends off death.
— Gustave Flaubert

Maybe there's an underpinning of misogyny in every little girl. There
is a little girl in me who is intensely unhappy not to have been born
a boy. Unhappy and filled with self-hatred. Maybe this is the origin
of my hatred, my continual dissatisfaction, with my body and with
my artistic potential. I don't love myself, yet I have an endless need
to be loved. I am tormented by a frantic desire to be loved. The
more intelligence and prestige a man has, the more interesting and
out of my league he seems, the more admiration I have for him and
the more I want him to love me. It's as if I believe that being asso-
ciated with such a man can make me feel better about myself. And
when he rejects me, I become so despondent I feel like I'm almost
dying. I write poems to him, and look for ways I might persuade
him to love me. Writing poems calms me down, if only tempo-
rarily. They work as prayer, magic spell, and exorcism. The poem
gives me the power to refashion my life, and comforts me with the
thought that if I cannot have his love for real, I can at least have it
in my imagination. It's like I'm two people; one feels the need gain
the love of some ostensibly prestigious man in order to have any
worth, the other is self-assured, proud of my talent, and loves me
for myself. In other words, there is both a woman and an individual
inside of me. The individual is artistic and free, the woman is dissat-
isfied and dependent. Endless, awkward, and self-destructive desire
comes from the woman part, pleasure from the individual. And the
individual is constantly seeking to recuperate the woman through
writing, to use her alienation as a source of creativity. I write so as
not to destroy myself. I have always felt that my condition of being

a woman threatens my artistic capacities. I have been told so many times that femininity and genius are irreconcilable, that the fulfillment of the one can only come about through the total destruction of the other. I told myself that there was nothing in the world that would make me give up poetry, and femininity felt like a burden, a barricade between me and that fulfillment. As I have gotten older, and ideas about women have evolved, my views have changed. I now think that these two sides are totally reconcilable. Nevertheless, there's an entire childhood inside of me that is still filled with self-hatred, wishes she hadn't been born a woman, and puts men above her in a universe of achievement and passionate possibilities, all of which she is denied. This is why I can't help but love Paul, and why, when I imagine myself at his side, I see myself as successful. The more I think about my past, the more I can see that all of my passions have been founded on this same assumption. But alas, the way alienation is constituted, nothing about my desire or the way I love can change. (When Pierre's prestige tanked, I stopped loving him.) Despite the fact that I know I can, through hard work, write my oeuvre, and, by delving deep, discover the woman inside of me and learn to love her, I can't stop loving Paul. An endless desire not to love, but to seduce. Who am I, then, underneath the burden of this onerous alienation? Nothing will stop me from getting to the root of these various alienations, because, for me, that's the best way to get over them, to break them, and to bring about, on the other side, the reunification of the woman and the individual through the creative act. I want to create my life as much as I do my poetry, and my poetry from my life. I don't believe that by avoiding our weaknesses, rejecting them before exhausting them, we can become free. Rather, we must delve down into them until they become clear. Not by suffering through them, but by owning them. But how am I to take ownership of this oppressive, relentless torment? By journeying to the very heart of my passions? Didn't I already start this with Paul, a few days ago, by letting him know how I felt? But I didn't tell him the extent of it. I will have more to say. Yesterday I was stuck there, burning in a timid, taut silence. I've already stood by silently for an entire winter. Maybe it's better to at least say out loud what won't happen by other means, to let the words exorcise this fierce thirst. But what kind of love does he feel for me? Is his rationale that because he is responsible for me it wouldn't be right? Does being in love make you an irresponsible person? Isn't he just trying to protect himself from the possibility of getting hurt by not really dealing with me?

———

I would like to live through a springtime that can make up for all my winters (and for the accumulation of all these awful days, all these moments lost in dreams of a bright tomorrow). I would like to stop dreaming about you, and in that regard, I've come a long way. Why won't you do the rest? But your obstinate silence, your wisdom, your reason, and that little regret in your voice: "I'm not indifferent, believe me, I think it would be very pleasant. But there are not only my responsibilities, there's also the matter of your age, of both our ages." What a sad little novel has ended before it even really got started.

Here I am, mutilated, worried about no longer being pretty, no longer attractive, and you, tenderly gazing at me from so far away.

———

March 29, 1978
I wish I could write about something other than this awful alien-ating reality, which tomorrow will be even worse. Now I have to fasten this armour to my body, a heavy and deforming artificial

scaffolding that makes it possible for me to walk, but makes me far less pretty. I came here to see Paul, but he has gone away for several days. The terrible suffering returns. An outrageous pessimism, a sad desire. Stéphan told me that I was beautiful, but I wanted him to say it to me, *him*. But why?

———

I'm crying. It feels like I will never come to the end of my suffering. I dig deep, I grab hold of what little taste for life I've got left. I feel as if I'm moving through a tunnel, my eyes obsessed by what seems like a light in the distance, probably more imagined than real. I've created it, this light, in an attempt to give myself a chance to move forward, if only a little. I don't expect anything from you. Oh, I will get over this new obsession. Happily, I still have Stéphan's sweet love. Yet I retain my right to be inventive, to take my desire elsewhere. I do not want to stop living at twenty-two years old just because I am no longer physically the same. I will always be deformed by this artificial leg. I will never be pretty, not anymore. I'm in a lot of pain. This evening, in this dead little apartment, I feel so alone. And Paul, who has left for the ends of the earth without calling, and this life devoid of even one iota of beautiful folly, passion, or sun. Only continual mediocrity, winter, uncertainty, and rational sadness. Prudence is a virtue born of old age and sadness. What pitiful words have amassed in the hollow of my spirit and my soul. Poetry is dead in me tonight. It would take a lot of love and hope to bring it back to life. Rediscovering, surprising, and revivifying myself by saying what can't be said.

Your face has been overlain by tumbling skies for quite some time. Here there are sad stones, ditches and roadways, your eyes lost in the useless grandeur of a vast pink and grey evening. Here so many collected dreams have gone away that nothing is left at the end of time but an expansive summer, smoky and nonchalant, a dazed aimlessness, a hesitant dying refrain extracted from a night without you. The choleric rainfall ceaselessly echoes your absence. But you laugh.

[*Prose poems*]

I don't want to hope, anticipate, wait, or delude myself anymore. I want to learn how to appreciate the almost nothing that is the present moment. I want to be satisfied with what's immediate, me, who never stops thinking about tomorrow, him, or going on a trip, or a to poetry event, or new literary friends, a fling, or a film. I think constantly about the poem yet to be written, it's what keeps me alive, shakes me up, animates me. I would like to produce more, and to judge myself only by this (the poem), written in the present moment.

I am constantly dying of everything.

Is there a sun I could name that could return my capacity for joy, and when will he leave my thoughts, this useless man? If I lived in the moment, free of worry, perhaps my pain and anxiety would go away, as well as this fire which keeps burning me down.

The desire to know men, to love and be loved by them, the desire to live in different natural surroundings, other places, to smile and to love through new conversations, under different lights and for different projects. To live.

Gold vagabonds on the walls of dawn

———

THE LIFE BEYOND
OR
DESIRE ENVIRONMENTS

My eyes fall on things at the exact moment when they appear to breathe. A certain whiteness catches my eye, a certain silence inside the whiteness, a certain desire (the three conflated). Mediocrity, poverty, sadness of the real; desire's path toward pleasure: flight and invented romance.

Moving across life. The writing represents desire, the environments are the landscapes, places, and faces of this desire. Stéphan will photograph the environments, because if desire can be written, it can't be shown. It's up to Stéphan to identify such ambiences, such textures of the real. Those moments or places when life is transformed into a strange celebration, a rupture, an ambivalence, a momentary intoxication. They don't last long.

———

LOVELY IMAGES OF RUNNING AWAY

Sometimes I imagine long highways under manifold skies electrified by lightning. The road opens out, surrounded by wastelands, fields, rocks, suburbs in the distance, and always a sweet void, an endless anonymous space under a darkening sky, summer's humid shimmer. The wind is odourless, the car hurls forward without stopping. It feels as if it will never reach its destination, as if in the distance there's nothing, which is to say, nothing but endless road. There's a certain calm that marks the scene, a lessening of anxiety, an approximation of happiness; an absence of emotion and desire. There are no more goals to achieve. I feel a hunger to write about the serenity of this absence, about the well-being of these places shaped by modernity, perfectly empty non-spaces which can absorb whatever you project onto them, the whole of their surface awaiting your reveries. The suburbs with their cloudless skies and low, identical houses; their concrete supermarkets, their wide black roads made mirror-like by rain, reflecting the red-and-white tail lights of cars.

I want the next desire environment to be more connected to Montréal and its suburbs, and to the entire atmosphere of North America. I love the Maine coast, and I dream of seeing New York again. I feel an avid thirst for an asphalt summer, for raw sun and never-ending spaces. A hunger not for beauty, but to encounter life in its swarming, shapeless, ugly state, miserable like mine, fighting bitterly like mine. Abrupt, violent, metallic, artificial-looking. I feel hungry to say what my culture has never said. To know the United States all the way to Mexico, air-conditioned hotels, highways, all that once shocked me, but with which I now identify.

The conviction that there's nothing you can change or hope for is like wearing sunglasses while walking in the rain. I love bus stations and their whirring music, I love a road lit up by tail lights when driving on a highway at night, the smell of fried food at truck stops. This is the trip I want to take, even here, at home, starting with my own town. I feel a hunger to roam through its seasonal expansions and ethnic neighbourhoods, through its chrome gadgets, neon, and warehouses, its demolitions, and I also have a hunger for luxurious things, unfinished places, and giant buildings with tinted windows. I want to talk about rocks, stones, and concrete, things that seem unassailable and incommunicable.

———

My only savagery is a dazzling harmonious golden dawn that has but an hour remaining to shine on a unique countryside, and every desire gives me the illusion of being at the origin of creation, before the inflexibility of old age has set in. A baroque colour is filling the room, awakening all my dreams, all the lost rhythms of a perfect song. (Beauty's spectacle is exhausting.) If I gave away my eyes and my hands I'd have nothing left, the other side of desire isn't serenity, but nothing. Nothing.

[Prose poems]

———

April 6, 1978

You pass a handsome stranger and are moved by his face, you conceal the feeling like a secret happiness, a ray of April's gentle, silky sunlight. You romanticize the encounter and tell yourself the most beautiful stories. A mere glance from a face, so fine, so faraway, can take me on such spectacular voyages. Ignorant of the life behind the face, I am free to imagine and invent it. I like to watch men, watching them brings me a kind of ecstasy, a perfect abandonment to pleasure. I like noticing a man's attractiveness or his charm and imagining, from the way he moves, looks at things, and the clothes he wears, the shape of his life and hopes, what it would be like to touch his body, what he would look like when making love. I remember the way I felt when I first set eyes on Paul; his smile was ironic and discreet; his eyes were cold, almost expressionless. He had a refined elegance, a serious and intellectual allure in his movement and the way he spoke. I so wished I could know him somewhere other than that hospital room. His manner was always lofty and arrogant, but also contemplative and restrained. The secret sensuality of his hands, his repressed passion. He said to me: "You are sensitive and passionate. We have a lot in common."

———

April 10, 1978

I must risk writing about my alienation. Now that I don't see him anymore, nothing feels real. All the joys I create, day in and day out, evanesce, leaving in their wake the gut-wrenching sadness of wanting to see him and not being able to.

And this beautiful spring day, and my elegance in the mirror, all for nothing. My taste for happiness slowly drains away, evaporating in the vibrant April air. I want to rid my mind of his image, but one part of me keeps maliciously cultivating it. I feel hungry to work on my poetry, as if it's my last chance at happiness. To explore the strangeness and spontaneity of desire. The way it collaborates with both our deepest weaknesses and our greatest strengths. The associations we build between it and particular places, particular lighting. When unsatisfied it grows monstrously large, dissolves into the real, becomes impossible. In quest of the unobtainable, we magnify it, but the minute we have what we want, it turns banal and elusive to that part of us that is sustained by the dream. I want him to love me. He will love me. Why am I so obstinate, so determined? I am a Taurus, we are headstrong, determined, and heedless, the ones who charge that deadly red thing waving in the distance.

Desire was iron in touch with the most beautiful images. A cutting edge, a door opening on the world and all its wounds, a heart, pensive and forsaken. I want to be welcomed by all the trees, the remotest lands, the suns too, gathered up by them all and put to sleep. All the nights are perfumes and you are the sad secret they speak of, to me alone they speak, and of my sole desire.

[Prose Poems]

I want to go away so I don't have to see him anymore. Seeing him only reawakens my suffering. But I won't be able to muster the courage to break with him, and he, because my love flatters him, isn't interested in putting a stop to it. Despair has no wings, nor does happiness, nor desire. Desire is an anchor, it prevents you from sailing, a cord, it prevents you from breathing. It is an ambiguous place, precariously uniting great extravagance, confrontation with the self, and the exaltation of self. The object of desire is always an object because desire's drive exists only in the self, not in the other. My reasons for loving him are wholly internal, the result of a pathological sense of lack (ontological). I'm not satisfied with myself, with my image, with my few qualities. My desire for him is a kind of approval of self, a glorification. To possess him would associate me with a wealth that I cannot attain on my own. I would be beautiful, not in the mirror, or in such a way as to draw attention, but by virtue of his approving look. I need to forget him, though he's only recently left, for feeding on his presence-absence (invented presence) will only drive me insane.

I must free myself from this kind of love. Otherwise, it threatens to play out again and again for my entire life, returning with each new fascinating person I encounter, triggering this suffering all over again. Relinquishing myself to the impossible, to the inaccessible. Shameless research on suffering? No, I fell in love with these men simply because we crossed paths and they were kind to me, not out of some foreknowledge that they wouldn't love me, that they were incapable of loving me. The entire problem comes from the fact that I do not love myself enough, so I need to be with someone people admire in order to allow myself to be who I am. Talk about alienation.

———

Today I saw the swallows arrive, flying through sheets of rain, and a feeling of lightheartedness came over me. I savoured the air, as I had a couple of days ago sitting all wrapped up, my face toward the Laurentide sun. I told myself that I absolutely must get myself together, grow up, live for myself. Live, yes, and stop letting the weather and my dreams weigh me down. Learn from everything, be open to everything, stop just sitting around, imagining what my life would be like if Paul loved me. Instead, I must build my work from every moment, gesture, and thought. Take, embrace the present moment, no regrets, omissions, or hurry. I can sense that I am between two writing projects. From this moment on, I must seek out my words and desires more rigorously and bring both to bear. (Pleasure of words, pleasure of the body.)

———

With the rhythm of baroque singing and the resplendence of a violin, the birds cut across the window's grey perspective. Their flight is so lively and elegant, and in me (my soul?), my spirit or my heart, I'm not sure which, the same springtime enthusiasm grows. I am happy to be alive. I feel life, bruises and all, but also the promise of the future. Suddenly, in this moment, I can imagine my future.

Terrible birds monopolize the possibilities, resplendent and resurrected they protect our exiles, our torpors. The moment following your lips is like my attachment to the place I was born, a reprint of my desires.

[*Prose poems*]

———

The sea is dying and far above there are meagre blossoms from whose weather I reconstruct your eyes. The sea dies at the feet of these labyrinths, my fantasies, while your withheld body is the Minotaur slowly destroying me.

[Prose poems]

———

The systematic, irredeemable madness of loving you even though I don't understand you, and today, it doesn't matter, I'm burying myself in your absence without regret. I've decided to work on cultivating your words, on translating my pressing and illusory desire, and to play my fantasy out as far as it can go, no longer suppressing it. Allow it to completely take over, as I did little by little with Pierre. Pierre called yesterday. He talked about spending his vacation with me and Stéphan, and I felt stunned anew that after fruitlessly obsessing over him for four years, I no longer feel any love for him at all, only a kind of tepid sympathy. All fires go out (that one had no real basis, and wasn't truly serious). The object of desire is, therefore, always an object, a fixed point on which to focus a powerful emotion. Something in us, in order to express itself, needs an object, but the name of that object is incidental. My love for Paul came out of several "environments." My desire is connected to these environments: the present moment and its conditions. I wish I could seize the real texture of the luminous present, insinuate myself into time passing, give all my attention to Stéphan, day in and day out.

———

I'm back in my emotional hell. Two-hundred-year-old alienation, to say the very least: the search for my identity is connected to love. How utterly stupid. But this is what I'm facing, and I should at least try to learn from it, to make what I can of this ontological truth. The person you love is everything, and you are nothing. I can share the sweetest moments with Stéphan and draw sustenance from our life together, but there's still a part of me that cannot accept our contentment. To accept it would be false because I am not satisfied. A part of me (surely the *main* part) feels superhappy with Stéphan. He's my best friend, a skilled lover, our tastes and our dreams hugely overlap, but other men answer, secretly, to other needs. But Stéphan is the most precious person to me. (The only man who is not, for me, an "object.")

I want to slough off all this sentimentalism and quit obsessing over my sexual frustration so I can dedicate myself more earnestly to thinking, and to writing. Though I'm well aware that, until I've put an end to this war with my body, this will be impossible. It pains me to think about being mutilated. Will it affect my independence, obstruct my projects, my energy? I stagnate, and sometimes feel that death is calling to me, yet I am looking for life with the whole of my conscious self, searching for it in a man, a landscape, a feeling.

I love the fact that Paul is older, I love how dependent he makes me feel, his ability to heal, what he knows about my illness. The strength of his understanding helps my will (sometimes weak) to survive. We live, every one of us, in a socially determined mould.

———

Tuesday [April 18, 1978]
I feel happy. I placed some poems in the journal *Estuaire (Estuary)*[2]. *The Life Beyond* continues to come together. Stéphan has already figured out the photographic piece. He knows what he wants to do and has several ideas about the overall design. Me, I remain superfocused on the text. Several poems are prowling around, but

I haven't had the time to start them. Yet the more I wait the clearer they become, even though their real form will only emerge when I start writing. I think about giving a poetry reading. Either solo, or with Jean and Alexis.[3]

————

Step-by-step I'm learning how to love myself, trying to live in such a way that my mind doesn't veer toward some far-fetched future, some time I think will be so much better; I'm learning to leave each insight to its rightful place, and to understand the strange ramifications of the way our thinking relates to what's outside of us, what surrounds us. And yet, my mind constantly wanders, and without trying to, gulps down thousands of arresting images, images that fill me with as much happiness as a tempestuous ocean. The ocean, the subtle fragrance of spring, the returning light. All things, the abiding desire that I feel for Paul, and my conviction that he is thinking of me.

I want to pin down the precise location, the root, of this premonition. I'm aware of the fact that he is a cold person, inflexible, and rational. How do I manage to convince myself that at this very moment, while completely caught up in something else, he must be thinking of me, or that the power of my daydream could bring us together just a bit? No, my sense of well-being has a deeper source: the absence of regret, of suffering, well, heartache really. Even if I can't touch him and despite the sclerosis of our social roles, the distance separating us, and the impossibility of what I feel, thanks to the pure freedom of spring I'm holding onto the pleasure of being in love with him, without any commitment, in a less obvious way.

Sometimes I think that, if he knew about my obsession, intangible though it is, Stéphan might pull away, other times I tell myself that we're so good together he can't leave, not anytime soon. My problem is that I'm afraid of being left alone, of solitude, and of not having access to a man's body. I can't go very long without making love, and now I am so anxious that I'll never get to be with any other men. Of course, these fears are not why I remain deeply attached to Stéphan, but something better, our great friendship, the familiarity I have with his body, affection. But now my lack of physical autonomy distorts these feelings, it humiliates me and provokes my sudden fits of impatience, followed by guilt. I'm afraid of being a burden, but with time things will improve. Little by little my spirit is finding, anticipating, and cultivating its sense of freedom and, little by little, it will catch up to my body. It's been a long gestation, I'll admit, but each day I can feel myself pushing toward the surface, feeling good about myself. There are sudden setbacks, plenty of incoherence and babbling, but I'll get there soon enough.

———

Marguerite Duras on desire:

> Desire: country of transgression. Her eyes were filled with "the light of madness," allowing her to go in search of her truth.

Desire: a possible road to my freedom.
  I shouldn't point fingers, who even cares about the motives behind this desire, it is life.

> Non-existence, indifference, inertia, and unstable signs have been associated with the name of woman: but in this case it's associated with a story and the potential ownership of a desire.
> From that point on what she rebuilds is the end of a world.

The dawn of her creative power.
She tries to listen to the commotion inside of her, she fails,
she is overwhelmed by the realization, even if incomplete,
of her desire.[4]

We are alive because we remember. The presence of desire, a strange breath. It's not important to know my desire's motives, for it encompasses something much greater: a path to "him," and to the world, a thirst, a hunger that will never be satisfied, a sort of existential quest for the other, and, by the same token, for myself. To stop being an object, to become a subject. Desire has occasioned this revelation. Not by undergoing it, but by living it. The ownership of my desire.

Desire: madness, memory, texture of the real

Desire intimately connected to meaning and memory. Possible ownership, venture, vigour.

Paul: *catharsis, floating seafoam, the first caress always tastes of snow.*[5]

———

This morning I'm listening to my favourite kind of music, a sort of delicate and solemn march that evokes a sprawling countryside in springtime. A rose-gold light, a thin dusting of sun, and poplars. I feel the melancholy pleasure of being engulfed by my solitude and have a very strong sensation of being completely open to the world. I see the light glinting off ocean waves; the smell, the sight, the sound (oh! these birds), transport me. I'm the only finite thing in an infinite world, which fills me with regret, for I cannot melt into it, I cannot become one with this beauty reborn. I can sense death, but it is a sweet death, like a ray of sun inside our being. I wave at life: these trees, these sweet-smelling breezes, this sun, splendid at dawn and dusk. I am somewhere in the south of France, or in Italy. I wave, but I am a stranger, so I content myself with seeing without being seen. I have but a single desire: to be in this place, either alive, or dead.

———

Today, April 22, 1978, I'm 23 years old
I haven't gotten very far. The door is open. From now on I'm only going to take care of myself. My aspirations, my projects, my pleasures. I'll do everything possible to succeed, to achieve what I want to achieve, to become what I want to become, who I am. I don't need any man. I have decided to stop acting differently around them. Wasting my energy over absences or accommodations, just because I like a man. It's stupid. I'm done with trying to please at any cost. I must simply, and primarily, please myself. No longer wait for what others can give me, but give it to myself. Give myself (work for) what I want. I must learn how not to fear being alone.

———

In the park, April 24 [1978]
Saw Paul. Emotion and distance. For all my suffering over him, only the physical attraction remains. He wants to talk to me about my poems. Fine, but I really don't care if he does or not. They are enigmatic to him, he didn't really seem to appreciate them, even though he claimed to have liked certain ones. But criticism doesn't affect me anymore. I feel confident. Some people like them, others not, but in the end, what does it matter? Spring, here in the park, the smell of the earth, of the sun on the earth, a luxurious sparkly sunlight, first red buds. To feel life, welcome it. I feel poems emerging, the birth of a style, and a great sense of calm. More and more I know what it

is I want, what I love. In poetry, woman's reclamation of her desire (not the other's desire, nor the desire to desire the other). The reinvention of her sex, or maybe just the invention of it, she who has never had a real form, a real life. The daily rebirth of poetry in me, like my non-stop rediscovery of the sun, the sky, the trees, and the earth. Constant astonishment, being open to people and to things. If only he (and they) knew that the only reason we exist is to come together, to exchange our essences, as different fruits grafted on the same branch intermingle in order to produce something fantastic. We must constantly reinvent our nature, be astonished by everything, touched by everything, be gods to each other. Discover and preserve it all; the beauty of soil.

But what's the point of loving, or even being interested in someone, who is so different from me? There's not a single shared thing between us: age, sex, sensibility, taste, etc.

Yet I'm pigheaded, I love him violently. Nothing can be done about it. Every time I see him, I give in again, overtaken by the same appetite. Appetite for life, for living. Would that my inner life could be turned off for a spell so that I could experience the pure pleasure of looking around at what's on offer, available and shimmering. Crowds in cafes. The work of hands. I think up projects for myself to do as soon as I can walk again. Going out with Monique, looking at handsome guys, finding ways to meet them. Doing lithography with Cécile. Going to the ocean, and to New York with Stéphan, and maybe with Pierre, and France. Buying beautiful dresses. Looking pretty, in spite of everything. Writing, becoming a member of the writer's union, planning some poetry readings with Jean, Alexis, and maybe others. Who knows? Publishing in magazines. And if I get a grant, learning how to fly an airplane.

———

Desire O my beautiful sailboat at sunrise my cartography of night

————

I'm having one of those fits of sadness. The house is suffocating, the dust of Montréal is suffocating. I wish I were somewhere else, at the ocean. My love for him is like wanting to run into the waves, to embrace the sun, the sand, the trees. I look in the mirror, I look pretty, it's a pity he can't see it.

Behind a window someone cautiously smiles
At noon spring makes more racket than a blue jay
And love heads out in a white blouse
The entire street is a buckling of blue
We have no history and the weather is better than ever
[*The Life Beyond*]

————

Everything moves away from me, no landscape accepts me, no place sets me free, only walking, only doing something, can release me from this long, oppressive silence. These poems, O, all these words I'm failing to plug away at that they might become palpable and set me free. I am obsessed by my passion. O, I would gladly give up the burden of this moment to hold him in my arms.

Patientia!

————

What I love about poetry is its complete freedom. There's no fixed theme (no topic or story), the words are free, and there's no restriction on my inspiration. I feel so happy when I think that tomorrow's poem won't resemble today's, since it's bound up with the unfolding of time. Tomorrow, all is possible, tomorrow any poem is possible. Each time I write a poem, I put my life back into the world. Each time I write a poem, I give my whole life shape and switch up my lovers. When I write, it's always summertime. I've always hated forcing myself to do something, no matter what it is. Homework always killed my inspiration. What pleases me today, might bore me tomorrow. Also, I don't like starting writing projects that might drag on for several months. I love changing moods, magic, finding unpredictable places, being alert to the seasons and to people, accounting for all of it, letting nothing get by me. Each poem is an opening onto the world. For a poetry collection to be coherent, it needs to be completed within a set amount of time, given that after two years my life changes direction. I love the extreme rigour the poem demands. I'm not a master at the language, or grammar and syntax, but centre the poem around a few precise lines with infinite possibility. What matters is the emotional power of the words in a line, their power of evocation. It's the way visual artists work. Maybe poets are more like painters than prose writers. Those who are fluent in both "languages" are so lucky. The poem reinvents speech, the music of the words at each instance, it regenerates language, astonishes and mixes, transmits an entire world, an entire understanding, and an entire dream.

This is exactly what seduced me about Japanese poetry, the haiku's power of evocation. I wrote *Sign and Rumour* with the wish to condense my vision, my words, to the equivalent of a hand gesture. To give birth to a feeling with just a few touches.

———

I think about France every day.[6] And not just any region, but Provence. I feel like I know it from reading, paintings, and photos. A particular light, a fragrance.

When I go, it will all be familiar to me, and I know that I will say to myself: "Here's where I should live and work." Maybe a sort of chromosomal memory has given me this love for Granddad's birthplace.[7] Granddad's things, his way of living (especially summer on Perrot Island), make me feel passionate about the idea of France (a particular France), also some of Colette's books, Éluard's poems, and Cézanne's paintings.

Sometimes I have the feeling of being trapped here, as if in a prison, of suffocating, of not being someplace where I have access to words. Even more than words, sights, sights that can carry me joyfully into the heart of my being, that can give me the world. Oh, summer, summer, filled with the sea, wheat fields, barbecues, cicadas, chickadees, white stone, and nights as warm as maternal bellies, with the complex fragrance of burnt grass, sweet flowers, rare herbs; everything that's in the garden Colette writes about in *Sido*. I don't want to die before having experienced all of these things.

———

Next collection: Prose poems, anecdotal.
                       Simple language, clarity of insight.
                       Strange coincidences.

———

Missed a meeting with Paul. Weird, unfazed, indifferent. Yet, at the thought of seeing him again, everything in me leapt up. I saw that I was pretty by the way people looked at me. Sure of this one thing:

being attractive. But to others if need be. I know that all desires fade, every story moves forward. Don't wait. I don't have the time to wait. Louis said: "There may not be much time left to live. You should live life to the hilt."

I don't have time to wait for Paul. Everything feels urgent. A thousand seductions, places, faces, hands. But with Paul, I feel the same certainty about my love for him as I did for Pierre four years ago. Pierre's coming over to the house tonight to eat with us. I'm still amazed that I don't feel anything for him (after having desired and suffered so much over him). My head is filled with trips, with imaginary departures. I know that in writing the last poems of *The Life Beyond* an entire period of my life has ended. I feel strongly that I am between two worlds. Two universes call out to each other. Right now, I'm feeling anxious because I'm going through a period of change. The weather is changing. Spring isn't in any rush. My heart is hiding, my body reorganizing, new sensations are surfacing, there's a new reign ahead, my days are working on it. I do not know where my strength will come from, but it will come.

He's unaware of being looked at
isolated verse unlikely miracle
there are no environments for us
His body is a fixed point
a proliferation of landscapes

The beaches flowered during the night
He places his incredulous hands on my face
He is on the edge of dizziness and ignores the fall
His lips father my days
Other loves have come and have gone away
And he never dreams in the light of day

[The Life Beyond]

———

I must learn how to live, how to be enough, how to believe in myself. Be independent, self-sufficient, passionate about my solitude, my freedom. And to not be these things with the hopes of earning his love, or because I must live without him, but to do them for myself, *myself*. To create myself. Open your eyes. Create.

———

I've been thinking about François Truffaut's film *The Story of Adèle H.*[8] It's about a woman who puts all of her energy (her genius) into the pursuit of a love (desire) she imagines. This grandiose mystification over a man drives her to madness. Her writing, crushed by her father's, remains blundering, inconsequential. She propels her creative energy toward this preposterous love. (The banal man becomes everything to her.) Alienation: to see the quest for love as the only possible avenue of self-realization, to give oneself to another to the point of self-destruction. Adèle H, a genius assassinated. (Her father: "the Father," a reigning power in the literary world, which has made him wealthy.) A world she can neither renounce nor attain. She feverishly writes in her crazy journal. Her entire quest for perfection, her life force, is channeled toward a man (who he is doesn't matter) to the point of madness. There is no escape from this useless waste of energy.

———

Freed of Paul, of this affair which was good for nothing but fabricating a fantasy. From now on, my time is my own. The May light inspires. Concrete travel plans. With my grant, Stéphan and I should be able to live for a good long time in France. I'm going to throw everything into contacting French publishers. Spending winter, our too-long winter, elsewhere. I will be reborn in a place where summer lasts a long time. I will get out of this desert of whiteness and finally walk in the places that live within me: Paris.

———

And yet, I have this very strange feeling, that through this rupture, this disarticulation, life itself has been returned to me, or maybe it's just that now, slowly, I'm learning to embrace it with more gusto. Maybe this is because death is so close.

———

The days are so long, and so beautiful. They astonish me with their beauty. Church skies, wind as cool as tresses, May's spring light softer than love itself. Everything gleams and glides, freshly washed by sudden downpours. I have an unbelievable hunger to live. To work on myself. I am learning all over again how to get around on my own, to be autonomous, and in my mind, everything is opening out, overwhelmed by emotion, and I am starting to realize that I never before really took advantage of the freedom I used to have, I ignored it, because my mind was manacled. From now on I shall put all my energies into living, into working on myself, and into becoming who I am. I am coming out of my shell. This spring is a real spring.

I love, and everything pleases me. The earth offers itself up, sounds, colours, and smells in conversation. I have intimations of different faces, other hands, so many places out in the country, and I feel capable of writing a book. (Will I succeed?)

Right now, there's a lot of talk about the psychosomatic ori-gins of cancer. Cancer comes from a mental deficiency. Anxiety? A refusal to live? Emotional excess? Solitude? Financial problems? The refusal to fight back, to show anger? What's the truth? Where does this leprosy come from?

A split personality, one normal, the other searching for affection. Maybe, in my case, the feeling that I can never really live my life, be in it, as a subject, has transformed into a hatred of my body and a desire to destroy it.

But right now, spring is sparkling inside of me. Poetry presses against my temples, asks to come out, and laughs. The source feels inexhaustible, a steady sun-drenched inebriation. I look at Stéphan, my beautiful love. I look at all the handsome men smiling on this afternoon, I follow their bodies with my eyes. They make me want to live. I have never before felt so moved to see the gold of early morning, to feel the grass come up, O, this light breeze, to hold a book of poetry in my hands and to believe I am holding the very heart of the earth, or God himself.

———

Monday, May 22, 1978
The Life Beyond is completely finished. I'm already thinking about my next book, *Environments*.

———

June 2, 1978
The scent of the earth after a rain shower washes the senses right down to the heart

———

CIRCUMSTANCES OF A TRIP, OR ENVIRONMENTS

Passionate return to writing. I have been silent for at least a month. I am learning how to walk again. I vacillate between being super-discouraged and dimly hopeful. I'm getting ready for my trip to France. I dream about it every day.

I'm no longer interested in the kind of poetry I've been writing. I'm more into hybrid texts of prose-poetry, a kind of unclassifiable writing, rigorous and, most importantly, free, written in an almost single burst, a creeping ivy over my daily life, one with it, a tool that can help me live better and more intensely. With my senses open to every delicate and vibrant sign the world has to offer. O, a long journey to write.

May the long branches of our sad thoughts be driven into you.

———

Love stood there like a timeless pillar, unassailable and passionate, and the days may well have been unconscious pearls polished by dreams about travel, clothes, and faces. I always came back to it: the thought of seeing him just once more after being apart for so long, the same irrational excitement, the same unnameable desire, the same pain, the same sad and pointless feeling. I would have wanted to get through to him with my whole body and soul, to know the truth, so that his feelings could be clarified. But he lied to me, just as Pierre lied to me, he was just as brazen, just as elusive. He slid away from me and I loved him. I had stopped imagining us together, I no longer believed in anything, though my mind continued to circle and be filled with strategies. He wasn't handsome,

I didn't like his arrogance, there was nothing of the dreamer in him, nor did he possess a social conscience. He was a man of science, with all the dryness that term implies, *not* a philosopher. He felt no concern about the direction the world is heading in, about technology, or the power specialists have over our fate. Given that everything I believe in was antithetical to him, I have no idea why I was attracted to him. It must have been his prestige and indifference. I fought against my feelings of dispossession, pounced on my confusion, no matter what form it came in, and when I sensed the onset of this malaise, I interrogated the root cause and dismantled it. Slowly I learned how to walk again, I sat down in the mall and flipped through books and brochures about France and Paris. I dreamed of being there. I enjoyed doing nothing this summer, going shopping for a new dress, eating out, having friends over. It was a humid and mild summer, filled with smells that reminded me of being out on the porch during my childhood. The future felt full of possibility and pleasures. I felt confident that Paris, that France, would give fresh inspiration to my poetry, that it promised to give my work a renewed energy and hopefulness. The days had a rosy feeling and I kept things light, at a surface level, like a convalescent slowly recovering her taste for food, the lovely feeling of sheets resting lightly on her ailing body. My spirit had been shredded and needed to breathe in comforts and do nothing. I asked my misery to take its claws from around my throat. Stéphan was a sweet companion and I loved him without constraint or reserve. There were times when I felt that we were no longer distinguishable, the one from the other.

Whenever I looked at my body I fell into fits of despair. I found myself hideous. I couldn't imagine taking off my clothes in front of a stranger. Also, my ferocious desire for Paul, it was baseless, a bit idiotic and off. I wanted him as if I was someone else, as if I would be a different person in his arms, with a new body, and with a completely different background. A young girl without ties, who has her freedom of movement and inspires boundless passion. I should have written a novel for him, and maybe I will write one. I wanted to give him the gift of my face, and I was sure of nothing but him. Sometimes he struggled to look at me, but I strongly doubt that this had anything to do with love. More likely it was his own image reflected in my eyes that flattered and troubled him (the way that a look registering discomfort at the other's love can be mistaken for a look of affection). Going to Paris, that will be my way of untying myself from him for good. I won't see him anymore, my desire will go dormant and eventually evaporate. Then I can discover other desires, less complicated and more delicious, desires that won't scar me or leave this bitter taste in my mouth. While I wasn't looking the stones have built a temple inside me. It will soon take its place as part of the catalogue of faces engraved within me, this love choker I wear, which at times can feel heavier than death. I was mute in his presence, overwhelmed by my confusing feelings. What does he remind me of? What makes him so attractive to me? What I imagine. What I imagine ...

———

June 19, 1978

I'm here, and then suddenly everything becomes a part of me (this is how it feels). I think of the many distant places I know well. I am but the mark these places and the people I've known have left on me, and the mark that I have left (in even miniscule, unintended ways) on them. I no longer have a single regret, I watch from the shadows, I witness your body and its absence.

A day of wonders
stones and secrets

———

The faces are fading away.

What if Paul prefers young men? Some men feel such contempt for women that even if they have sex with women, they might as well be homosexuals. I feel incredibly tormented by this idea, seeing as everywhere I look, I see that women have absolutely no say over sexuality, so male homosexuality seems like just another aspect of masculine power. In this case, men aren't even our partners. They create clans where desire moves exclusively between them, chasms in which female desire is completely lost. And as far as all those who are not homosexuals, how many actually love women? I see the sexes as two unbearable solitudes. Since I've been sick, I can see it in some of their eyes, a contempt for my body now that it has lost its charm. But Stéphan is still as in love with me as before, and his example helps me to have faith that the solitude of the sexes is not without remedy.

But who is he, this man who has lived with me for more than three years, whom I think I know so well that I no longer feel any need to write about him? He is so *here* that I cannot imagine him. I don't use words as a substitute or a trap to monopolize his love. His love is a gift, like the wind, the sea, a peach. He is sweet and familiar. He has the inexhaustible body of a teenager. My desire will never deplete it. He is the "one," an indescribably secure partner, always on offer, never fulfilled. His deep love is like life-restoring waters. He is the companion of my dreams, my most intimate friend, my sure thing. When I'm with him I never feel bored. I can be myself, just as if I were alone and not ill.

———

I write nothing, perfect nothing, live nothing. I busy myself with the laundry and think about the weather, then your image intermixes with thoughts about poetry, reminding me of deeper things. But I run away from this synonym for pain and unsatisfied desire, at least I try to.

Madness O major sea of desire

Writing closely connects me to the present, to what's lived. I am the unknown curve of hours. To construct a text from the roots and the sap. When my life stops and my dreams face a dead end, when my life stagnates, I experience this vague desire to write a novel. To let my imagination write the life I have been refused. Now I want to write texts that do not partake in any known system of writing. Close to poetry, without actually being it. A text both narrative and musical.

———

I can feel that I'm in the middle of a transition. I will no longer put up with the slightest grief or constraint. I don't want to think about Paul, that's a sterile desire and I don't want frustration to be the source of my writing. Sometimes I have a vision of my sad little child self sitting on the porch, just like a little make-believe boat.

———

I wait for my departure date as if it were the second coming. The longer the wait, the more it feels like it will never arrive. *The air is so sweet it fends off death* ... To at last discover life's sweetness. To be filled with wonder.

———

At times there's a certain coolness in the woods of the town's with-
ered countryside. In spite of the crazy commotion, a certain silence
of wings. It stems from a miraculous breeze that moves over our
feet, as enlivening as a burst of sea water. The leaves turn over and
display their silvery underside, and I see another sea breeze filtering
through the sky, which glides by the chain-link fence, hides shyly in
the curtain, gives ordinary objects new breath. Absence is forgotten.
This morning there are tears in my eyes, which I have not let fall, in
my stomach the feelings of a dream I failed to achieve. Your hands
on me, your hands. And the air with its flower-filled sweetness is a
living source, reanimating textures, crystalizing the light, teaching
me about stones, the secret breath of the material world. Life seems
eternal. (The pleats of the chair's fabric turn into a sculpture, the
colours are a painting, the wind a watermelon. The dream suddenly
comes into being, my love for you contains all the summers.)

[*Prose poems*]

———

1. The cool air like the sea in the leaves reawakens all my dreams
2. The cool air like the sea in dreams reawakens all the leaves
3. The cool air like the leaves in the sea reawakens all my dreams
4. The cool air like dreams in the leaves reawakens the sea
5. The cool air like the leaves in dreams reawakens the sea

Return Trip Ticket[1]

Poetry as a fixed point, almost religious (cultural), the sacred centre around which the world was built: Paris.

Disillusionment: inspiration made profane, and by extension "the place" of writing.

Places of remembrance: place made sacred (poetry).

Disillusionment about Paris: a profane place, meaning I did not receive a single "vision" there. Abrupt feeling of being in the presence of something sacred the first time I saw the ocean, and New York. None of this is connected to anything, really, except to an emotional way of looking at things. For I have made these places sacred to my inner life, enhanced by the fact that my experience of them was so fleeting.

Montréal, a sacred city because it's filled with memories. My former haunts, places where I may have once formed an impression, had a conversation or encounter, even though they have nothing inherently magical about them, move me. I should keep my distance from these sorts of exalted feelings from now on, dig into less fugitive depths, "religious," but rational, lucid.

———

December 7, 1978
A meeting with Paul. Kisses. His manner was different, more expressive. Surprise.

———

It continues to snow. The silence disturbs me. Every side of me is walled off. No movement inside of me, nothing reaches out toward another world. I see the universe fragmented into a million insignificant places (or bearers of the same message, of the same pain). I do not want you to confuse your silence with mine. I know that my hair, my hands, my eyes have only one chance to cry out. You, you are a flight into chaos. I am a secular paralysis, desire's relentlessness. Don't run from me again, don't stay an enigma. I dare not ask a single question, I stand at your threshold as if on a threshold that admits no trespass. Gripped by a ludicrous shyness, the fear of driving you away by making even the slightest wrong move, of insinuating myself somewhere I'm not wanted. I'm on the verge of you as on the verge of tears.

[Prose poems]

———

SECRET LOVE

When I think of him, I remember our night walks through the hospital's corridors. I was frightened by some of the rooms with their doors ajar. I turned away from those exposed bodies, stretched out, wounded, curled in on themselves with insomniac fear, or asleep, faces marked by a rediscovery of an original sadness. The hospital was a dark labyrinth, punctuated at regular intervals by little reddish lights. At every turn a Caryatid kept watch under her lamp. He seemed so majestic when he walked, so at ease in this funereal maze. We talked but did not follow the thread of a conversation. I was too preoccupied by my desire. My feelings ennobled the bleachy smell of the floor tiles and the morbid lethargy of this place, through which we alone seemed to wander.

The hospital is the last place my memory has made sacred, now I absolve every countryside, every atmosphere, and him, I deny him everything he wants, theoretically. I want him to be anonymous, ridiculous, hungry, alone, and unsuccessful in his ambitions.

There are times when I have this vision of thousands of women walking. Their solitude is so vast and so moving. It is so much like my own, and mine like theirs. It gives me a strange feeling of being swallowed up by the universe, as if the whole of the cosmos is moving through my heart, making me completely transparent. In point of fact these crowds of women are dead, engulfed by a never-ending oblivion. Whenever I have a feeling of infinity, or eternity, I think about the solitude of these women. God didn't just abandon them, he killed them. Their solitude goes deeper than our memories and will never come to an end.

———

To make love profane: abolish the mystical idea of the other's body, make it profane, penetrated, known; exalt the differences and maintain the hidden (profane) character of each human being. To demystify the other, making their body a sign of nothing more than itself. Body and self indistinguishable. So that love is hidden, by which I mean inside of us, and ongoing. So that the body and thoughts of the other become one. Those places that our fundamental fear, and our desire for a spiritual safe haven, have made sacred, would no longer be mysterious, they would merely be hidden. Fear of the other would recede. We would want them to keep their secret, not to subjugate them, but to enter into complicity with them. To make them profane, to accept them as different, but connected to us. Not to base our relationships on some notion of mystical possession, but on the rationality of what's hidden, of desire, of words exchanged.

Mystification: fear, which becomes mystery (wish to subjugate).
Hidden secret: recognition, modesty, the desire to love.

———

Now my poetry is coming back to me in wave after wave of despair.
I want to run away, to become familiar with sunny places, far away
from here, on my own, to start my life completely over, my exis-
tence. To sever myself from memory and forget all these shadows,
the people I miss, the cold, the vast tombs all around me.

———

Friday, [December] 15, [1978]
A short derailing conversation with Paul. I feel like everything
around me is coming undone, disappearing, scattering. I feel myself
becoming a stone, bizarre, solitary, and recessed, even though out-
wardly ebullient. I used to notice the slightest atmospheric changes
(wind, light, oh sea, you've been so good to me!) but now I am
becoming increasingly oblivious to life's changes (colours, sounds,
shapes), and even love had lost its wondrous aspect. There's noth-
ing but cold desire, naked, lacking passion, lacking "ambience."
Yet I still have the melodramatic feeling that I'm bearing the entire
burden of desire on my own. The men are careful, petty, super-
pleased with themselves, static, depressing to see and depressing to
love. And I blame myself for being divided, for loving several men,
each differently. I, too, am a *Spy in the House of Love*.[2] But the
house of love is a rigid tomb, ancient and labyrinthine. I hate all old
things, things that bring back memories and attachments. I wish I
didn't have a past. I want to be constantly in the present, changing
myself each day, changing my world and continually remaking who
I am out of this dismal solitude. Poetry used to be my ground, but

now I'm completely exiled. I have nothing more to say, to live. Despair stalks me, for I know that I am out of tune with myself. But who am I, with whom can I find a rhythm, who can I connect with in this insomniac night where I now reign supreme? What do I want? Who do I love? And why am I so listless about doing any sort of work, so disappointed in my love affairs, and why has my heart gone cold? Since September 1977 I have been destroying myself bit by bit, I am descending into the unknown. What am I afraid of? What is suffocating me? Why do I feel so terribly alone even though Stéphan loves me? And why doesn't love fill this wound, and why does the entire world, life, and my very self disappear into this wound? I feel as if every day is an uphill struggle. Yes, every day is impossible, every day I fall farther. Death doesn't frighten me. It would give me sweet rest, at last, no going back.

———

What a dreadful feeling of precarity, and how disconcerting to realize that the man I love unapologetically, hopelessly and therefore absurdly, could lose me in the crowd for three weeks or longer if he so chooses, can, if he pleases, sever our connection, cut off all communication and leave me crying out in vain with no hope of reaching him. He has total control over when and if we see each other. I have no power over him whatsoever, especially not the power to make him forget himself, nor to make him love me more than I love him.

I had the strength to break with him for four months, but find myself in the same place as before I left, except that he takes one more step toward me, then stops at a safe distance, indecisive and cruel. He has no idea the extent to which I am dependent upon him, so much so that I've become speechless. Sometimes I love him to the point of wanting to die. I hate this dependence. No one knows how close to the edge of madness this desire has taken me; if he knew the extent of my suffering, he would laugh at its childishness. But I want him, tenderly, cruelly, stupidly, my appetite for him is like a thirst never slaked, the flavour of burnt grass.

At this moment there's a diffuse light over the Place des Nations. *We are alone, isolated in our disquiet. Alone before silent galaxies on imperfect and circumscribed nights. Around our faces the city creates muffled clearings. And already you've nothing left but the shadow of his two greedy hands, my eyes fixated on the impossible. We are no longer mad nor the divine breath of infinity, questioned in our bodies by the elements of pleasure, night for us is an underground lake and dawn is the stone it polishes. We wander through the springtime on overload, lowering our eyes toward our dismantled legs. Our world comes to an end and we are shaken by so much solitude. Speak to me before the sluice gates of despair open. As the hours progress I welcome you more and more, like a breath in the extravagant middle of April.*

[*Prose poems*]

———

Demythologized: a world of chaotic signs, yet at the same time a love of one's surroundings. A love recorded in the quickness and fragility of the moment. Always destroying the recognizable signs, except when seeking knowledge of words and of the real, otherwise always.

Knowing without memory, to break free of the chains of the past, destroy history, accept the precariousness of eternity, its dreamworld and illusion. To invest writing with a new freedom. Purify the language, give it song, rhythm, destroy its carapace, its armour, make it orgiastic, vegetal, in symbiosis with the body.

Raze it to ruins, reach the sand, the water, the wheat fields, the wind. Listen to the contemporaneity of snow or sun.

———

[December 26, 1978]

I feel sick to have left Paris, not because I loved it so much, but because I left a part of myself behind and, now that I have returned to Montréal, I'm four months older, and my time there seems so unreal. When will I ever find the Marie I was in Paris again, so that I can walk down the cobblestone streets, cast my eyes on the glow of the old stones, those flaming ruins of memory and evening?

My illusions and this torment are making me obsess over Paris. But I wandered through those months like a sleepwalker, and now I'm doing it again. But only Paris can create this feeling. When in Paris, I tortured myself with thoughts of the hospital and my past lovers. My mind became entangled in a whole sequence of images, which is happening again with these thoughts about Paris, since it too has become part of my past. And my present is nothing but waiting, horrible waiting. Stuck between two moments of inspiration, two stories, I have become nothing. I am neither she who tried, yet failed, to find out who she was while in a hospital in Montréal, but especially in the French countryside and the streets of Paris, nor am I the person who I will be when I wake up tomorrow. But who is this woman, where is she, who I am running to find? I cut my ties, I drift outside of the world and myself. I think of the things in my storehouse of landscapes, atmospheres, and faces, they grow dimmer by night. I can only see fleeting glimpses of them now, which tear me to bits. Why? Why I am so drawn to running away, to being elsewhere? I want to embrace my life to the fullest, but right now I can't figure out how to go on or where to go, what life might be able to give to me, or even springtime.

I can no longer take this mediocre little life. It's December 26. We haven't seen each other since December 15. The words I use are too old, the way I use them is so tired, I'm not finding them, nor my sentences, or rhythms, and my images are as tired as hackneyed films or those atrocious surrealist paintings. I want to cross everything out.

———

December 28, 1978

I can no longer stand the hellish whiteness of this country, nor my life, nor myself. Night mixes with day in the same singular white horror. I am no longer anything, I no longer do anything, I am but the shadow of what I could have been. If only I could make my life as vast as my desires, break with these tormented thoughts destroying my every attempt to think differently about my life, my surroundings, and myself. I'm the mirror of the icy sun streaming between the dry branches until it crystallizes into a yellow death. Everything is always on edge, about to fall into terror, pure babble, drooling insipidity, the absurd. Everywhere I look, my life is made up of nonsense. Neither this world, nor myself in the window, have a single reason to exist. Every second of every action is stupid. I constantly ask myself how I can possibly go on. The hours weigh heavily, like tombs. My existence is weighed down with the ennui of the entire world. My life seems so mediocre to me and the future so much like the past I draw back from it, panicky and dizzy. I want to invent my life, to enrich it with vistas, experiences, and passionate love affairs. I want it to be a fascinating, mad enterprise, burning with encounters, a long sentimental adventure, but it stretches out before me as colourless as my mother's life and the lives of all the other women I know. Silence is castrating, men are antique statues, dismembered, decapitated, pitiful in their ephemeral splendour. They are handsome, without secrets or nervous energy. And daily life, my source of enthusiasm and pleasure, crumbles in my hands, disintegrates before my lips, and disappears. My source of smells, colours, and memories has dried up. No matter how hard I try to stay myself, I retrieve only tatters from my mind's kingdom, skeletons, fragments of images. I am terrorized, immobilized, voided, dispossessed. No country, no mystery, no love affair arrives to fill this void, the vast destructive operation of desire, its implacable torrent, its mad and useless entreaty, reverberating through every second of my time and every corner of my space. The sounds and voices coil in on themselves, gestures are left unfinished, the eyes have fallen asleep, everything is just this waiting and the struggle against this waiting. I know that it can be a trap, a shackle, a prison, a well from which I might not emerge tomorrow, fierce and moving forward, filled with attitude and energy. I fear that this waiting is siphoning off my lifeblood, my intellectual strength, making me shaky and neurotic, filled with hate for myself and possessed of but one word, already so insistent within me: destroy.

Yes, the wisdom of destruction ...

——

December 31, 1978

Now one city replaces another, but their walls breed the exact same light. Here, just like on the embroidered and embittering Paris streets, I feel like I'm being suffocated by a conspiracy of cold empty space, buried beneath the same deleterious gloom under the same stone sky. All around me life closes off, as if facing the horror of death or the end of the world. Here, as elsewhere, the flesh is closed, wounded, in every sensitive fold and crease, the slightest shudder of its dreams, the shallowest breath of its beauty. Pleasure has deserted our faces.

When I woke up this morning I was confronted by my age. I saw myself through the eyes of my twenty-year-old self, having just published my first volume of poems. I was so proud. I told myself that by the time I turned twenty-four I would have accomplished so much more than I have. I will turn twenty-four in April. Suddenly spring feels so near: awkward executioner of my love affairs. Twenty-three winters, every one of them has been the same nightmare of sleeping and waiting. It's been three years since my grandfather died. His shadow follows me, so familiar and yet more and more distant. It's been a year since I crawled out of my tomb, utterly crushed, secretly in love, and here I still am, confronting the same heartbreak, incapable of changing the grotesque and petty trajectory of my life. My life has become uninhabitable, limited, with no common measure between my trembling hands and my ever-growing desire. I dream of a sultry winter, filled with gleeful secrets and intermingling, and of a springtime drenched in profound renewal. The windowpanes were pierced by pale yellow and delicate blue, it was noon, my love, when you turned to me, just for a second, and in that sudden vision I saw your face betray your love for me. O, the joy I felt was like a pointless premonition (a premonition that we'd have another springtime filled with passion, pointless because we probably won't) and my pain over this beautiful moment, forever wasted.

———

In these times maybe there's nothing else, neither within us, nor throughout the whole world. Our provisional and rigid modern constructions and the endless suffering going on in every country have made everything go dark. Sickness mounts, freedoms are shredded, and the frail face of love is lacerated by the thousand hatreds of fallen man.

———

January 5 [1979]

I've never seen someone's eyes so full of desire. He wants to keep me at a distance, because he's afraid, and at the same time he doesn't want to, because he wants me, I think. He is domineering, resolute, egotistical, and careful. I don't think he loves me, he is just experiencing some form of desire. Everyone says he's honest. I think he's dishonest, but well meaning, in other words, mainly dishonest with himself. Because of this situation, I am alone and he is alone too, maybe. It's a struggle between my pride and my alienation.

All poetry has pulled away from me, all the words have left. Suddenly nothing seems important anymore and, day or night, there are no insights to comfort me. I am like a semi-blind person, sudden bursts of light hit my iris, yet I cannot make out any shapes in full. I am disoriented, at loose ends, worried (financially and emotionally), and all possible futures seem boring and mediocre. In the hospital, I made up powerful dreams to keep myself alive. I imagined that when I got out an entire life of passion awaited me, a life of chance encounters, of emotion, exchanges, stimulating apprenticeships, of writing. But nothing has changed, just the opposite, ever since I was released everything has become colourless. I've accomplished absolutely nothing but this arduous and tedious re-education in how to live my everyday life: learning how to walk again, to move through the city without being afraid, the return of the old problems of money, of having to get a job.

I am perfectly useless. Who reads poetry, who cares about what I create? No one. So, what use is it? Should I do something else? But I love to write poetry. I hate novels and I don't have the meticulous, peremptory spirit of an essayist. I wish I could take courses in theatre production, but I doubt I would be able to find the money.

———

How is it possible not to recognize that it's what we share that makes us who we are, not some extraordinary and never-before-seen mystery? There's an outward uniformity and an inward conviction that the self is everything (alienation). Yet each life is but a record of other lives, as well as our shared words and concepts. We are all using the same code, inscribed by the same vast silence.

We see the journey and backdrop of our lives through the exact same lens: well-worn habits, clichéd love affairs. In this shared room, anticipation and kisses lie dormant beneath our emotions. (Exoticism and sad passions.) In every movie, novel, and picture our emotions are fabricated, reproduced, guided, spelled out. Our encounters with each other are no longer imaginative or strange. We don't really know anyone, walled up, shielded by our ennui, our fears and our sleeping eros.

———

Nightly rate: the price of a hotel stay, from noon to the following noon.

NIGHTLY RATE

poems written on the typewriter

———

January 8, 1979

I'm wandering down a highway cutting through fields, low snow-covered suburbs, undifferentiated wastelands blanketed in heavy whiteness. Then there's nothing, nothing before me but my death. There's nothing more I can do, I don't want to fight, I want to stop trying, to shatter my dreams, drown the images, put the faces to sleep. To be transparent to infinity. To be the mirror, water's reflection, implacable azure. All my hungers have vanished, all the light, at times I hear a distant music, reawakening a shadow. Like a filmic sequence, my love's desire loops on replay. He leans over me like a man leaning over an open precipice, a well, a ravine, a river, the vastness of glaciers, of destroyed cities, barricaded buildings, the open maw of death, decomposing nights. I am from nowhere, from wastelands, from anonymous American suburbs, monotonous seasons, faceless landscapes and crowds. From poverty, from despair.

Last year his eyes were grey and now they are a very pale green.

———

[January 9, 1979]

Visit from Paul. He holds back, wants to stop everything. Says that he doesn't love me enough to answer to all I ask of him, yet touches me deliciously while saying this. He won't speak to me anywhere but in the apartment, alone. He says he's afraid that having an affair would cause us both to suffer even more (him especially), despite claims that he has no particular feelings for me. Yet I think he loves me more than he knows. Before leaving, he couldn't bring himself to let go of me. Kisses. Said to me: "You are beautiful, you are sweet."

He couldn't stop looking at me, hugging me, pressing himself to me, tenderly, then suddenly very forcefully.

———

NIGHTLY RATE
poems

traces of wolf tracks in the snow
in the field of lickety-split
in the field of my memory an open wound
an open wound
— Jean Charlebois [*marie marie*]

———

January 10, 1979

I'm afraid. I'm stuck, castrated, frustrated from being in love with a dream, and suffering like a mutilated beast. Once again, I am fighting against despair and death. Again, I am completely alone. It was no longer possible for our bodies to be apart. (What a pathetic soap-opera sentence). Yet all of this is really happening, yesterday again, and I can no longer give him up, but he has no problem being apart. He is smitten, then puts me out of his mind. He is hard and distant. I feel exhausted from wandering through this labyrinth, just as I felt a fall ago when I was lost in that labyrinth of bodily pain. And today, fixated on him, I face the same death, and I'm battling through a sleepless night, an endless night with neither rest nor dreams, hoping to bring forth my life, so it will still exist, so it will remain strong, naked, invincible, daring. My passion has fitted me with these strange blinders, and now he has gone away, back into the silence of his power, the comfort of his age, his family, his fame. I would like to take an axe to that watertight world, closed, sure of itself, mediocre and workaday, that sleepwalking universe sinking into smugness, fear, and ennui, filled with hatred for the heart and the other. On foot in a landscape of freeways I feel alone, my pain a suburban wasteland, a road blindly leading from one city to another. I fall to pieces, I sink further down but don't give up. I cry out but no one hears me. I know that he loves me, though he won't admit to it. I write like a fool, like a neurotic teenager. I am having a crisis of words, of images, of sounds. Poetry is dead in me. Nothing can fill its absence, nothing can relieve my distress. Yesterday, overcome, he said to me: "No more talk between us." And I responded: "It's you who keeps talking." And he acquiesced. My words, useless and absurd, caught in my throat. He says I'll forget him, but I haven't. I will never forget him, and if he chooses to be with me, he will never be alone. He thinks I'm just going to let this thing go. He is afraid of me, of suffering, he feels no passion for me. Says he doesn't love me as I love him. Yet, he becomes so passionate whenever we embrace, he looks at me, finds me beautiful, his face betrays him. He trembles at the thought of leaving me. He promises to return, but I know that these absences work against me, for there's no place for me in his normal life, and I become more abandoned than an orphan, more broken than a dead child. My days stretch out before me like a block of solid granite, solitary stones, my nights sickened from reliving this nightmare of desire. I write like an imbecile so I won't go crazy, so that I won't freeze to death, so that winter won't become a cage with no exit. I write to bring on the spring and make summer a saferoom to protect my world from total collapse. I am in the middle of a labyrinth with no Ariadne to guide me, because I am not Theseus, but Ariadne, confronting the monster that is herself. Fighting. And even if I kill the monster, and get out on my own, it must not be for any light but the light of his face, for he has created this shadow, frightened and upset by the intensity of my love. Twenty years ago, he says. Who was he twenty years ago that would have made him love me more?

I don't give a damn if I love him more than he does me, I love him enough for the both of us. I'm going to ask him to let me love him, just to let it happen. To give us a little something. I know that he doesn't want to give anything, not even a chance. Yesterday I pulled out all the stops, rocking his world, I couldn't have done it against his will, this man who kept insisting that he had to go, yet took me in his arms and let me touch him, touched me. He promised to love me, but I know that he doesn't keep his promises and yet I'll keep waiting, so long as there remains even a little bit of life in me.

———

Haven't I been living as if tethered to him for months now, partly because he's been encouraging me? And wasn't last night confirmation of what I always suspected he was feeling when he looked at me? And I'm not just imagining how many times he's gone from being frosty to affectionate. After my four months away, it was he who sought me out, who wanted to rekindle these feelings. But as soon as he did, he pulled away. Maybe he's not aware of the game he's playing. That must be right. He loves that I love him, that's all there is to it.

The light is cold and blond, reminding me of the Magdalen Islands. I see the alluvial fans, the large, lonely dunes, the hard colour of the ocean, the obdurate winds, the tempestuousness, the examination of form and matter, the sad mystery of those last birds trapped by the tides. I've wasted my life. I've never let myself go really wild. I've been resigned and miserably sad. I haven't loved all of the men I could have loved, nor have I laughed enough, seen enough, tasted enough, loved enough.

It's too late to learn how to live, I no longer know what to do, where to go, what I love, or what I want. I have no idea what might make me feel passionate, if not my love, which expands and devours me without pity. I can't even write, all the words about love have been used to death and my spirit is broken.

Everything in its place and each hour in its secret building. The shadows accumulate around us, the days keep us apart. With every thought my hand is back in yours, I glide my face down your body again, surprised by your shortness of breath. I return your caresses. With every thought I make love to you again, with the same deep moan, the same desertion of the world in our eyes.

[*Prose poems*]

Nightly Rate

Waiting — Forgetting[1]

Some nights the light hitting the bricks turns red and the frost becomes a violent, nuanced, superb blue. It's almost unreal. Everything floods with solitude. The city turns geometrical and aggressive and the colours flooding into the rooms make the wood gleam, the lamp's light soften. Making love becomes a struggle, more urgent. Absence bites your eyelids, long and hard.

———

I suspect that there are two different kinds of nationalism. One is connected to the lover, the other to the mother. So, one is erotic and liberating (in the Reichian sense of the word), and the other is castrating and repressive, turning country into "homeland," into "motherland." The first is invested in keeping the country among the living, the other in maintaining the homeland's power. This latter speaks the language of the dead. Therein lies the difference between fascist discourse and nationalist poems such as Gaston Miron and Pablo Neruda write. The "lover" nationalism opens itself to the world, and to the other. It makes language erotic, multiple, and free from all formal constraint, while in the "mother" version of nationalism, language is castrated, underdeveloped, reduced to its fears and silences. The face of the whole world is hidden behind all that isn't said. The important thing is to be open to the other, to accept his or her secret. It's not by dominating the other that we affirm the self, but through convergence and exchange, in other words, eroticism. To know is to live. Fascism is control, a state of death. Fear. Fear of the other: sexuality. Fear of passion, fear of responsibility, fear of solitude. A true nationalism is the living affirmation of the self as a social entity. Memory is also inscribed in the body. Solidarity with those of your sex and of your country (sharing the same culture, habits, language, and fantasies, maybe also the same terrain, history, and future). Not being afraid of the other inside of you. Of the woman sleeping inside the man. And this is precisely why men, afraid, have always hated women, and sometimes the other, the Jew, the Black. Don't ever tell them that they are "sensual, perverse, jolly, nonchalant, stupid," in other words, not calcified but alive. And all the phantasms and fears that man projects onto women, Blacks, Jews, the devil, and so on, are merely the part of himself he doesn't want to acknowledge: his erogenous body, life. The devil is a part of life, but in his ignorance, man contemptuously calls this the "animal part," seemingly unaware that therein lies the very essence of his existence.

(There's that sad music again, coming from the empty room.) Miron does not conflate the love of country with maternal prohibition, but with desire and the other, the body of the beloved, a woman filled with the promise of life.

———

The life beyond is when you are no longer *in* life, but looking at it, trying to find a way in. Not dead, but on the brink of life, near birth, in the process of being born, perhaps, in the middle of that journey beyond borders and outside of time that is characterized by desire. Desire for the other, desire for the world. So that your life pours out, as if from a bloated wineskin, yet you still remain at a distance. The life beyond in the sense of *beyond* the sea or *beyond* the grave. You must go past preconceived notions, prejudices, fears, and habits, move beyond obtuse reality to a reality both more painful and more pleasurable: the unknown, the hidden, the contradictory. Open the senses up, learn from them. Move through the opacity of silence to a place where nothing is predictable or fated, a place where we can really invent our lives and our loves.[2]

———

January 17, 1979

We finally slept together. After so many months of wanting to, it was *more* than about time. I've dreamt for so long of being close to him, and now I feel both a sense of clarity and sadness, because I feel afraid for the future. I know that I love him. I miss his body already. But what can he give me? Nothing, in fact. I am reduced to an intolerable solitude. Either I must keep lying to Stéphan or forget about *him*. At least pretend to forget about him. Go on living after this new defeat, this heartbreak, I must live with all of it. But I'm what's important here, my survival. I wonder what's going to kill me. I have to start writing again. And why do I feel like I'm suffocating, like my mouth is filled with snow? The weather is atrocious, this winter intolerable, deadly. I feel trepidatious because he's made up his mind never to leave his family, and I don't want some half-way thing. I don't want to be the one waiting around for whatever time he can stop by; I don't want to waste my time waiting, alone, longing for him. And yet, if I don't have him, and I keep on living just like before with Stéphan, my body will feel so hollow. I am caught in a trap. I want to run away, but I can't stand being alone. Why can't I manage to write anything except these dumb scribblings? Could it be that I'm dead already, my mouth shut and eyes closed because I'm so totally miserable? And above all why, why can't Stéphan satisfy my body? Why doesn't he answer to all my fantasies? Write …, write … Translate this malaise, this slow death, this painful contortion into life, into love? I never want to fake it. I hate myself for lying. But I *need* his body. His smell still lingers on my hands. Me, I've rushed into a tunnel and I can no longer see a light at its end. If I at least had a decent job, I would be spared all this time lost in misery and thought ...

I've become like a block of granite. I don't want to lose Stéphan, he's my best friend, and I've always shared everything with him. But for now, I can't share this thing. This chill. I refuse to be anyone's mistress. In all my love affairs I want to be a woman with a man. Everything must be equal. I will not give more than I am given.

Why does nothing appease me, no place, word, or dream? And why is my desire for the impossible so over the top? I want to be a poet, completely and transparently, and never lie. The calm suits me, welcoming each new day as full and alive, a gift of light. I must choose to be happy. It wasn't so long ago that I had cancer, and could have died, it was just a question of a few weeks at most, and here I am, alive. I should sink my teeth into every moment, every colour. Not zone out or let things get to me. All loves are possible, so why can't more than one face fit into the heart?

Even though I'm stuck in this room, I still stroll through Montréal. I see giant curtains of cold hitting the brown and red brick, a faint calligraphy on the windows, giant blind eyes of the occasional car probing whichever streets are still passable. How hostile this city seems to me, with its metal and neon facades, nothing but silences and solitude, how ugly with its port concealing the river's whiteness, its fantastical factories like black palaces behind the squalls of snow. Wastelands, bituminous construction sites, naked light bulbs, waiting rooms, and the horrible lunar glow of the street lights. How can anyone stand a city of such hardness, humiliation, alienation, exhaustion, renunciation. I see the trapped expressions, crushed from the emergency room to the hospital, the open wounds that never stop bleeding, and I see the blank expressions, mute in the cafés, the brasseries, staring out but no longer seeing. Expressions mutilated by abrupt gusts of fear, of prejudice. Hated city, mirror

of myself, I will never be able to part from you. I resemble you
with your bad neighbourhoods under gap-mouthed skies, resem-
ble you with your seedy buildings, your cracks. City sacrificed to
the comedy of madness, theatre of my meagre memory and lame
regrets. I hunger for you down to your entrails ... but aren't you
the one who is devouring me? Aren't you the one disfiguring me,
bit by bit, more each day? I've lost track of where I'm going and
what I want. I look at apartments, check out your neighbourhoods,
and I imagine what it would be like to live in them. I invent lives
for myself based on nothing more than a street corner, a scene of
intimacy seen through a window, the seasonal play of light. I am writ-
ten into you, a bizarre symbol of your sorrow. You are unbearable
Montréal, with your fragrant streets winding through the moun-
tains, and those other streets, corridors where your heart beats in
the dust of contempt and ennui. In July and August, you rot inside
a pressure cooker of humidity, then your frozen cry lasts all winter
long. Your January bite chaps the soul. Nothing moves in Febru-
ary, for you have become chiselled in marble. In March you spill
tears of rage. You've no shame as ugly April, completely naked. In
May, yes, in May alone you lift your skirts and hit the lights with
your slips and smiles. (June: a poem). All the hopes you allow to
be raised by autumn are smothered to death under the weight of
December's ornamented ass.

———

The memory of what I've known and lost is so painful to me. I
always wish I could relive the experiences I loved. We attach our-
selves to people, to places, to moments. Aging is loss.

———

January 18, 1979

There are birds flitting through the powdery morning snow. You can reduce a bird to just a bird, but you can also look for their true nature, a composite of arrogance and illumination. A bird is a parcel of air, its wings are whispers changed into song, and even the little village sparrow makes music with his chirp. And the snow, why the snow, he asked me? But he already knew the answer because snow is the prettiest skin. It's hard when you have to fight just to survive or to live, to simply enjoy life. If I have battled against the intolerable fact of my death, at present I am learning how not to turn every love affair into a defeat. Love is not embittering, contrary to what he thinks. If love only makes you frustrated, if you fight in vain and never reach communion, it's alienation's fault. For in order to really live you must live moment by moment. We forget our loves and that's fine, the important thing is on the horizon, the one that hasn't shown up yet. You have to know how to routinely recreate your life, recognize your pleasure, and never miss out on it.

> *You're the death of me. You're my remedy.*
> — M. Duras

Why is it that everything I write now is so clichéd and totally obvious? Nothing moves me anymore, nothing except the same old feelings, impressions, and colours I've already described, and which have grown stale from repetition. This new affair has to stay super-secret, super uncertain. It lives inside of me in secrecy and silence. I can't live clandestinely or in shadow. I'm okay with it for a time, but only a very short time. What will become of me?

———

January 19, 1979

Over the ruins of our cities lies desire's clairvoyance.[3]

I have travelled through the blind corridors of bodily suffering and fear of death. I have travelled across, though I had no wish to, the forever unyielding country of death. Why must desire stage the same life and death struggle? And doesn't death always win, over everyone and everything? How is it that every action, word, or place can be emptied of all sense, all delight, by death's offensive ambition, by the void? (After giving me a chance, he pulls back, and now I've stopped expecting anything more from him. I am cast out of the world, numbed by unbearable pain. When my body was broken, I had to put it back together, rebuild my equilibrium, find a new way forward, use different strengths. And every time he hurts me, I grow another carapace, learn anew how to survive suffering, fear, and pain.) But why do I always feel so sure about this thing, like the advent of spring (and why can't I let it go)? Is it a dream? Am I suffering from a mad illusion I can't escape, blinded by an indestructible desire? There are times when his eyes become walls. I can see it when he folds back in on himself, when he closes the door to me, because his irises turn blue-grey steel; when he opens up, actually sees me and lets himself live, they turn green. Why do I sometimes say to myself: he *will* love me, it's inevitable? From what subtle indicators do I construct this dream, this stupid conviction, this useless belief in our future? I'm perfectly aware that we are separated by eons. Galaxies worth of history, light years of feeling … what path forward is there, if even the bodies refuse to accept each other? On one side my singular will, on the other his predicament. He said to me: "Can you teach me to be free?" I should have said I can only teach you if you want to learn. But do you really *need* to be free? And the less free you are, the more abusive, insolent, and irritating I become.

———

Why am I not writing? Have I come to realize just how little power words really have? Haven't I believed for far too long that they could remake the world and create love? Nurturing some private superstition, I bet everything on their power. Now I can see what little hold they actually have on the real. I'm sinking into a hard and inflexible reality that stifles all words. For any poem I might write would be but an incantation to make you love me, or a catharsis for my pain. But I know now that, from here on out, no word will assuage my solitude or my pain, no word will get through to you. I am reduced to silence, for I don't understand why I love you.

I realize that I have nothing to offer you but myself, and that your life's full. There's not one bit of space left. I feel so poor. My wish to give you everything would cause you to lose it all. It's funny, don't you think?

Why snow? Because snow covers the world in complete absence, is the supreme epidermis. What could possibly be more naked than snow, more open to being stared at until there's no more ugliness, no more distance, and all the banalities of our quotidian universe are eaten away, leaving only a perfect sensual form, a shoulder, a hip, maybe a stomach. Why do I want to know you so deeply, so much so that your memories would become conflated with my own, such that I could no longer distinguish the two? How strange to believe you can give someone something so essential, yet feel yourself to be superfluous. I try to imagine what your kids are like. Will they turn out to be freer, crazier, more exuberant, and alive than we are, than the people we pass by each day? And is there anything more important than the many-coloured beatings of our hearts? Right now, I can see you tensing up as you read my letter, furrowing your brow. You're always shocked when I can't figure out what's going through your mind, when I ask you to tell me things you think are too personal. In fact, I shock you often, for a ton of reasons that escape me. Also, why am I so sedentary? Why do I love it here in this sad, small, and sclerotic province that you don't even know? My roots in this place overpower both my will and my outside interests. Miró said that he inherited his vitality from the Catalonian soil. When I'm realistic with myself, I can see that this province, with its yawning gaps and colonized mentality, eats away at me. Even if I leave, go be a writer somewhere else, I'll carry it inside of me and keep coming back to it, as if it holds the key to what I'm looking for, a secret that long ago, in a time immemorial, gave birth to me. And this is also how I see you. I love you as if you could open some essential thing still sleeping inside of me, as if you too could give birth to me. (You're still furrowing your brow.) I love you in a thousand other ways and I could discover a new way each day. But what good would so much solitude do me, right?

Before the age of twenty-two, I was unacquainted with death. Now it's my double, yet I still haven't gotten used to it. Before the age of twenty-two, I was young, but now a flood of murderous water has filtered through me. Is aging just a process of becoming entrenched in absence and incomprehensibility? What use are the things I learned to believe in as a child, now that I'm being absorbed into this giant, unformed mass called time? But I am bothering you again. In fact, I will always bother you, even in defeat, even in oblivion.

———

To be gentleness all set to become violence.

———

January 27, 1979

I divide this city up until there's nothing left but impalpable suffering, yes, the dirty framework of its birth, the fragile root of its vitality. End of January, the city relaxes beneath a very gentle wind, atypical. This ephemeral April fragrance suddenly fills me with hope. (I hear the sparrows chirping at my window, making the sweetest music, such joy ...) My mind drifts and suddenly my too-narrow life, beaten down by this infernal seasonal cycle, flowers into superb visions of the future. I am no longer time's prisoner. Like this sudden apparition of sweetness in winter, my life feels suddenly sweet. My past, this nightmare, collects in every present gesture. All of a sudden, I wish to live without memory. For in my desire *not* to forget anything, I have chained myself to outdated feelings and old desires. I have become the person society wants me to be, rather than myself. I am a collection of the world's prohibitions, frustrations, and fears. I set out to overcome the alienation caused by familial fears, but now I must also leave behind society's strictures. I am victimized by my ideas about the seasons. It never feels like I decide anything, everything is imposed on me from the outside by others, by the weather. Every single winter I give up on the world and on love. I feel rejected by everything, subjected to a strange and bewildering emotional devastation. Spring is always my superficial deliverance. I use it to trick myself into fruitless dreams of one day being happy and famous. I don't feel free. I feel enslaved to delusions I did not choose. Last night, thinking about my masochistic passions, I asked myself where did I get this taste for the improbable; it prevents me from working, robs me of all well-being, all sense of peace. My reality collapses, all reasons for living are thrown into question, doing anything other than what pertains to my love seems needless and tedious. I become desire, impossible to gratify. I want those who don't want me, and those who do want me I couldn't care less about. Is this all the fault of alienation? Or is a combination of factors at play? A present I feel increasingly closed to the world, indifferent to what's around me, all I think about is escaping and the most secret of pleasures. I've been too-successfully taught that women are supposed to love others before themselves. I'm feeling less guilty, little by little ... learning to find pleasures within, not in the other, and to stop thinking everything's my fault. The only thing I'm obsessed with now is a premonition of my rebirth. The other can do nothing for me and I can do nothing for him. I'm learning how not to expect anything from anybody, but to welcome everything *freely*, without asking anything of my life and other people. Especially other people. I have always wanted to bend destiny to my will. In fact, it's a problem having to do with faith. I've always been sure that God doesn't exist and that there's no such thing as fate. As a consequence, I believed that man could master his life. But now I see that everything is subject to ineluctable laws. Sickness, love, death: I don't control anything, not even these words showing up in my head. They move through me, but I decide nothing. We have to accept that things are out of our hands, even though I have always resisted the idea that man is a victim of his times, his misadventures, his sufferings. The creation of a body of work comes from the daily creation of your life. That's what I believe. I used to tell myself that we are responsible for everything that happens to us, and that by will alone we change the course of our life. But I was wrong. My will to heal did not save my leg from amputation; my will to make the other love me did not make him do so. War, death, hate, and stupidity could descend upon the society and nothing that I might do could change that future. What I know now is that every moment is a tomb. My generation is called individualistic and egotistical, but how can we possibly maintain our illusions? Man cannot be changed, there is no way to fix the prevailing imbecility. Poetry will never have the audience of a hockey game. Life cannot be changed. How can you stop physical pain, or pollution, how can you change the obtuse mentality of men, how can you prevent some people from being victims, others masters? How can you have the nerve to talk freedom to a man subjected all year long to the infernal rhythm of a machine to "earn his living." The entire past must be destroyed in order that anything of life be saved. Humanity is too old to find the strength to start over. And then, to what end? Our destiny is not inscribed in our genes. Who knows what biology will teach us one day? Do I understand only a quarter of my drives, my desires? What iceberg, seen as but a surface sliver by my conscious mind, might lie beneath the network of my nerves, my veins, my brain?

I've always felt the misfortunes of others as a wound, the clampdowns of the world's dictatorships sear my heart, uselessly. I've always wanted Québec to be liberated, felt sickened to death by the piddling amount of dignity we have as a people, but my feelings changed nothing. It's better just to live out your life's purpose, as long as you remain true to yourself. I will never participate in the alienation of others, not out of concern for them but to remain true to myself, to love myself, out of respect for life.

What good is loving someone so ardently? I should feel passionate about myself. Why not? As Jean put it so well, it's really the only thing I have. But it seems I cannot manage to believe in myself, to love myself for real, and that I need someone else (someone chosen out of some irrational space of admiration) to have even a modicum of self-esteem. If he loves me, doesn't it prove I'm loveable? And just like that, he gives my life meaning, and his body arouses my body, gives it true dimension. I'm trapped in the Prince Charming paradigm. It's so obvious none of this has anything to do with real love. In fact, I know nothing about love, what I know about is the tenacity of my desire. Why him? Because of his seriousness, his maturity, his self-confidence, and his reserve. He's the type who never gives in, I'm the fool who thinks I can bet on him and win. It would make more sense to tackle a wall. I must resign myself to the fact that there's no hope, he doesn't love me. Yet I keep insisting on this craziness. Sometimes I calm myself down by telling myself that I'm the only thing that matters, and that I will never love again. With everything in my power, I wish I would no longer feel such attractions, only pointless and momentary passions. I would like to rip out my heart and love only myself. To no longer be subjected to the fluctuations of my feelings; to become a purely sexual being who needs to be satisfied, period. To have a spirit free to create, to be strong, superior to others. To stop feeling intimately wounded and devastated by someone. He couldn't even begin to suspect how much power he has over me. He has made me into nothing. He should have given me everything, yet he has never given me anything, not even a little tenderness, not one true confidence, not a single release. If he doesn't love me, there's no hope; if he loves me, I might make him realize it by acting indifferent to him. It's my only lifeline. But why even keep trying?

———

January 30, 1979

I want to celebrate life in all its minute subtleties, but in order to do so I have to get my body back; it may take awhile, but I must get it back. I want so much to feel a renewed interest in life, I want a non-stop eroticism to permeate everything I do and all my relationships with the world. To feel and translate life, right down to its smallest quiver. I want to write again, something completely new. To bite into existence, no holds barred. To be filled to the brim with all things tender and enchanting. And I can make up a lover for myself, sweet as the grey of summer afternoons after a storm wind lifts, hot and menacing, scratchy and soft. A wind that relieves the day's oppressive heat, that opens night to its cool refreshments. A current of air, a door creaking, the big flat sound of raindrops beginning to fall. All the paper in the street swirls up. The sky turns violet, though part of the sun sinks under the storm a few rays remain, moving the stones and trees with their play of light.

———

February 1, 1979

Note

> ... *the unconscious is structured as a private mythology. You could go even further still and assert that the unconscious is not only a "mythology," but also that some of what it contains is replete with cosmic significance; in other words, that it reflects the modalities, the processes, and the destinies of life and of living matter. You might even say that the only real contact modern man has with the cosmic sacred is through the unconscious, which acts through dreams and the life of the imagination, or through creations that come out of the unconscious (poetry, games, theater, etc.).*
> — M. Eliade [*Myth and Reality*]

———

February 2, 1979

A kind of very intense, nebulous pain has seeped into me. The pain of a weeping hawthorn tree. I hold the power of the unbelievable over you, from now on you will go away and I will shatter you.

Big suns overcast, a great blank repetition of days. We will never again be alone together in April's flights. The winds laugh in our

face, despair sneaks away. On doorsteps I see the moons interlac-
ing, sharing a beat, their breathing disrupted.

[Prose poems]

——

February 3, 1979
Your body is an elaborate mise en scène and I can no longer tell this
desire from desires past, nor separate it from my destiny. There are
too many risks, rekindling in me distant impressions, unrealized
hopes, primordial fears. It was there before I was born. This desire
expands all the others, predating my liveliest anticipations as if
from the most forgotten corner of my childhood. Now I am afraid
to let your face drift through my memories. I cling to the difficulty
of maintaining you with this ever-present desire. In each thought,
my love is immediate and ephemeral. You are ceaselessly born and
die in me. Your body is both a fixed point and a proliferation of
landscapes.[4] *My love is a dream inside a man who will never under-*
stand the extraordinarily silent mythology of little girls.

[Prose poems]

——

TOPOGRAPHIES OF LOVE

——

... there is an original fault, that of having an origin; which
falls short of the glory of atemporal being; such that the self
is not awakened to stay true to itself, but expects to learn
about the nature of light from the world of darkness.

> *Time has only one reality, that of the instant. In other words, time is reality narrowed to the instant and suspended between two voids ... the instant is already solitude ...*
>
> *... through a kind of creative violence, time demarcated by the instant isolates us not only from others but also from ourselves, because it separates us from the past we care most about ... time appears like a solitary instant, like the consciousness of a solitude.*
>
> — Bachelard, *Intuition of the Instant*[5]

It is always in the instant that life finds its first reality, *"time's true reality is the instant; the duration is but a construction, lacking any absolute reality. It is formed from without, by memory, imagination's power par excellence, which wants to dream and relive things, but not to understand them."* (Often, I project my past onto my future, looking to relive old feelings, or dreams I wish I could realize, to give myself a taste for life. My instant is unreal, sudden, because my thought is completely caught up in imagining, remembering, and projecting.)

"Thus time could be adequately represented by a white line — pure potential and possibility — upon which, like an unforeseen accident, a black dot is suddenly inscribed, a symbol of an opaque reality." (The poem inscribed as black on white.)

"We remember having been, we do not remember time passing." (My memories are clichés, of every specific thing I did.)

"Memory, guardian of time, can only store instants; it conserves nothing, absolutely nothing, of our complex and false experience of duration."

"The complex of space-time-consciousness is the essence of a tri-partite atomization, the monad affirmed in a tripartite solitude, from where it communicates neither with things, the past, or the souls of others." (This is an exact description of the misery love makes for me. Love (desire): acute consciousness of the instant. In facing the past, the future, the space which separates us, all things become unreal, my life becomes unreal. This nothing, along with an acute consciousness of myself, sucks me in. My solitude is atempo-ral and infinite, instantaneous.)

Because we can only see our lives moment by moment, nothingness is the only continuity. I would like so much to feel the sweetness of the sea and sand once more. The only time I've experienced life's full-ness is in the presence of that rhythm and light. My desire vanished; I became one with the utter softness of the coastal light. Identifying for all time with that instant, feeling no need. All past and future abolished. I was the very gentle nothingness of a continual moment. Engulfed forever in space, as if time didn't exist. There's nothing to match the ocean for evoking eternity, the edge of the world, its shore of subtle unchanging colours, its continuous heartbeat. From the beginning of time, wave follows wave. From the beginning? In fact, it is not time passing, but the same instant repeated to infinity, from the birth of a wave until it crests and dissolves on the sand. The ocean is the essence of pleasure, of life. (*Gymnopédies*)

"Matter forgets to exist, life forgets to live, the heart forgets to love. By sleeping, we lose Paradise."

"As for thought, it's through irregular insights that it makes use of life. Far too few instants make it through the three filters to con-sciousness! So we have a sense of muted suffering when we go 'in search of lost instants.'"

"You must desire it, you must want it, you must extend your hand and step forward to create the future. The future is not that 'which comes to us,' but 'that toward which we are going.' The sense and the carriage of the future are inscribed in the present itself."

(I am starting to realize that our sense of space is the same as our sense of time. We think of space as a continuity, when in fact it is a discontinuous series of locales and landscapes, as photographs show. If you freeze a film sequence, disrupting the illusion of continuity, you can see that the action takes place as a series of instants, and in a sequence of separate places, similar to the way that a melody is just the development, the gathering up of a series of notes. My memory connects certain instants to particular places, one setting at a time.) This is the true profanation of the world, to see the universe as no longer a single entity (religious thought), but as a spatial-temporal fragmentation, infinitesimal.

———

February 7, 1979
We live in a state of constant "distraction," to the point of forgetting our most basic roots, almost to the point of for-getting our instincts. Everything around us is artificial and false. We continue to lug around laughable superstitions, a vain heritage that alienates and enslaves us.
— Tàpies [The Practice of Art]

It's strange, for several months now, when having a conversation, or listening to readings and songs on the radio, anywhere the voice is being used, certain words have been detaching from their con-text, singly, alone. They astonish and fascinate me. Even words that I hear all the time. For a few seconds, I can grasp them, can suddenly access their meaning, which I find astonishing. They seem both common and rich. They seem filled with other words, images, colours, and music. Then I forget them: out of arrogance, emptiness, circumstances, etc. They come, then they go. I wish I could seal them in a vault, in my head, stop them from disappearing. I wish I knew how to manipulate them, how to recreate and share what it's like to be suddenly captivated and astonished by these words.

LICKETY-SPLIT

———

February 7, 1979

I'm seeking a form that is different from poetry as it is currently understood, what is read right now. I'm looking for a true atonal song. Words without lyricism that correspond perfectly to the present. But what exactly is our contemporary reality? I don't know. It seems to me that the world stands on an anxious threshold between past and future. But the present has no texture. Sometimes we're living in the retro atmosphere of the last war, other times in science fiction. But who are we? And why is there the same anxiety, the same despair, in every city all over Europe and America? Into what silence is our universe sinking? Why do I experience these premonitions, these visions of desolated landscapes and of silence, these hints of fascism, this smell of rot, prejudices, old superstitions, racism? Of everything getting old and the gangrene spreading. And why has this exhaustion taken us hostage, as if there's nothing left that needs changing? We're in the grips of an overwhelming and deadly sense of helplessness. My love affair is an image of this reigning desolation. For some time, I have been obsessed with wanting to destroy everything in my memory. I should forget the past world of my old passions, fears, and words. I need to lose my old habits, clear everything out, discharge the old ideas. I want my outlook to be one of astonishment and discovery, so that secrets open and questions pour forth, so that new desires can make me part of a new language. I want to destroy the harmonies I've inherited, I didn't create them and they suffocate me. Bit by bit I am emptying out, but it's still not enough. I am still not empty enough for my spirit to open and my intelligence to wake up to a clairvoyant contemporaneity. My love for Paul has caused a marvellous destruction, forcing me to question all of my attitudes, my dreams, to interrogate my feminine alienations, let go of my fantasies, and open my eyes to our society, to the codes that rule over it, to its horrors, to realize how deeply I've been forged by this society, how unfree I am. Yes, this love affair has revealed to me a death much worse than physical death: the non-lived life, a death lived day after day …, the death of others, the death of the self in a dead universe. I'm learning about silence, discovering how ignorant and silent I am, to what extent I'm nothing, and that this nothingness is not a death knell, but all possibilities, all openings. I'm learning about the shadowy power of being nothing, the creative power of oblivion. You must forget both history and your personal story to create a world you can finally breathe in. I suffocated so much in Paris, and in Montréal all during December and January, deprived of discovery, stuck in old feelings, old ideas, in one single, unchanging desire. I thought that, like the seasons, my old self periodically returned, never evolving, but now I really want to break free of this infernal cycle. I want to blow it all up, my old frustrations and facilities, annihilate myself until I reach the perfect vertigo of words, so I can at last experience what has always been hidden from me: the real taste of blood, water, wine, and sweat.

———

THE LAST VISION

The last premonition that I had, the last lucid vision, was at the Opera in Paris, during an evening concert.

DESTRUCTION IS OUR DELIGHT

They were right there, sitting in front of me, and I suddenly became aware of something they themselves hadn't realized, something that hadn't yet happened but was on the brink of happening, and, for their sake, I wished they might take a risk and do something crazy, because they were so rigid and so reasonable, so dead. Their necks were in my sightline, clenched, their well-coiffed hair; he, older, elegant, wearing a straight, bright white collar, and she, his daughter's friend, possessed of that mournful elegance typical of little girls from good families. They reeked of reserve, wealth, taste, ennui. There they were at the Opera, nodding to acquaintances, creasing their programs, but just a little, while they waited for the concert to start; the chandeliers gleamed, the perfumes hovered, their clothes were fine. It was before the evening meal. Outside, autumn was not only dazzling, but subtle, adding a little chill to the air. I knew exactly the kind of hushed interior they would retreat to for dinner following the concert. But when he bent his head to speak to her, in an indifferent and polite tone, I thought he might crack, and that he might see how young and beautiful she was, hear the music, let its sound expand their souls. Maybe his heart would skip a beat, he'd hesitate and feel a kind of melancholy, an artistic emotion that would bring them both back to life. They were on the verge of falling in love. In fact, I felt certain that they were *already* in love but, blinded by habit and fear, hadn't yet become aware of it. I stopped watching them: their heads were so upright, so stiff, without the slightest tilt or softness to their necks. They didn't even brush shoulders, yet I could still sense the closeness of their breathing, the feeling of oppression they shared. After we exited the concert hall, I saw them again in the front courtyard. They were surrounded by the magnificent blue of the Paris night. There was a festival on the grand boulevards and a dense crowd of people heading out for the night. I could clearly imagine the kind of chic Paris apartment they were going back to. They would put on a beautiful record, eat from gleaming plates; someone would pull the heavy velour curtains over to conceal their reasonable intimacy. It made sense. Which of them might realize, I asked myself, that they were already as one, that desire has already begun its delicious destruction? Yet, should they listen to that desire, they would threaten the society they represent. They would be hunted, lost to our world, a threat to the established order. I doubted that they possessed the artistic aplomb to embrace such an adventure. I told myself: whether or not they loved each other, society will eat them up. Unsure of their right to life and to love, they will not succeed in vanquishing it. And though I wished the impossible for them, watching them mistake themselves for the bespoke crowd of the Opera, I expected nothing from them, not even a juicy scandal.

———

TOPOGRAPHIES OF LOVE

———

Our destiny is in play: we can allow ignorance and deceptive myths to survive, and therefore oppression, or we can look for knowledge and happiness.

He is nothing who dares not piss on the stiffest altars. And he who doesn't know how to remove the mask covering almost every face is also nothing.

— Tàpies [*The Practice of Art*]

———

February 10, 1979

I want to outline an exact plan for my next collection, *Topographies of Love.*[6] To sketch the locales and the inner harmony of my love affairs. The empty moment, free of memory and dream. Banality, to the point of smothering all signification. The conflation of misery and desire. The body of the other, upon which all existence is written. The primordial landscape.

Beginnings: everything must be created; and endings, the way that all existential aims become obliterated by this painful abundance.

———

Last night I saw Liliana Cavani's film *The Night Porter.* It's been a very long time since I've been so bowled over by a work of art. To me, this film is a poem, a devastating reflection. I understand why it has provoked such a scandal. The right thinks it's a sex film; a surefire way to see nothing. The left freaked out because it upset its convictions; hardline feminists understood nothing about the relationship between the torturer and his victim. After having read Reich, and having interrogated several of my own fantasies, I can see how far this film goes, it calls everything into question. Increasingly, I believe that passion is the supreme weapon for toppling a rotten society. I need to explain. Liliana Cavani doesn't divide her world into good people and bad; people's relationships and intentions are more subtle and less divided than between antagonisms such as "good" and "bad." But, on either side of the equation, those who reject the game of silence, hypocrisy, and the mask, who reject tranquility, and are not afraid of their passions, do not sink into oblivion. They are the present and the acute conscience of a society that is asleep, the very same society that must kill them in order to re-establish its contemptible and death-like composure.

> *Too many similar plans aim to "cure" us with a well-chosen environment and design, with the "mechanization of culture," without any other purpose than to throw us into a quiet somnolence, when what the artist seeks is insomnia and disquiet ...*

> *White. The colour of the origin and of the end, the colour of whatever is on the point of changing condition, of absolute silence which, as Kandinsky said, is not the silence of death, but that of the preparing for all the possibilities of life, for all the joys of youth.*
>
> — Tàpies [*The Practice of Art*]

(White: clairvoyance of desire)

REMARKS CONCERNING LILIANA CAVANI'S FILM
THE NIGHT PORTER

Ambient fascism, Reichian theory of sexuality.

Relationship between man-woman, Aryan-Jew, etc. Fears and prejudices. Society of false omissions and of silence. Sex seen as scandalous, especially when freely accepted, lived, and passionate. Those who express themselves and refuse to wear a mask are neither better nor worse than others, yet because they refuse to accept mediocrity or to compromise, they are a threat to a hypocritical society. The same precipice that brings them alive with feeling would throw others into a panic. The artist or the poet is someone who refuses to wear a mask. He isn't dead, he isn't sleeping. He is the acute awareness of the instant. He is worry and pain, the guilt of others. Max is the guilt of others and the young girl is Max's guilt. The others want to become comatose, they are the living dead, they lull their crimes to sleep and go about their lives without remorse, convincing themselves that they are cleansed of guilt. Max accepts his guilt, and lives it to the point of despair. Max knows who he is and the young girl knows who her torturer is, they have chosen each other deliberately.

———

February 11, 1979

Excerpt of a letter to Monique[7]
Since the last time, no news of Paul ... it would be better to forget ourselves even more. Since the beginning of this stupid story, I have thought and read a lot, and I can report that this desire has made me relive, to the point of exhaustion, all of my old desires, from my earliest childhood to the minutest dreams and fears of the twenty-three-year-old woman. I have become conscious of my alienation, and not just my own, but that of others, that of the society I live in and have to deal with. Society lives in fear, and passion is a threat to it. Passion is neither good nor bad, but it doesn't lie, it's an uncom-promising excess, it is life, sexuality, and it terrifies people. Our entire society wants to shut it up, because it represents disorder, creation, and the destructive awakening of memory, the agonized magnificence of the instant. Passion (along with death) is the most profound experience we can create out of solitude, and this makes it powerful. Unknowingly, Paul established between me and the actual society a queer dialogue. He is the prototypical straight *dude,*

integrated, efficient, reasonable, in sum: dead. Now, when I look back on the many talks he has given me, they ooze with mediocrity and fear, he has understood absolutely nothing about life, about love. What shocks me is that there were times when I adapted to his vision of things. To him, I can only ever be his patient, or his "girlfriend." His relationships with the other fit perfectly with the models our society has forged. He is incapable of imagining his own life, of creating a new understanding between himself and others, of creating his own relationship with a woman or with love in whatever form. Before it was even born, our relationship was already dead, already had a definitive shape. It was schematized, codified, and, as such, insignificant and boring, it was not supposed to threaten or scandalize others. It was built on lies and fear. He didn't want his wife to know, he made sure to remind me to be careful around his secretary and his nurses. He had already warned me about his lacklustre feelings. Poor guy! But I know he wasn't reducible to just that, that he had made a choice to transcend his limits. He asked me: "Will you teach me how to be free?" That alone proves his lucidity, but he panicked. Me, who is learning to be free, with difficulty, slowly, how was I supposed to show him in spite of himself? Finally, I saw the most intelligent film of my life. A masterpiece of clarity. The Night Porter. While everyone hides their desires, mutilates their imaginations and hearts, blushes from their fantasies, this couple lives them: they push their extremes to the end, embrace their pleasure without guilt or regret. (Everyone has been struck by the film's representation of sadomasochism, when in fact it's very discreet, the relationship is for the most part a crime of passion, exalted, a connection of possession and tenderness.) Some people ignore all the passion and think "sexual sickness" ... This couple is a living reproach to those who want to forget everything and lie to themselves ... this couple is scandalous. They have no masks: they love each other. They are neither good nor bad, nor better than others, they are just real, they refuse to forget. They are shot down!

———

Excerpt from a letter to Yvette[8]

I've grown accustomed to using certain images and words more than others, and now these images and words, previously a source of wonder, have become traps … A poet develops a sound, but when it becomes too easy it stops being alive, that's when you know that you've started to plagiarize yourself. I must avoid making a pastiche of my own work. It's always during difficult times, this waiting and searching, these moments when I need to surpass the self to rediscover it, this is why I've become more fragile and more anxious by the day.

———

My dear sweet,[9]

This evening I reconnected with my poetry. It won't surprise you to learn that it was about as far from transparent as possible, a complete shift toward the unspeakable, the obscure. Also, what time more delicious to reconnect with poetry than that frigid mauve hour, when Montréal (you remember this frightful Franco-American city the way I do) makes us dive into memory, shreds the metronome with its well-gardened windowsills and the facades of its buildings pierced by fire. Every hamlet of my love converges in one lyrical epic about an aged doctor entombed in the belly of a woman.

There's no longer a single thing I like about myself. I have become my former feminist awakenings turned inside out. Centuries go dark inside of me at the termination of their sorrows. I have reconnected with the most elementary of poetries, a poetry of oblivion and indeterminate night, rays extending out from blackness.

———

February 14, 1979

I like affirming Montréal's reasoned-out ugliness, and have found that I am deeply rooted in it, that I draw something from it (but what?), which makes me want to live. Montréal is ugly, I delight in seeing it, in saying it, because to me this ugliness is akin to a great gentleness, a frightful welcome. Everything seems to have been designed for efficacy and cost-effectiveness, nothing to please the eye. I feel at home in its grinding need for productivity. I find Montréal relaxing, because its ugliness never asks to be admired. Though this city has no new pleasures to offer me, I still find ways to make new discoveries. Yes, I'm still capable of being astonished by an expanse of sky reflected in a window, or by the way a city street can sparkle at nighttime, and feel like I'm discovering something for the first time, because such beauty is neither culturally sanctioned nor called by the name of beauty. It's a way I have of looking at things, and as such is subjective, ephemeral. Neither cathedral nor museum, Montréal is an anarchic and ridiculous place. At least half of the life here is happening behind closed doors. My love for Paul has the same existential structure. It's an absurd, improbable, and ordinary love founded on feelings that are the opposite of love. For in fact, everything I like, Paul lacks. I find his way of thinking baffling, even shocking. There is no reason for this love to exist, and yet it does. His absence, the awful burning it made me feel, has mutated into non-stop thought. I think about him all the time, but I'm not in pain. I have grown free of him. My desire persists, but it's no longer cruel. I feel good about my solitude, it's no longer a burden. All the moments and locales from these past months, December through January, have taken on a feeling of extreme unreality. I had stopped being able to exist without him. But now it's as if, having come to the end of a nightmare, I am retracing my steps in the opposite direction. And now each moment, each locale, is deliciously tangible. I haven't a clue as to how this transformation came about, what mental break is responsible for alleviating my distress, but I no longer idealize Paul, nor desire him. (Did I really idealize him?) My future has sunk into indifference. I know now that he was just a fragment, a tiny part of an idealized love. Each man makes up but one part of the beloved. Love is dispersed throughout all possible men. I love knowing that my desire for Paul isn't based on anything beautiful or reasonable; it is free, a little gesture, a useless speech, a poem written only to be ripped up and thrown away. This desire is a creative act, by which I mean that it doesn't answer to any imperative, leads to nothing, serves nothing, doesn't conform to any notion of happiness, nor answer to any of the things we ask of love: fulfillment, joy, discovery, etc. This desire receives nothing and brings nothing, I love its ephemeral colour. I love the idea that it has no reason to survive, that nothing feeds it and yet it keeps on going. It is each instant's drive toward meaning (the drive coming only from me), it exists by virtue of my will alone, of my ability to keep it alive. Through me alone. *It's my freedom* ... What road has taken me from love's alienation to its freedom? Why do I feel intoxicated by feeling (and being) free in Montréal and free in the other's desire? Montréal opens a fissure for the spirit, this desire opens a fissure in the mind. Neither the one nor the other correspond to what's learned or known. Because neither is settled nor committed to memory, both must be constantly reinvented. They continue to be a great font of discovery. I have no clue what I'm looking for, nor if there's anything to find, even their very existence remains uncertain. I can form whatever impressions I want of Montréal, and of my desire the images and the sounds that chance offers. Hidden in every place and body lies an imaginative source. With Paul, I'm no longer going to play the role of sufferer. And as for Montréal, I no longer know what I think, the cultural memory of its corners hasn't drained me, all I have is a life of experiences inscribed in stone. Montréal is the cartography of my history.

———

THE TOPOGRAPHIES OF LOVE

———

Our kingdom is east of the city

———

February 17, 1979

Saw Paul before he leaves for three weeks. I won't see him again before March 9, and I'm trying to fight back the terrible anxiety I can feel rising in my throat. He's convinced I idealize him, that my love for him is like my idealization of Paris, but I feel certain it's just the opposite. In fact, it is the one thing I'm sure of. He's not my father, instead of comforting me he keeps plunging me back into a world where nothing makes sense. He's a comforting figure, for sure, but my desire for him destroys this aspect. It's all chaos. I don't expect him to reassure me, nor to be reassured by this love.

I become aware of the depth of my naivety, and in so doing its layers peel away, alas. I lose the simplicity of my ways. Thinking back on my feelings, I twist their truths and complicate them in an attempt to fit them to the rules and norms of our society, to make them admissible. I told Paul that when I checked into the hospital, I knew nothing of its hierarchies, or of the social codes that held sway over that microsociety. I interacted with the staff in a spontaneous way, which upset them, because they weren't accustomed to such behaviour. I can see now that the way I responded to my cancer was completely atypical. I allowed my intuition to inform my actions. I acted like a person who had never learned the ways things are supposed to be done, or the right thing to say, or felt the fears that oppress us. I didn't experience my cancer as my destiny. I wanted him to see me as different, for him to create a completely new kind of relationship with me. To be neither his patient, nor his friend, nor his woman, but as a thing apart from all rational paths. His double. Something new. He is not my doctor, nor my friend, nor my lover. He is the central character of all my silent mythologies. He is the fecund myth of my despair. It's through him that I now dream. Through him I feel a freedom akin to that felt in the depths of pleasure, he is the intimate debacle of my words, in him I dip into all the dangers, I destroy all destinations. In him my love is a gift of the instant which is born and disappears with each pulse of my memory.

Sometimes I act instinctually, which is to say "poetically." I manage an original act (natural, spontaneous, free, and fertile). Sometimes I act reasonably, that's when I act according to social norms I may not agree with. But for me, it is desire that leads me to this instinct, this sentimental intuition, this obscure and ineradicable liveliness at the source of all creation.

I've never been so much, yet so irrationally, in love. Nor have I ever felt so completely overwhelmed. That's the complex brew. All he has to do is come toward me a little, and I can sense what he wants, and if there's a hope I might be able to see and talk to him, everything else just falls away. From the tone of his voice I can tell if he wants to give in to me, just a little, or to say no. I'm pretty sure I can see things he can't, tender little acts he's unconscious of, and everything inside of me tells me that these feelings are more than just vain imaginings, or illusions. I can make my story into something quite ordinary, approaching the denuded perfection of a work of art, or I can fashion it into something intricate and mythological. He is an entire world; I am an entirely different one. He represents the hard reality: my death (and the fight for survival), bourgeois order, the nuclear future with its oligarchy, its repressive power. I'm like the artist who feeds off the very public that would like to assassinate him: he gives to me, he feeds me, he is open, attentive to what I'm going through, but he is also the one who is killing me. There's nothing he can do about it: *He's the death of me and my remedy, he's my remedy and the death of me.*[10] I am still convinced that, though he couldn't save my leg from being amputated, he did save me from death. His affection toward me lends an allure to his medical care. Though it's probably just habitual for him, for me, because I live entirely in the realm of feeling, this care feels like love. He just doesn't get it. If my body has healed, or at least momentarily escaped death's clutches, my spirit, for its part, has only been able to avoid going under by grace of the tenderness and the attentions of a fifty-year-old man, and all of the wonder his presence gave birth to in me. Of course, I feel gratitude for the doctor (and I know that he is not infallible, that tomorrow death could easily prove the stronger of the two), but I feel love for the man. All these things inevitably overlap, and this is why it is impossible to turn my desire into contentment. But I love him more than anyone in the world. I don't want to change his way of being, because it is his way of being that pleases me and is the revelation for me of an entire world filled with differences and discoveries. And, like the artist and his public, I want my indestructible solitude to become mixed up with his at least once, for his whole being to penetrate mine and for this to be the source of a new language. Because even if the artist and his public are two irreconcilable entities, the one draws his life and power from the other, draws his dream and song, draws his future and past, his darkness and his light.

———

February 18, 1979

THE FIFTH SEASON
(possible story)

A love story, set in America and Montréal. A mythological story of desire. In a specific city, a specific winter, a woman in love with a specific man. She knows that he is leaving to spend some time in an American city. He has left, she decides to follow him because her desire has thrown her so off balance it has dismantled all of her inhibitions and fears. She knows that in making this decision she will lose him forever, because he doesn't love her enough and has run away from her, but she decides to perform this act of total freedom anyway. She wants to respond to all that's humming inside of her, to be close, to be absolutely true to herself. Her decision is an act of pure futility, of freakish freedom, for her despair will not be alleviated by it, because he probably won't allow her to see him. This story will be a strange journey into her own self; with descriptions of the airport, the plane, the departure, like a strange journey through a mouldering society, a journey through facades, the facade of quotidian reality. She leaves Montréal in wintertime, a Montréal filled with memory, because her past, particular memories and feelings, are etched into various places throughout the city. She leaves for an American city that is similar to Montréal, but it is unknown to her, where she finds herself immersed in the moment, completely, without past or future, on account of the fact that she's just passing through, a stranger, rootless. And, for no apparent reason, she has managed to disrupt the infernal seasonal rhythm to find herself on the timeless and infinite moors of feminine desire, her love like an overwhelming, dizzying light, a void both weighty and painful. Suspended between life and death, she wanders in search of this man whose face, little by little, seems to fade away, and suddenly, skinned of her old identity, she no longer really knows why she is there, she is no longer certain of being in love and begins, bizarrely, to disregard her own desire. She wanders, completely emptied of herself, having become a sort of silent abstraction, until, more or less by chance, she runs into the man in a public place, a hotel restaurant, for example. She watches him from afar, unable to find the strength to approach; it's not that she has suddenly become passive, but rather that she has penetrated a new dimension of life, a fifth season; her desire has shattered the limits of all intention and her love is suddenly like a living power. She hasn't yet discovered the next level of intensity. In fact, I have no idea how this story will end, because I myself am this woman wandering in a familiar yet indecipherable universe, indescribable, in an old world in need of reforming, in a winter sadness gently rocking toward a seasonless absence. A fifth season like another life. I am this artist working toward the total destruction of her history with the end of refashioning a world where it is once again possible to breathe, this woman plunged into an extreme solitude, touching the bottom, the limit of desire. Her desire is therefore both nothingness and eternity. Her desire is more hopeful than death, more difficult than life. Her desire is the end of an old order, of an oppressive state of things. She wanders in an exterior "no man's land" which is the incarnation, the image, of her interior "no man's land." It's always been this way with me, dream and reality, body and spirit, no definitive borders, the waters intermixed, vast waters dispensing joys and pains. I love Paul to the point where all of my memories go extinct, without his body, my body wanders in total night. It is obvious that a sadness so extreme looks like idealized love. But only drives of such extremity can give us new life.

————

May every so-called custom be a cause for worry.
— Bertolt Brecht quoted by Bison Ravi

————

Yes, she said, this actual man I've gone after, is exactly the one I'm looking for, exactly the one I love, with a face I long to kiss again and a body I long to hold again. I have lost him inside of me, a victim of my intense desire, a desire transformed into all desires, this man into all men, my useless love for him turned him into an abstraction, into the Aeneas who abandoned Dido, the Theseus who abandoned Ariadne, the Ulysses who abandoned Calypso. And I have become nothing, all of my memories went with him when he vanished. I'm prepared to be reborn into my desire, to reinvest my power in this absence. I turn against my old skin. My desire is my freedom, it leaves me alone. It stands before me like granite, a wall I have collapsed against. The woman who loves him can no longer survive, another is born and who loves him differently.

[*Prose poems*]

————

I pitch from one extreme emotion to another. I thought I had broken free of my too-big pain, but here it is. It has returned. I refrain from calling him up, him. Once again everything grows distant. Sometimes the anxiety that ruined Paris for me comes back. It's here, right now, because of the following: he's not here, he won't be here tomorrow or the next day. I love him, how stupid and useless it all is. Just like that, an entire year wasted because of this pointless love affair. It must come to an end, one way or another. I must write about something else. I must get over these feelings once and for all. Of course, we idealize love (wax museum), if we didn't, who would put up with this pain? I've got to get over it! I'm getting out of this wax museum where everyone is striking poses and no one moving, stuck in a set place by the world. I wish I had the strength to go completely crazy. I'm trying to force myself to look at things in a non-customary way, to see life differently from how I have always done so, because that is the one, the only way of changing. From the inside, not from the outside. The exterior is nothing but an age-old paralysis. You don't recklessly attack a rock. A rock will not move, you will die first. But you are only movement. (Finally, my erratic heartbeat has stopped. Since yesterday my heart has been pounding, made anxious by absence). Nothing can change the four seasons, yet a fifth interior season is a real possibility. You just have to want to create it. Flee my fatigue, let it fall away like an old coat, forget it so that I can find laughter. Rediscover and never let go of my insouciance. My little love has gone to sleep in the waves, the very soft waves of night, the many beams of blackness. I would like to reconnect with that young girl of seventeen who could make love without breaking her heart, and for whom every man was but a brief, unencumbered wonder. It is clear that I want you with me all the time, you are the precipice of my existence, I make my way toward you with a secret desire to be destroyed, and when you don't destroy me, I do it for you. I'm a dead ringer for Hedda Gabler. I would like to see you be uncompromising, passionate, and heroic, but I must be these things for you. I am the real hero of my love, and you, you act surprised and don't understand anything about this barrage of pleading. Unsatisfied desire has driven me to the worst stupidities. If you had simply slept with me every once in a while, I would not have been so fanatical, but you, you probably risked losing something. We are two monsters of pride and egotism. We want to succeed in everything, lose nothing.

One day I'm free, the next I'm not. Everything is hard to control. From one hour to the next I am sad or happy, conscious of or dazed by sadness. This love I'm feeling is at the point of annihilating all limits. I want to love with a wild abandon, with an impulsive ease. I want a love built out of the conviction that someday everything will be fulfilled, each instant will become a measure of light, a reinforcement of solitude, and everything will be useful. What use was my feeling miserable over being apart in Paris? He was so far away, my terrible love, that the streets felt to me like giant furrows, enormous rivers about to engulf me forever. And those hours that unspooled in the French countryside, while we drove toward some point on the map. I dreamed that he was with me. Why these cruel convictions, these senseless projections that destroyed that brief moment and all the joys it might have held? Why does the present moment fail to make me happy, such that I project all sweetness and pleasure onto an uncertain, unknowable future? Each instant is round and full like a delicious efflorescence, but we cannot escape the massacre of the actual day. In order to live, we must capture the multiple nuances of darkness. Every day is a different breakage and every night is the same serene and continuous flow. All nights form one single night, but the days are detachable, the one from the other. They have their own winds, their own colours, smells, and temperatures. Nights are different in their makeup, they are oceans, their tides ebb and flow, but from each night whispered into the ear of the other the same clairvoyance, the same fragile innocence. Nights make up the "no man's land" of my life, they calm me. I love their bouncy cheeks and the secret sweetness of their skin. Nights are welcoming to seekers, they have no work imperative, they are left to those who do not know everything, who have no answers for anything, to those who are sick, who are alone, to those for whom pleasure is the only reason to live, to those who have true friends, the sort of friends with whom one can discuss things until dawn, and who are stimulated by exhaustion, rather than quivering with ennui. Nights are perfume and gemstones, they are aids to understanding, nights know nothing of lies and masks; lovers' voices tell no lies in the intimacy of the darkness and dreams are the most accurate mirrors. Nights undress us, and you, my love, already you are almost plunged into night, though you think yourself a master of daytime. While you think you are controlling your life through the clarity of your work, night has arrived to invade your skin. Night is the loss of memory, night puts our eyes to sleep so as to awaken the other senses. Sight is cerebral, but night is sensual, and a place for senses linked to passion and life. The night is a perfect fruit, a musical sound, a maternal flood, an open ground. Night has slipped under your eyelids, you are drunk with its unknown tenderness. Day persists in lying to you, night is an echo, it frees you and your words return, obliging you to listen. My love, while you journey toward the apex of a mystical solar America, profane and stateless night pierces your body, in the laundromat, the airport, the hotel room, already a twilight of coarse familiarity closes in, forcing you to face your fear, opening you to the destruction of your orderly world.

When a memory really comes to the surface, isn't it to abolish itself, to destroy itself? Don't those moments when we try to remake our lives occasion the surfacing of memories? All of a sudden, we want to forget, because we want to remake ourselves in a new way. In art, in poetry, isn't it when we start to remember too much that we feel the urge to destroy it all, the imperious need to forget everything so as to make a fresh start, to reinvent ourselves? Isn't it when

I start to imitate myself too much that I cease to live and to create? For the last several months my life and my work have evaded me because I am repeating myself. I am horribly empty. But this emptiness is a promise, because if I am empty, it means the old way of feeling is no longer working, it must be changed.

———

I attempt to psychoanalyze my suffering and by doing so drain it of all poetry. Everything I read I see through the lens of this habit I want to destroy. Destroy the person I've turned into at twenty-three years of age so that I can move forward. To deepen the sleeping irrational, smooth the edges of my angers. I use Paul to resurrect all of my obsessive fears. I can no longer find myself except through him, he is the thread in the labyrinth. In one direction lies death, in the other, love, and I don't know which direction I'm going. I'm fighting blindly, my imagination gone dark, and my instincts are way too intense for me not to be wary of them. I no longer fear contradicting myself (something that made me so ashamed in the past; to be caught in a contradiction). Now I contradict myself constantly and feel a lively pleasure in doing so, as if the mind, incapable of seeing things in a clear and definitive way, sees them always ambiguously, and that in itself gives them value. Things are double-sided; one day I see one side and agree with it, the next day is different. This love affair has been good for me in that it has made me rethink everything; I can't grasp it. I see it from within and at the same time, from without. I suffer through it, feeling both sensual and hostile, then I feel free to choose. For a love to exist in the most honest and true way, it must constantly be recreated. Desire is the bird of fire. We must die and be reborn constantly in order to feel the creative power of love.

8:20 p.m. I am in the brouhaha of Concordia University, around me people are speaking English, I can't help but feel that I am in a city other than Montréal. How I love these flash trips through my own city. This town is really divided into two parts. To the east, our kingdom, to the west, that of the stranger. Paul belongs to both, he is both the known and the unknown (the kind and the hostile, freedom and alienation, the brother and the colonist, the double and the stranger). The topography of the city corresponds to the topography of my love.

Understand the word 'love' in the sense of a very gentle and very violent state of mental confusion.

———

February 21, 1979
From one man to another, the city, from a promised pleasure to the promise of pleasure, the city and all its ethereal twists and turns, its interlacing of uncertainty and excitement. In the steel wall that is mid-February April's mad wind blows through a giant structure of baroque buds.

[*Prose poems*]

———

Our spring is a springtime with the right idea.
— Éluard

———

February 23, 1979

Now that I know that my love and my death share the same trembling and peaceful gaze, how can I not implore such dark sweetness to reconnect with pleasure forever?

On my body, in my body, I see and I feel the stigmata of death. I recognize the signs as those that invaded my grandfather's body.

———

I will number colours that will never sleep
and for which blackness is the apotheosis and prism

———

February 24, 1979

Poems the form of which would be based around rhythm, around beat. (Drive, rhythm, breath, beating, pulse). Breath is the essential thing, the first living sign, the movement that goes from you to the other, from the other to you.

And now, stuck in this metropolitan cage, my dreams bite the dust. I don't know where my profound sense of emptiness is coming from, from Paul's absence or from something else. From this thing Paul awakened in me, and which I can no longer put back to sleep, this part of me that wants to live intensely but is prevented from doing so? This physical need burning through my senses? The relentless taste of horror in my mouth that I can't seem to shake? This ontological weakness from the absence of creativity and intelligence? My life is completely bogged down, I can't see a single sunny patch up ahead and it's terrible. No patch of sun shines through the opacity of the real, no outpouring of joy. Even my happiness about publishing with Gallimard[11] didn't last long. It's because daily life has become intolerable to me, frustrating, painful, and this good news only creates another thing I'm waiting for, another weight to my days. My life is made up of nothing but stupid periods of waiting, I can't make up my mind about anything, not about my love affairs, nor my desires. I can't leave. (Where would I go? Here, at least I'm home.) I'm miserable staying put. I wait for a sign from Paul, without much faith, I wait for the confirmation from Gallimard, I wait for the release of *The Life Beyond*, I wait for a job, a little money. I wait for everything and absolutely nothing happens. I'm a sad tightrope walker with an erratic heartbeat. My heart is plagued by a bizarre flutter. My breathing is uneven. My mental anguish has never affected my body like this before.

A mix of poems and prose with, first and foremost, a rhythm I can feel singing inside of me, poems that console me like an ear pressing against a heart. Once I perceive this original pulse, this metropolitan chant, everything will be able to burst out, emerge, the images and the words. The universe will once again be decipherable. No longer will existence be hostile or sacred, but every instant desecrated, all the way to its core, its central void, its deep black regenerative nakedness. Existence overrun by self.

————

February 25, 1979
I love short fragile nights filled with secret acts that renew our hope.

————

Last snow: skin's first startle

———

To wait for nothing and forget everything — the opposite of subjectivity — the absence of all centres — a correlative for this change in expectation would be a night without anticipation. They are together, but not yet. The language of poetry: a language that contradicts itself. The claim is that when the beloved draws near, desire is frustrated and gutted. Proximity of the beloved distances desire.

———

February 26, 1979

Whether I write or not changes nothing about the disaster that is my existence. In fact, given the fragmented, contradictory, and pathetic nature of my writing, writing right now only serves only to accentuate the disaster.

———

February 27, 1979

The only reality I'm interested in is the body of the other, for it's the site of perpetual reinvention. The body of the other is a continual profanation. Desire transforms it into a sacred object, pleasure desecrates and fulfills it. A pendulum between mystery and insult. Through the body of the other the universe becomes demythologized, the best remedy against alienation. Pleasure is the act, the fulfillment of my freedom, pleasure beats a path for me back to myself, alleviating my alienation, demystifying me.

Montréal and North America, profane city and profane landscapes *par excellence*. Avoiding the cultural frameworks around beauty and admiration. Banal places without history. Everything must be fomented in one's own memory. Everything must be created through one's own will. Places without preconceptions, or transcendent meanings. Yes, not one iota of aesthetic, virtual, divine, or cultural transcendence, etc.

———

This totalizing thing that love awakens in us, the lack of which is as bad as death. This murmur, this suite of sad and fragile voices, this crack which keeps expanding, engulfing the entire universe; am I not already dead, mutilated by absence? I don't even love him anymore, I am without him, that's all, I hope for nothing, I dream of nothing. I am forever destroyed, forever denied. And no such likeness will ever be reborn inside our lips. And no such face will ever embody so much desire. I am indifferent to everything and all poetry has left me. I no longer have the courage to love. How small he seemed to me that last time that I saw him, and tired, and almost old. For a year everything has been subsumed by him, all that has happened or been undone is because of him. Why have I given him such power? How could I have agreed to so little, and accepted so little, and kept on going in so much pain? No one comes near me anymore, and I don't go near anyone. I am silence, blackness before all words, the ideal void, I have sucked down the entirety of the real to put a stop to its ringing.

Topographies of Love[1]

for I only came here yes to possess the darkness
of you   only the darkness
— Jacques Brault, *Four-sided poems*

Happiness O very light rain on my lashes
a harmony between skin and night
this silken look of darkness

———

Recopied from February 13, 1979
(My sweet dear) This evening I returned to poetry. It won't be news
to you to learn that this new work is about as far from straight-
forward as possible, a complete shift toward the unspeakable, the
obscure. Also, what could be more delicious than to reconnect with
poetry during the cold's mauve hour, when Montréal (like me, you
have a good sense of this frightful Franco-American city) becomes
but a plunge into memory, a torn metronome above well-gardened
windowsills, the screaming light of buildings. All the locales of my
love affair are concentrated into one intimate epic, about an aged
doctor buried inside the belly of a woman.

I feel no more self-pity. I am a wineskin emptied of all the old
feminine awakenings. Centuries go dark inside of me at the termina-
tion of their sorrows. I have reconnected with the most elementary
of poetries, that of the oblivion of the most diffuse evening, that of
the tender rays of blackness.

Last snow: skin's first startle

This is exactly what I've been feeling for several months. This
poetry of banalities, this ongoing fragmented writing I'm moving
toward, where my will and my suffering have become one and the
same. Barrenness and profanation. Topographies of desire for love.

Desire for love has always served me and serves still to embody the much greater desire that my work holds. An indefinable desire, a source that feeds but will never be fully realized in the work, even though it's through the work that it (desire) fulfills itself.

> *The more pure the inspiration, the more the one under its pull, closer to the sound of its source, is diminished, as if the richness revealed, this superabundant source, is also an extreme impoverishment, is above all the superabundance of the refusal, that turns itself into something that makes nothing, that wanders through the heart of an endless unravelling [...] there is a point where inspiration and a lack of inspiration are confounded, an extreme point wherein inspiration, a movement that is beyond tasks, of learned forms and sanctioned language, takes on a barrenness, becomes an absence of power, an impossibility that the artist futilely interrogates, which is a nocturnal state, both wondrous and without hope ...*
>
> — Blanchot [*The Space of Literature*]

———

I saw the distraught bodies of cancer patients. I can't just get over such a vision of pain. How am I not supposed to cry out when I wake up to such horrors, inspired by a God who always forsakes the most humble and gentle people; our world is reflected and dies in such ocean-sized eyes. How am I not supposed to cry out when I wake up to the indifference of some and the gentle powerlessness of others. And the white and very slow death of hospitals, the cavernous solitude of antiseptic beds. An old woman mutters: "I have never suffered so much." But the sky is a stone and the people around her are dreadful stones.

———

March 4, 1979

Everyone cheats. He, the artist, he doesn't cheat, doesn't dupe anyone and isn't a dupe. He is outside. No one can understand him.

—Van Velde quoted by Charles Juliet

Here's my therapy: never lie to myself, never mask my real feelings for others. Though I feel passionate about this position, I know it's extreme, and somewhat intolerable, for everyone lies to themselves, is afraid and wears a mask. But I am always coherent, because real, I'll never fall prey to schizophrenia. Not lying keeps you lucid even while undergoing the worst suffering. The worst suffering, the most frustrated passion, can make for moments of incredible lucidity. It is easy to become consumed by society's morals, to assimilate its values. I am constantly inclined to lie to myself, to hide, to go to sleep, to be assimilated. You must keep a constant vigil on the self in order to conserve, preserve, and make your "originality" (in the sense of origin) spring forth. You must resist becoming habituated to whatever it might be, for becoming habituated is like falling asleep. Our senses, our capacity for astonishment and revolt, are put to sleep by habits. Habits are the passive acceptance of the real. The artist must invest the real with his will, gamble on the impossible. Only this umbrageous power can force reality into becoming an inspiration, generative of words, of forms, of colours, of sounds.

When I say reality, I mean real stories. Not the form, the look of things, that kind of reality is illusory and fluctuating, belonging only to the gaze. I am talking about things that actually happen, about things done to us by others, by chance, or by our biological condition. Actions, statements of fact. All that is not shaped by our gaze is reality: the social situation, illness, death, eroticism. The misery of Saint-Henri[2]: undeniable reality. The old woman, dying of cancer, undergoing the worst pain: undeniable reality. The physical presence of the beloved: undeniable reality. Someone hits someone else, kills them, someone kisses someone, caresses them.

———

March 5, 1979

How can I hold back these giant waves of hope in my heart, these flutters of optimism, of crazy certainty, of empty hopes? Why am I suddenly flooded with the memory of so much love? As if Paul were here, as if he had told me he was on his way over. Yet, I must keep a clear head, and not hope for or expect anything. Meanwhile, something futile is unspooling inside of me, my heart leaps up, a softness fills my eyes, infusing the everyday with strange signs, a holiday mood. There's no source for any of this, unless, perhaps, it's from the fact that I'm going to see him at the end of the week. What's more, it's not a sure thing. But I know he'll come back. Montréal looks like him again, Montréal will be made sweet with spring and with him. But he will not be mine. I dream and I dream that I am dreaming. *Topographies of Love* is so dependent on him, the danger weighs heavily upon me. This development could destroy the manuscript's vital intuitiveness, and I could find myself, once again, facing the castrating heartbreak of starting all over again. When he comes near, everything begins to look like him. I am in love, but should not expect anything beyond this fleeting, ordinary pleasure. I must savour and draw life from it, so that being denied his body doesn't totally wreck me.

———

As long as it remains light we'll keep watch
afterwards I can't promise anything

———

March 6, 1979
Waiting, the pink reflections made by a nocturnal downpour seduce
my mind. And the wind becomes a tongue on my eyelids and cheeks,
moves down my neck, tells of other nights. Some are sheets pulled
over the secrets of children, over smiles, involuntary guardians, and
others, beautifully wrinkled, are first secrets, first wolves. The city
unfolds itself and turns into rainbows from the ample loosening of
air. Waiting has no more importance and night confides in us before
we fall asleep. Night is the mind's amorous confusion. And at day-
break your scent is in the sheets.

[Prose poems]

———

As long as it remains light we'll go on watching
afterwards I can't promise anything

———

A rigorous, systematic, raw, and lyrical exploration of a city through
its commonplace connections with love. Not finding this by using
flowery baroque images, but through the efficacy of words, the
lucidity of language. Finding oneself in this place, in this instant,
and in the movement from one transport to another that charac-
terizes love.

———

I have conflated the words 'love' and 'desire' for too long, and this epic mix up has brought me an absurd amount of misery. The word love calls up an entire mythos, and I moved this mythos of love onto desire. I was in the midst of building myself a mystique of desire, the way that our society makes a mystique of love. Desire, unmythologized, is livable; desire, mythologized, is unlivable. There's nothing infinite or eternal about love or desire, these are well-worn quotidian realities, commonplace niceties.

But what then have I always felt for Paul? A mystification? An idealization of the other, to the point of creating an exceptional being through whom the universe is revealed? Or simply exacerbated desire? But why does desire become fixated on one person over another? Who creates desire? A phantasmagoria formed in childhood (such as the love of heroes), chance, or a free act, that is to say freely chosen? But to what degree is 'making love' reduced when the other is put into the totally ordinary reality of being just one traveller among others? Making love like eating, for example ... I'm like those homosexuals who are endlessly wiped out by desire, and for whom the object of desire takes on both immense and ephemeral dimensions. But, educated as a woman, I was taught to conflate love and desire, and I believed that each desire was the end of the world. Now I've really reverted. Maybe love and desire fundamentally have the same face, but each wears it differently. Some desires are rekindled, others go out, certain people arouse more desire in us than others, and we call this love. Paul is the embodiment of a great desire, but that's the mystery, and I can't figure out what causes it; I must savour it in the instant. All mystery leads to destruction. Consciousness comes about in those instants when we are conscious. Consciousness and the instant are one and the same, but all of these dreams about Paul were mystifications and all mystification is alienation.

There is nothing habitual to the instant, but all mystification is an eternal return.

Instant and consciousness.
Mythology and unconsciousness.
Writing begins when the unconscious makes its way toward consciousness.

———

An instant of heat swaying though pines. That moment when an entire universe hid behind the rocks, grasses, and burning trees in an intensely ordinary landscape. I would have liked to have been able to penetrate it, this place that held the creative mystery of Cézanne. Creative mystery, an energy I lack, the power to get up each morning and find your way toward the same astonishment. To find a multiplicity of forms in the real. Cézanne is like a miracle to me, Cézanne, who completely abandoned all of the forms and laws of our world to seek a new language: leaving everything in order to reinvent it all. Cézanne, the same desire after a century of disruptions. We stand before him as if standing before evidence, before clarity. Cézanne goes further than all of those who came before him as well as those who were more successful than him in his time. Cézanne built the real. His quest was of such an acuteness, such an intensification of consciousness, that even the freest formulations of the unconscious can't touch his powerful newness. Why don't we feel more passion, why are our words aimless, without madness or urgency to get into the world? Why do we journey forth as if our lips had been seared by a burning fatalism? This indefatigable odour of rot, of death. What's causing this slow surrender? Where have the beautiful enthusiasms gone, the disasters, the hopes? Nothing can stop this giant metronome hammering at our heart and ribs, leaving us to grow old in boredom and disgrace.

———

March 8, 1979

So, after this long discussion with France, I took note of just how alienated I really am. Instead of trying to become a realized person through work, creative pursuits, and new experiences, I've always attempted to realize myself through the *other*, through men. As if love was the only interesting thing in life. Instead of using love as just one of the multiple ways of knowing oneself and the world, I've lived it as an alienation; to realize myself through the other, to enjoy his power. And therefore, I do not love myself (am ignorant of and inadequate to myself). I need the other to love me in order to become loveable (this is the source of my foolishness in always wanting to seduce). To exist through the other's gaze (alienation), and this leads to the worst kind of will to destruction. A ton of poorly directed energies.

———

March 9, 1979

O the beautiful days at once foam-filled and sooty when the mountain turns around us and the white page is stained with the black salt of March. All of the city's malleable materials have entered our consciousness, all of the odours through the mouth, and our kisses followed the strange debauchery of brightness. Ethereal blossoming in the dream of shadows. We have been seduced by distress.

[*Prose poems*]

———

When you come near me I am released from these destructive emo-
tions, freed of this projection into the void. The child in you that
I didn't know, the child inside us who doesn't yet know us (who
still holds all the barrenness of your past and the candour of these
future tides).

[*Prose poems*]

———

March 10, 1979

Robert Desnos's last poem, written right before he died. It's the
copy of an old prose poem he had written eighteen years earlier:

I dreamt so much and so intensely of you,
I walked so much, talked so much,
Loved your shadow so much,
That I no longer have anything left of you.
All I have left is to be a shadow among shades
To be one hundred times more shadow than shadow
To be the shadow that will pass time and again
*   over your sunlit life*

Desnos, dead in Czechoslovakia in a German concentration camp.
See the relationship between Love and Death, and the indissoluble
thread which weaves the poet between them. It's as if all reality,
even the most atrocious, can only be spoken of through love.

———

We are assaulted constantly by ecological tragedies and wars. It's frightening how fast our society is becoming technological, how we are increasingly alienated and directed toward a future that rejects us. In the face of this drama we can still find our suffering, our alienation, and our freedom in love, love is our last instant, our last genuine landscape. Writing is the search for a lost paradise.

Topographies of Love

a lot of shadowy work is needed
so that the stars will turn green
— Pablo Neruda, *The Hunter of Roots*

[June 1979][1]
The days of summer when the waters rise up to assault the walls.

———

[August 31, 1979]

Montréal is still my negative imaginary, a captivating dream.

June 8, no one was around and the summer resounded like a gong.

You crossed the street in the direction of the houses with pastel carpets.

July 27, skinned alive after the blue crops of the countryside.

A man near a beach is proud of his vacation.

You are inert in the establishment of souvenirs.

8 o'clock in the evening, it's cold, I know that you are coming back, but I keep quiet.

Montréal's greatness is like an all-purpose mess.[2]

August 31, my arms flail around with desires. The city has suddenly become crystallized.

Your body lingers on, the east where everything happens to us and the west where you listen to the familial tick-tock. (What a disgorging of luxury and of greenery.)

O Montréal, is there no way to clear a path for our lives?

———

Note

There's nothing I can do but wait for this pain to pass. I can't read, or write. Today is September 2, 1979, what, then, is up with the weather? Why is my heart so fixated on his promise to love me, so much so that everything else is annihilated? Where am I going, who will I talk to, if I can't speak of the person who's living inside of me and ripping me apart, making me feel like an idiot? I have no more thoughts, no more tears or laughter. I have been laid into my desire as into a tomb. Others are but wild-eyed passersby. The disembodied things crumble in on themselves. Love has turned bad. It reveals nothing, if not its own limits, if not our innate desire for the absolute, which is but a metaphysical form of sex, of pleasure. The body seeks fulfillment, responds to its destiny, and from that we deduce a whole new world. But it's a terrible illusion that harms the soul. There is no absolute, no eternity, no infinity, there is only attraction, only indefatigable attraction which flattens us just like hunger or death.

———

we have seen the nameless forests file by ...

[*Self-portraits*]

———

there is this relentless desert of colours
and then the uncomfortable magnificence of desires
one must limit sleeping waiting sleeping some more
I closed the windows and brought the chairs indoors
cleared the table and telephoned no one was home
made the bed and drank the water left in the bottom of the glass
all the seasons had been crumpled like bad copies
our shadows held themselves still
it was the start of the demolition

[*Self-portraits*]

———

I write you on everything that isn't me ...

[*Self-portraits*]

Note
Write poems with a striking precision without anyone being able to detect what is being clarified. Such that the words would be porous and the style both astonishing and familiar.

———

September 20, 1979

Everything has become mythic, fantastical. My desire for him is becoming exasperating. I am on the edge of madness. In silence I call to him, implore him. Sometimes I see him as my master, sometimes I wish he would hit me, and that his contempt for me over these past two years would change into some form of terrible violence. Anything other than those tepid feelings. Other times I dream of enacting revenge, of making him take a turn at being humiliated. I flee, he needs me, he looks for me. These are all just the rantings of a frustrated woman. The truth is, I love him to the point of vertigo, to the point of dementia, but because I'm in love alone, and there's no way out of this situation, the volume gets turned up and I suffer like a beast. I fear myself. Once more, all my writing sucks, because I am unhappy, uncertain. The entire universe has withdrawn its signs. I am no longer an individual with a world, I am a devasted and alienated woman. I thought desire would be my weapon of liberation, but instead it has become my straitjacket.

How do male writers manage to write major works about their passions? Are those passions made up rather than lived? Is it because I live mine too much that not a single word comes from it, and I have no control of my mind whatsoever? The onrush of feelings, my mind's discombobulation, my memory of his body. Stupid, I am completely stupid, ever since knowing him I no longer understand myself. I wait for him, but he will never come. I know I will accept whatever he gives me. It's horrible. I shouldn't lose sight of myself. I want to be an egoist and only feel passion for myself. But he is there, he is always inside of me. I question myself about him: he is the unknown, the pariah, and the master all at once.

Strange arsonist, unconscious of himself. He doesn't know himself, has lost sight of himself. He will never give me anything, though I know I am prepared to accept any little crumb. But no, I will not accept only crumbs, I know I'm too good at writing for that, I love him too much for that. But what is loving him? Believing in him, knowing he can be as generous as a king, but that he lives a circumscribed life and must respect its borders? He can be generous, but not toward me, if I love him I should forget him. No, forgetting him would be contemptuous. But me, me! What is best for me? What should I do, where is life? The debauchery of the heart or the control of the mind? Where is my creativity? What, I mean to say, is poetry, true poetry? Isn't poetry a form of rebellion, and isn't love a form of rebellion? But shared, you idiot! You woman alienated by myths, Ophelia still slides her long veils in your waters. Wake up! Shared love ...

———

collection
this hunger this exhaustion
as if surrounded by this pull
the hours sprout
blind and passionate
we imagine saving ourselves devouring ourselves
your shoulders impassable night
(at the edge of tears the way of the world)

the waves scrub our memories
and you an unknown destination
(you recognize a series of lightning strikes)
cry out

[*Self-portraits*]

———

September 21, 1979

Excerpt from a letter to Marie-Claude

... writing isn't easy for me ...; My work on my third volume is intense but slow, I am trying to find a rhythm. Sign and Rumour *had its own rhythm, and the rhythm of* The Life Beyond, *as you no doubt noticed, was distinct from it. Now my life is vibrating in a different way and I must find the exact pulse, the deep primary beat that is guiding my thoughts, my dreams, and my actions. Every new book is a question, not an answer. Everything was clearer in my head with* Sign and Rumour, *with* The Life Beyond *these certainties went away, and now I haven't a single one left. Contrary to what is believed, sometimes the deeper an artist goes into their method, the less they know of themselves. This is perhaps what allows us to find new forms, but what an endless misery! In fact, the older I become, the more miserable I feel. This is not a smart way to proceed you'll say ... It's true. My adolescent crisis was nothing next to the riddles now forming all around me and inside of me. I'm not even sure what I want out of life. I know that I value writing over all other preoccupations, but what kind of writing? Why poetry? ... I spent almost a year not writing anything good because I questioned myself. It's absurd. I realized that in order to write, I sometimes needed to stop questioning everything and let myself follow whatever came spontaneously, and "superchargedly." I would like to harmonize my life and my thoughts and my feelings. But my thoughts sometimes*

conflict with my feelings and I don't always act in accordance with what I think or feel. There's a fissure, I'm not sure where. It's a lack of freedom. I mean internal freedom. I want to transcend my limits, pull back the borders of my consciousness, sink into the realm of words, and pull out all of the tastes and colours I can, the uses, but some sort of laziness or weakness, frozen, (an ontological weakness?) holds me back. Often when I try to write, nothing comes. Hours of work ends up in the trash. Sometimes it's stomach-turning. So, I say to myself, what good is it? But I know I can't succeed at anything else. At seven or eight years old I started writing, this activity monopolized my mind, never leaving it for a single day. To give up writing would be tantamount to giving up on myself, yet at the same time all of it is so difficult, so demanding, and what good is it, finally? I no longer know ...

Loving and this chalk silhouette at the window ...

[Poems at the Margin]

MASTER AND PARIAH
THE REBELLION OF THE ANGELS

If I remember correctly, one day the angels rebelled against God. God sent his army to quell them, they were beaten and thrown into hell. Did they commit the sin of pride? Maybe it is more that they committed the sin of choice. God was their destiny, their fate, they lived in his kingdom and were subject to his law, but they rose up and wanted to create their own lives. They fought and lost, then fell into solitude and fear. All wise people know this lesson, those who work the entirety of their lives to abolish their desires and feel themselves to be like a leaf upon the water, provoking nothing, letting themselves glide through life without demanding anything from it and not wanting to control its course or flow. The angels became devils whose loud bursts of laughter were too rarely heard, because they had learned irony, and humour, they are those who have not given up on themselves. O beautiful dark angels with burnt wings, are there nights when you lay on the ground, look up at the stars, and at last feel at one with the world? Or perhaps the cry of rebellion is never quiet in you, the fire suppressing the supreme indecency of your desire.

Such is the destiny of those who love life passionately, of those who never give up on the impossible.

———

MASTER AND PARIAH
Outline for a novel

Every Angel is terrible.[3]

A meeting in the Louvre in front of the drawings and sketches of Lorrain, Claude Le Lorrain.

The café in the Photo gallery. He says where he practices.

She keeps still in her office. Silence. Refusal.

She thinks of the following: the feminine taste for annihilation. The abominable admiration of physical or social strength. Gabrielle decides not to pursue her fantasy.

David's anger. His comfort.

David looks for her throughout Paris.

Gabrielle phones him.

Dinner — Make love.

David flees, Gabrielle pleads.

Gabrielle returns to Montréal, Québec. Description of her fantasies.

Stay at the Islands at her sister's place. Spring. Description. Letter. Arrival of David. Summer, eroticism, humour.

———

I did really dream of you from morning until unhappy evening. Kneeling through the night in your imagined body, standing in your thoughts by day. And everything that went into the spark of the last two years was nothing but false fires, painful unconsciousness, deep sleep dressed up as desire. I dreamt of you and dream your shadow down to its bare frame, until I can see the forgiving softness of the dawn on the other side. I dreamt you into a thousand places in Montréal. You have become part of my unknown: all that I cannot decipher of the real, just as I can't understand you. In my attempt to understand you I have looked everywhere, in particular books, in particular places, in so many material signs, insignificant or fragile, yet there. You were a wandering thought, an unavoidable feeling, and often I figured you out, in spite of yourself. I was not guilty of certainty, I am certain of nothing when it comes to you or to love. But I don't hold with certainty, for it hardens the mind and the heart, is a prelude to death, because life is nothing but outbursts, questions, and chance. You, you are immune to answers. I made you wobble on your pedestal, but it was of no use, you didn't need me. Before deciding to chase after me you pretty much *let* me go toward you. Now that I've come around, do you really have so little need of me? Even when you push me away, it seems like you still think about me. Neither rejecting my love nor ignoring my presence will free you. The only way to be free is to love me. If you gave yourself to me, I would no longer be a burden to you. But perhaps you'll forget me through sheer will. Just by wishing to forget me, you'll succeed in doing so. Yet I believe (which is so irrational on my part) that despite the cruel tone you've adopted, you've fallen in love with me, a fact you're trying your best to ignore, but you're struggling, and it's your final struggle. But me, I have stopped fighting for the impossible. I've given up looking for you, you can come or go, begin again, forget, or be generous; my love won't lessen, or insist, or suffer anymore, because I feel you everywhere now. From morning until unhappy evening, I have dreamt too much of you. For too long I have kept watch for the slightest tremor of your skin, of your gaze, not to be able to deeply intuit you, as a pool senses the movements of the clouds it mirrors. The aim of my dreams was to just look at you, even during your most distanced, difficult absences. To you I seem like some one-off you've hallucinated, but if you loved me I would be an endless font of sweetness. In me you would decode your memory and your life. There are so many land-scapes within us just waiting for a sign to awaken. Will they wake up? Is this purposeful or purposeless? It doesn't matter. We think we are acting of our own free will, but we are obeying indescribable underground drives, and we cannot change the shape of things. It's likely that everything you're going to do has been seeded in your past, just as the person I once was couldn't help but fall in love with you the moment we met. Such as I am, you answered too much to my eagerness, giddiness, fantasies, tenderness, and knowledge for me to either avoid or forget you. Most likely I fell in love with you because you hadn't the slightest need of me, and thus you could push me to my limit. Now I love you in a different way, my love is no longer con-nected to suffering or to the death drive. I desire you less, I love you more. My mind moves in your direction as my body moves toward a fountain. So many beautiful seasons are poised in your hands.

Of course, my passion for you is primarily physical. We love physically. Because, without the body, how would we make sense of our loftiest metaphysics? We understand the world through our bodies, it's the body that makes the heart expand. Sensuality is everything. That is where happiness begins, there and nowhere else.

Montréal, you are alive inside of me, and every day more fiercely alive, and though not mysterious, you're awkward and difficult to describe. I have known your banks full of autumn and such gentle freshness, your transports so grey. My love lives inside of you and you ring like a gong in my immutable night. Him, from every corner he approaches me with you in his arms (or you approach me from every corner with him, my love, in your giant arms, your sad and almost docile arms).

[*Prose poems*]

———

TOPOGRAPHIES OF LOVE

We should no longer "abolish" chance, as far as words would allow, but on the contrary we should assume it, and the presence of others, to which we sacrifice the infinite, and our sense of ourselves, consequently, will open a possibility. Events, those that puncture destiny, will break off, signifying, in the field of mute appearances. Certain words — bread and wine, house, and even storm or stone — will do likewise, words of communion, words of sense, detached from the framework of concepts. And a place will be made of these assumptions and these symbols, which, even though nothing, of course, in its last substance, will be our completed human form, and therefore the unity of the act and the event of being, and its absolute. Incarnation, this outside to the dream, is a virtue very close to hand.

— Yves Bonnefoy, *The Red Cloud*

Poetry ... is the creator of language, that is to say, creator in the concrete sense. Where such creation doesn't exist (which might be, and, at certain times in history, can only be, a creation against *an existing meaning, a destructive creation), there is no poetry, and everywhere sense is made it exists, no matter the form.*

— Éric Weil, *The Logic of Philosophy*

———

AUTOBIOGRAPHY I

A rhythmical prose text that moves from me, my daily life, and my love, to the design of the city. The splitting open of these places, acts, feelings, the ones becoming reflections of the others. The formation of a kind of diamond from this constant carbon, my existence. "Transfiguration" of the poem, or more likely the crystallization of thought through the intensification of the senses. Sense and sexuality intensified leads to the purification of forms, the tool that aims to spring the prism from the darkness, the star from the night, the word from the silent mass of the earth. And yet, all germination begins with a wound. All polish is created through cutting, levelling, blows, and rejections; the object shines like a clear well-worked thought. The martyring of the object gives birth to the look that multiplies our lives.

———

SEPIA

Attempt to gather all of these disparate elements in order to figure out their meaning: fragments of days and of the mind, both conscious and unconscious. The sense lived or invented, not like an absolute reality, or a truth, but the way that a piece of fruit smells when you peel it, the taste when you take a bite.

And by the way, how can I *not* point out the beautiful similarity between the word 'sense,' as a synonym for meaning, and the senses, our senses, which show us and give us the world, which invent our existence?

We can always be certain of form, but not of the sense, it is manifold, vacillating, open to all weathers. Those who erect a dogma around it, who believe that they have definitively understood it, are always off, and sometimes by a lot. Meaning is a gift; it never runs out. It murmurs, and all the forms belong to it. It rebels, and all certainty runs from it, all the questions gather round: it is an ocean of laughter.

———

October 9, 1979

It snowed this morning, even though there are still green leaves, and red, and yellow, and orange. An impromptu show of what's coming. Inverted weather. Snow's dreadful show. The embodiment of our solitude. Body dispersed, disseminated. Pages torn up. Words flayed, rejected, shreds: memory blank. That way snow has of engulfing all sounds and absorbing all smells. A foreshadowing of death, but with the haunting of a strange desire. Snow flattens out obstacles, hides the rough patches, the ugly bits, the textures. It is strangely modern, snow, also musical, though we don't hear it, because it falls, rhythmically, perpetually, at times dense, at times light, discursive and modulated by differing winds. It is strangely religious, snow, because, kneeling and pious, it falls down in pure columns, unsuspected, from high in the sky, only to vanish, though we never know where, on the ground, or remain as sad petals. A cathedral where light disperses unknowingly, into which our spirit escapes, questioned by something endlessly open, inventive, and endlessly depressing, suffocating, steady. Snow gags like a pillowcase over the face, like arms in a too-tight hug, like something missing. Snow is known forms, sense lost.

———

I am not happy, I am not unhappy, unless being locked away in both mind and heart is a bad thing. Every once in a while, I am released from myself by the terrible confirmation of my need for you and my pleasure in seeing you.

I believe, more or less, in the importance of happiness. I'm interested in knowledge (to learn and simultaneously be born of this knowledge).[4] That's what poetry is. All apprenticeships and discoveries of self and world necessitate some sort of tearing. What I fear most is not the possibility of pain, but of having my life weighed down by certainty, complaisance, senselessness (that my life would become meaning-poor). But I don't think we share the same definition of what's sensible and what is senseless.

To me, something is senseless when it no longer has even one iota of mystery, or amazement, or tentativeness, when it settles into a single, fixed aspect. What's sensible is the thing rich in multiple meanings.

———

Calligram of stars when Montréal cracks open the door

———

I have dreamt so much that I feel as if my very life has been no more than a long dream. I have dreamt so much of you that it feels as if you are a long dream that must have begun the first time I shuddered with love.

[Prose poems]

———

I miss the Magdalen Islands so much. I suffer terribly from their absence. I'm referring particularly to the landscape, because it calms my anxiety. Large spaces opening out onto colour. Nothing but colour.

———

I don't want to think about destiny, the absolute, the infinite, I can't stand the sacred. I try to use words to create a place I might enter from inside, made of two bodies, made purely from the reality of conflict (Misfortune/Happiness). Where one, clashing ceaselessly with the other, would doubt everything, lose all certainty and perspective, about the world and himself. Beautiful things would become ugly, or would stay beautiful, it would make no difference, but this place would always lead to the self, the self as a laboratory of sensations, out of which he would try to reinvest in his life, life itself, with previously hidden or forbidden meaning. A place (the two bodies) that makes reason uncomfortable. To love deeply is an anti-social act. Passion is no longer the master of signs, of that code of dismal, factual communication that society uses to secure and delude. Passion turns us into a "wandering Jew," the butt of sarcasms, fears, prejudices. We become the hidden side of people, the side that frightens them because of its ability to throw their entire existence into question. And suddenly, all these "productive" and "alienating" values, which have been forcefully put into their heads since childhood, and for which they have lived up until this moment, can appear false, revealed in their true light, and that is what they fear more than anything, maybe even more than death.

Mad love helps us to unlearn. All must be unlearned in order to create, all must be doubted, looked at with astonishment. Destroy the forms and make a meaning that is multiple, fluctuating, and moving.

———

I can't bear people who feel sure of things. Those who believe in something that is unchanging, transcendent, religion or science, make me sad. Poetry is not empirical, but speculative, it walks on uncertain ground, for poetry all meanings are possible. It reflects the language, moving through it as through a forest; all dies and is reborn and nothing is ever really the same. There is nothing transcendent in the wording of a poem, it is the very life of the poet in and through language, autobiography in a vivid state. This place where the body and language play pleases me, it is a theatre of coincidences in which the actor and the spectator constantly change places.

———

These poor soft purposeless nights
and needless roads and nameless things
grounds absorbed by some internal burn

———

[November 1979]

My imagination as a transport to another world, but poetry is emi-
nently of this world. Yes, imagination as metaphor, a metaphor
which only serves to reinforce our perceptions of the here and now.

———

The silence of waves and desires like slow spheres

———

Writing is a way of knowing. The word 'to be born' [*naître*] is
within the word 'to know' [*connaître*]. To be continually born into
the reality of a knowledge that is always speculative, never intran-
sigent and dominating. Life is multiplied by living in and through
language, a space where everything continually comes and goes. It
deepens the autobiographical side of dreams. It is another form of
mad love.

———

A hand only just offered then retracted just as quickly

———

Is metaphor the imaginary, or perhaps just one way to shake up and
make more real what everyone else sees, without doubt or question,
as the real?

———

flowers on the patio table ...

[*Self-portraits*]

———

1.

Sometimes the imagination is thought to be like the encephalo-gram of a sleeping man. The domain of dreams and fantasies. But once we stop opposing dream to reality, the conscious mind to the unconscious, the imagination will take possession of its true defi-nition. What's very far is often so very close, just beneath our skin and intellect. The real multiplies its signs. No one comprehends the truth or essence of the real. Maybe a sense must be invented to find it. As it stands, a thought that is not empirical often turns dogmatic. Meaning is born and develops through our physical understanding of the world. From there, the richness of the poem.

2.

Is metaphor (in poetry) the only form the imagination takes?

And yet, if the imagination is the construction of "another world," located either to one side of or above this one, then poetry as I conceived of it is not a work of the imagination. Because poetry is eminently of this world, and I believe that the most tangible parts of the real are the primary sites of its investigations. Metaphor, therefore, serves to reinforce our perceptions of the here-now-this. But every poet works in their own way ... As I see it, there's noth-ing of the transcendent to the imagination in the poem, it is just the poet's life in and through language, with all the varieties of meaning that metaphor offers, a vivid autobiography, a theatre of coincidences, another form of mad love.

———

Dear Richard,

I was writing (finally!) to my friends Claude and Brigitte, when in a sudden flash I could clearly see a particular evening, very blue, very light, on rue La Fayette. At the beginning of September in 1978 it wasn't chilly like it is now, in 1979, and it's not as grey there as it is here (no matter what they say), and all the windows (there are even windows on the roof) allow a thick golden colour to filter in. You can see people working, and others on their way back home. The city of Paris glides under our feet reeking of humidity, pastries, frying, gas. One has a hankering to go out and mix with the dense crowd and become anonymous. Tonight I wish I was still there, in that almost violet sweetness before Paris swings into nighttime. "We should dream of truths that look like us," someone sings on the radio. How beautiful, I would have liked to have written that.

We should fight to get that sense of freedom and anonymity back, to be nothing more than that particular evening, so light, so misty-eyed, I can't even see myself reflected in the windows. To have so scant an identity as to no longer live through a sense of self, but to merge into the spectacle of the street. I would be a gaze that continually fuses with its object. Forever rid of my ego, without remorse, without fear, without hope, I would become everyone's dream, a kind of wind, a supreme evanescence. The poem being always located outside of me (a being, a landscape), I would become the poem itself. I love twilight, the onset of night. The waning light often gives me a feeling of anticipation, a delectable premonition of the end of the world. "Let the world go to its ruin, that's the only politics," Marguerite Duras says so vividly in The Truck.

At night people prepare their folly. They put on their festival masks, or more likely, they take off their masks and fashion their real faces, maybe. Tonight I regret being myself and for taking everything so seriously, for not being above it all, exaggeratedly carefree, filled with conviction and laughter. I would like to give fully and always, yet I give poorly. Only giving comforts me. To live or to forget myself, because I cannot be absorbed into the crowd. To give, without really knowing how. Writing is a little like this, the egoistic impulse to give everything away ...

———

The more I wanted to love, the more I lost what I loved. As soon as I asserted my will, the world evaded me. As soon as I wanted to give, I suffocated, and what was indifferent to me came toward me. I am alone, terribly alone, and yet something is lying in wait in the shadows, something is waiting, ready to rise up, some kind of great departure: myself. No one else. The ability to finally love myself without any need or presence of the other to reassure me. Me, indifferent to strangers, collecting memories, amassing images, living in what's ephemeral, temporary, the useless second, a moment seized, forgetful of promises. Generosity frightens, then repels. I will no longer be generous except to myself. I so prefer this solitude to the other. I will no longer walk beside myself, but in my own steps. I want to hear my own dance, to breathe in the singular pleasure of being alone. O woman, how you have been alienated, how you have been deceived into wanting to live off the other, with the other, through the other, and, like some sort of ghoul, feed off the love of men. I wanted to give, but only that I might get something back. O Paul, you are so far away. At last, I hate you, and how delicious it is to hate you, to be practically indifferent to you, to finally be able to laugh about you, about us, finding the whole thing so limited, small, and laughable. From now on, I'll be my own path, I'm not going to hang by this thread any longer. But, now that the thread is cut, the ground feels very close, the soil is about to open, it may already be loose and flowering. How distant they seem, all the wordless strangers accruing their ordinary experiences, their dreary escapes, their hollow gestures;

fragile, morose puppets who buy their happiness. How heavy it is, like a crate, a November afternoon, a commercial song.

O Paul, if only you knew how terrible it felt to have wanted you so badly. Yet, in the same way we can forget an intense physical pain, so too with existential pain. We can forget the pain of loving without being loved in return. The anxiety attacks that destroyed me. Like a phoenix burned down to ash, I now feel reborn from nothing. Paul, my last gasp of confusion, I wanted you to be a hero, Icarus, but already my sadness at being separated grows vague. O Paul, poor man without scope or language, your body was the end of my world, yet all it took was for another body to show up for that end to change form. It's pathetic. I only loved because I wanted to be loved, and only said those words in the hope that they would be said back to me. Now I want to cultivate a lofty indifference. Men are cowardly, pitiable, and tedious, and should be taken as they are, without fantasy or passion. When they wrap their arms around us, they do so like little boys huddling close to their mothers. Homosexuals, they shun the mother, that's why their love affairs are passionate, sexual, brutal, ephemeral, phantasmatic. These men aren't looking for a maternal refuge. It's their kind of love I would have wanted, not the romantic antics of weak males sleepwalking through life. They give nothing unless they're secure in their possession, they think only of protecting themselves, meting out their feelings, keeping track of their hours and orgasms. They like to make you wait, but they wait for no one; they leave. They love it when you're unattainable, no more lively, unruly or uneasy than a statue on a pedestal. Men are never central to our ideas about love.

————

This trade wind love swept to the forefront of fears ...[5]

[*Poems at the Margin*]

Wrinkles[1]

the exploded mortar-shell heart whistled its love song
— Apollinaire, *My Love's Shadow*[2]

1.

When I awoke this morning, the sky was a blue expanse across which floated smears of gold, orange, and light pink. Then, little by little, it was overrun by heavy white clouds followed by snow and wind. A storm. I got up, feeling "blessed," like I do when travelling, but lost that feeling the moment the sky changed. It's probably just because I am young, this feeling of intoxication, or maybe its source is some delicate mechanism intended to help our bodies wake up. I was filled with intimate, delicate, and delicious sensations. It was one of those moments of perfect illusion that give my life a feeling of immanence, a moment when everything in the world has a clarity to it and carries the weight of lived experience. My "soul" becomes a part of everything I see, feel, touch, and anticipate. Images culled from conversations, films, and books flood my mind and become a part of me. I know that everything is threatened by destruction and meaninglessness, that our world is threatened by chaos, and that behind its facade of eternal harmony, nature is plague-filled and out of balance, eroding, irreversibly disappearing, or at least losing what we've known as its tranquil and "divine" aspect. But on these routine mornings my mind sees only the beauty, and even chaos seems beneficial. I constantly gravitate toward pictures of sea, sun, plants, sand. I see myself leaning against a white wall where the softness of light intensifies. It neither burns nor blinds, but like a wave, floods my body with a primal sense of well-being.

A mildly stereotypical place (I'm not afraid to say) I'll never give up, because to do so would be to give up on myself. For it's not some exotic locale, it's sovereign country of my mind, part of my unrealistic hope for a definitive home in the world. In truth, this place moves inside of me, fed by the accumulated traces of it that my little diaristic life has recorded, like this morning's sky and wind, perfumed and caressing some tomorrow, somewhere else in the city's twists and turns. Planes from it are always taking off, heading for a kind of ambitious thought. It's in turning toward this last feeling that the poem sneaks in, allows me to sense it. (Like the way the Italian landscape affected numerous European writers and painters over the centuries.)

Because it has no describable reality, I cannot really represent this place. It's a lyric abstraction. The closest I come is via existential fragments, and my writing about those fragments. And still the poem escapes, only rarely showing up in a clear and definitive way. My haste makes it explode before touching down.

I hate all mystification in writing, the entire mythological universe; the poem should be sensual, material, just like everything that incites me to live is tactile, and all that *seems* abstract at first is really made up of actual elements that the senses can name and the intellect can easily recognize.

———

One day at a time each begins to disarm
the secret splendour of his art

———

2.

Romance has become the only "place" in the life of the individual where self-expression is still possible. I want to say, where you can still give and shape your own meaning through actions, impulses, and feelings; next to which the rest of the universe, society, and nature, are irremediably degraded and reified. The only power that remains untouched is man's very internal one of instinct, of sensation. Starting from what is left of freedom, of autonomy, it is possible for him to reinvent the imagination of his daily life. The quotidian, the private life has become the only possible domain for his investigations, his only power. In all other realms of existence, the individual is powerless. Economic power normalizes our existence and packages our relations with the world, political power turns us into its (passive) observers.

———

I began with the title *Topographies of Love* because that was the goal, to map places in the world that could, through the individual's internal, passionate impulses, become repositories of meaning. With *Romances*[3] I'm moving in the opposite direction, stockpiling things and places in the world that can then be reshaped by the interior life; emptying the social sense or nonsense out and filling it with created personal meaning. This to establish an erotic relationship with reality, even if reality has become completely frigid and the individual powerless, or vice versa. It's a hope.

January eighteenth nineteen eighty
The fragile parsing of rhythm
in the morning the lifeline moves from one hope to another
reflected in an album of images
the gusts the tastes the atmospheres keep watch
we know the promises by heart
we know that the night is a stone

[*Poems at the Margin*]

———

3.

Listening to Ernest Chausson's "Poem." I agree with him that death is not as scary as the idea of dying without having said and done what you hope to say and do. This is the obsession that plagued me when I was in the hospital. It has not left me. The fear that death would interrupt the dark work of my poetry. That a line would show up and, resistant to whatever harmony is haunting me, would never have the chance to become realized. Time would run out before I could find a way to move it across the threshold. Time seems to move far too quickly now, and my sadness at the thought of all I may not have time to write knows no end. But I'm not conflating quantity with quality. It's with quality that I want to conquer time.

———

4.

I don't know what kind of melancholy grace this man had, what ironic stance; next to him we were caricatures of ourselves. What is the source, then, of our desperate desire? A desperation provoking endless regret, endless pursuit? Things appear and fade away by themselves. We observe a strict silence, as if living on a beach where no one is allowed to look at the waves. And me, I am stunned and fascinated by this man, as if facing a body made of stone, docile before fountains, abysses. Inside the darkness that fills all men my thoughts are multiplied. I see them all through the lens of my desire. Long and seasonal, desire beats with the material heart of the world, it is the powerful instant, all possible and impossible signifiers. It must always be approached through the gaps. It persistently speaks to us of our selves. All the landscapes of the earth resemble it.

———

5.

Beauty ... beauty with its gaucheries and apotheoses, descended
from heaven, arisen from earth, an empirical form of happiness. I
no longer think of beauty as incarnated in any particular object or
nature, but exclusively in the body. Which manifests spirituality in
every gesture, smile, or look, and at the same time is a kind of ironic
angel or work of art in motion. The body of the other serves as the
first intuition of our creative work in the world. An immediate and
fleeting response, imaginary and likely to be disproved, a perpetual
consolation. To me, virile beauty is made out of words.

———

this intense music I can't forget ...

[*Self-portraits*]

———

*Some smiles deserve poems. From now on your smile will become
for me one of those imponderables which make life worth living.
From the old splendours only one kind of magic remains, particular
faces, nearby or faraway. A last irony, an ultimate sweetness, our
faces belong to the glances of others. Yours, it's a bit like* the sea
having fled with the sun.[4]

[*Prose Poems*]

———

6.
In the house no one dreams of contradicting the father
Outside the glimmering poplars gently sway
I think of the coded rustling of the bees

of the clouds' effusions
how life might not know how to feed us
all shudders will come after us

[*Poems at the Margin*]

———

February 22, 1980

7.

Three days ago, Paul informed me that I have a cancerous tumour in my lung.[5] He's confident we can beat it. Suddenly everything seemed so precious and fragile. Suddenly everything seemed to be rushing toward me without ever coming close. Paul's handsome face, the softness of the air, the bustle of the streets. I walked for a long time by myself, bursting with overflowing love and growing fear. The shock paralyzed me, no poems were left to numb my pain. Even though I had wanted to keep writing in the hope that I might secure myself some permanence in this world, I understood that for everyone else I was an unknown and unremarkable writer. And I asked myself: will I live long enough to write and make them all blush, plough it all through the fields of my words, distance them from their circle of shadows (enough time also to love, even those who despise me), to know where my texts will end up? Then, all of a sudden, being popular or unpopular seemed completely beside the point, and all that mattered was time, and codifying my lived experience in the immutable analogy of words. Living is as much about receiving as giving. How I had wanted to be taught the inexpressible form. Then the shock hit me at a deeper level, paralyzing all thought, all hope or desire.

———

what rhythm breaks so fragile a shadow

———

February 24, 1980

8.

By some sort of symbolic fluke, up until yesterday it's been a very mild winter. There was no snow and I was happy. Unlike during other winters, my mood was in lockstep with the weather, I headed into the hospitable city and wrote. Now, this awful, inevitable development and, as chance would have it, snow. My poetic investigations cut short by this stupefying, suffocating circumstance. I need air to write, my mind must be free when it comes to things and feelings. It will be even harder now that my life is to be divided, once again, by this same painful battle.

On the other hand, apprehensions aside, I've developed a sort of delicate, yet matter-of-fact, sense of humour, genuine. I'm not sure why or how, but it's a form of grace. Daily occurrences and challenges that used to seem huge have shrunk down, become absurd, almost artificial. The same thing happens when I listen to Mozart, or look at the sea; I can feel how small I am, yet at the same time I feel that this smallness is inserted into the network of the living universe and, like all living things, has a role to play, and that yelling and crying about it won't change a thing. It makes more sense to channel our energies into being open to what's best in us, what was inside us even at the hour of our birth, instead of wanting to bend existence completely to our demands and dreams of greatness. Like standing before the sea, or in Mozart's music, not remembering, waiting, or hoping for anything, but simply being present among the living, benefitting from all of life's aspects, and this fragile, expanding shadow.

———

It's not like I'm in a film where, after one of the characters dies, things go on as before. After me, there will be nothing more, because I am both the character and the film. After me, no one will continue the dialogue. There will be nothing, because I will no longer be there to note the obvious. My death will be my only eternity, my absence my only infinity. Everything that I say, everything that I write will come to a stop, only my silence will continue without end. It will not even culminate in a cry, or a sigh. It won't resemble a dying star, the disappearance of which unleashes a chain of events. It will be like an emergent thought engulfed by the void, which leaves no trace, not even a memory of the thought's first coming into being.

Ah! The sweetness of daydreaming, listening to Baden Powell. Am I not in a place I've always dreamt of being? The only place that suits me, by the sea, surrounded by the sultry brightness of its rhythm, under the white blaze of walls; a land dominated by summer's profusion of colour, its gentleness. Someplace that has returned to its origins, sand and water, bare elements. Am I not on the threshold of an indescribably sweet and accepting vista?

———

9.

I want to tell you that knowledge is not essential to understanding, that we can instinctually feel many parallel lives firing inside of us, and that we extend upward every time our thoughts draw from the readied perfumes, colours, and rhythms of abolished time. This isn't mysticism, this is love.

———

ROMANCES

———

*When the city appears to you like a crystal you no longer
hope for anything*

———

10.

I have rarely experienced so much desire to write and such difficulty
doing so. It's almost as if I'm not me, but a projection, conflicted,
artificially maintained between two rhythms. The embers of the
love that illuminated my past keep burning, and I call to the future
with all the meagre strength of my heart. I am kept off-centre by a
thread woven from a mix of my disappointment and love.

I have only just started to reject my old talismanic dream. My
improbable love affair, the book I want to open but which will
remain shut. How I would have liked to have easily found shelter
there. But the other is definitively closed. In my dreams, I made
myself a part of his life, but in the real it did not feed me, not in
that reality which, in service to the poem, must be so tenacious. I
feel nostalgic for his body, even though I had so little access to it,
at times this ongoing yearning is extremely painful, at times, if I
concentrate, calming.

There's no point in my wishing to stop turning the pages. They
turn on their own, and the text, with no help from me, congeals
under the stress of too many readings. The time has come to move
on to another poem, yet which one still eludes me. I believed there
would be a return, that both my illness and my love (the two
conflated from the start) were part of a cycle, but things are not

looping back to the same juncture, a little below or a little above, who knows? Even I don't understand my depression.

I must love him, this man, without any possibility, delay, question, or demand, I must love him in a completely abstract way, for myself alone, imagining this love elsewhere, at a great distance, in an existence that might have come before or after us. There's nothing to be done against the indifference of events. I must love him if only to be certain that I do. For the poem that redeems useless things. Though the poem hasn't fed me for a very long time, its writing could be like a magic potion to make his complete absence disappear. O you, ever since we met, I speak of nothing but you and shall speak of nothing but you.

> *The Word of woman gives birth to the unhoped-for much*
> *better than any old daybreak.*
>
> — René Char

But what's unhoped-for always shows up.

———

What reason did the air have to be so sweet
a tree stopped between flowering and empty space
before its life is multiplied in its roots
all embraces are prolonged haphazardly
give birth to other seasons and secrets
night deconstructs us by heart

[*Poems at the Margin*]

———

11.

Because my body is threatening me, I scrutinize it. It's as if I think its precarious state, its difficult battle, might teach me something about myself. As if, through it, I could know a little more about what is beneath the articulation of my organs and bones, the underlying structure. My body is being controlled by two extremes, on the one hand death, which ever since I've had cancer shows up day after day, even if I'm not aware of it; on the other love. I've never stopped feeling its intense beat. Sometimes I just *think* these extreme emotions, other times they show up as physical symptoms, which surprises me. Then I must exert all my mental faculties so I can recognize and name them for what they are. Their physical presence gets by me, and I no longer can discern any of my own will in them, or response, and it's from the questions they repeatedly raise that I'm born. It's as if my likeness, in some extreme way, could end by betraying me and, all masks having fallen away, I finally come to know myself before facing complete oblivion. To at least once know or see, to emerge from this long sleep, and to wake up wearing "seven-league boots," aware of nothing but laughter.[6]

——

[March 6, 1980]

12.

To feel passionate about one's life. A sudden premonition that everything needs to be written down, so that nothing is lost, I must relive it all so I can understand, deep down, the way things echo and fit together, the harmony or the sumptuous materiality of things, and also this strange maze of feelings, the outpouring of my thought and of my heart. The mind takes note, but the words erase themselves. How can I keep hold of them when they encircle me?

How, for example, can I translate the experience of dining out this afternoon? The city a smoky crystal, the muffled interior of white marble, pastel curtains, and sofas so big I felt lost in them. The heavy wall hangings absorbed the too-bright winter light; a few potted palms under the gold decor. Only one conversation would have fit the elegant comings and goings of the patrons: talk about him. But as a man who listens, without hiding behind the paper, to all I have to say. Speak about him: tell me about him until I can't hear anymore, until all the desires are quelled, all the places, all the bodies. When he left the hospital on a cold winter's day, what did the sad and confused look of the brick, the concrete and the windows say to him? What about the clouds unfurling across the sky and the solemn, intimate snow? What did he remember that made his body shudder with the image of my face? A wild and needless question. What good is it to obsessively return to these half-formed thoughts and perceptions, or to any such intuitions? They can't control any future, nor resolve any past, yet they won't let me go, so long as I am unable to determine whether this is a hope or a vision, or if certainty is nothing but another naive and final self-delusion.

The house is dark. I'm avoiding my image. I want it to be loving and free, I want it to be as alive as my preoccupations, so that I could feel, in this battle I'm waging, the promise, the fullness intended. The seconds fall drop by drop with the senseless weight of metal, and I have to fight for each one of them. Hard work is not necessarily rewarded. Contrary to everything that I was taught, the better does not necessarily follow the worse. It's a lesson I must learn. The worse hasn't stopped and were there to be a better *you* would be it, but I ruined that possibility by wanting and loving you too much.

A beautiful autumn day, very high up, perched among the colours, I thought I saw my life finally pivot, moving from its share of shadow to its share of light. My elation returned, the exuberance of all things. I thought that you had given in to me. I am sure that I never loved your eyes so much, your voice, your body, and that night has never trembled so with the breath of desire, with its breathing. I'm sure that no night has ever yearned so for daytime, as the retreating break of an ocean wave leaves behind a perfect ray of sun.

Where should I begin my life story? At the most terrible, my illness; through the facts, I am a poet, I am published, I am twenty-four years old, I have lived with Stéphan for four years and I love him, I am pretty and poor? With the melodrama, that I have another love, an impossible one. With my childhood, which was neither joyous nor sad, but like all childhoods textured in its details? There's nothing to say that hasn't already been said elsewhere, everywhere. And yet this is my life, and I have always lived it to the fullest and scrutinized it, and its insignificance never ceases to amaze me.

I have always felt pained by how little power I have over my fate, or to accomplish my dreams, or to choose people. I have always wanted to steer the course of my life, to predict its actions and accidents, yet it has all happened outside of and despite me, when not outright against me. I don't feel any resentment about this, because in my mind I am free and passionate, and things are beautiful. But I don't know to what extent life will wound me. The worst injury it could inflict would be to leave before I should wish it. It will, sooner or later, as life always has the last word. It does not respect our wishes or hopes, but it is all that we have and that authorizes everything. I'm learning to let it do what it must. Truthfully, I'm not going to write this self-portrait. Not yet.

———

13.

I often have this strange impression of having experienced a very specific kind of happiness somewhere, in some specific place, I feel a shock, or have a flash, and feel I can remember it. But the moment this very gentle, very clear, very oceanic feeling swims up, words escape me. One image looks a bit like Brazil, another might be from a movie, yet the shape flees, evades all telling ...

I feel a strong desire to write a poem, but the form is still fuzzy, still distant from my wishes, so unreal, so unremarkable. I want the poem to spring up casually and gracefully, to be a polished stone delivered up quickly, in an almost pulse-like rhythm, a rhythm that resounds in many directions, yet never breaks. But this poem turns in circles, the lyricism rings false, the idea evaporates, the sensation grows dimmer and dimmer. This poem is still far off, and yet, feeling pressed by time, I long for it, for its freedom, its extravagance, its fecundity. How can I give the poem what I don't have? Perhaps I hope that the word can transform my world. If I turn to face myself, I find only the desire to love and to live.

—

14.

I'm amazed at how limited my intelligence is, how incredibly circumscribed my freedom of thought. I am more thought than I think and more felt than I feel. And my life, it doesn't strike me as extravagant, but brainwashed and compromised. I have spent too much time looking, stupidly, for meaning, trying to corral it. This quest has torn out my soul.

—

Which whips up the flame
the path was pricked with azure
two took up the entire area all for themselves
and there was scarcely any love

yet each morning the universe hit the wall
the trouble continued

[Poems at the Margin]

———

15.

The Magdalen Islands have revealed more to me about myself than Paris or anywhere else. I deeply miss them. I want to live long enough to buy a house on the Islands and spend a few years there. Everything seems so important to me right now. I want things that are really down-to-earth. The Islands ... so much space to take in. The long beaches, the constant winds, the sea's many frigid colours and the swaying grasses mirroring the waves. I ache for this place as I do for a lost beloved, someone you're still in love with and can't stop missing. To have your very own house, where every object quivers with stories and serves as witness to something you've done at such and such an instant, in such and such place.

The wind snares the plain
the basement lamp sways
comfort me

———

16.

Light years separate us, my love, from the other side of the planet I think about you. There's an unresolved remainder that keeps circling back, cyclical, pathetic, firm, holding the stars we extinguished in its hands. A single glance can hold so many sighs. There is so much infinity in death. Death has large wings, I am certain that the dead don't forget, I feel sure there's no oblivion, that the earth consumes but never forgets. One day, all that we have deeply loved will be returned to us (so much expands that not even a single moment is lost).

———

March 20 [1980]

17.

Printemps [springtime]: the most beautiful word in the French language. The light returns, O what hope, the most beautiful season in the world, miraculous and mad for love. It makes you feel like incredible things are right outside the door. Tender looks and gestures, luscious moments, conveyors of words and of images. Yesterday such a great afternoon light infused a flower bed, a white veranda, a house made of stones. The feeling of love was tremendous, like a child beginning to grow inside of me. It was my poetry, begotten by this love. This is how it is. This too-quiet landscape suddenly murmurs and sings so many sweet things to me. My roots stretch out, so that one day I may produce as many fruits as spring does, as words do. Let summers convey them into laughter on its outstretched arms. The sap is forming inside the maples, you can hear the rumble of its umbrageous force preparing to feed us pleasure. This is the March maples breathing deeply.

———

Earth eaten by the root ...

[Poems at the Margin]

———

Here is the tree the prairie and hopefulness
here horizons are made ready like beds
the facades plumped by a luscious wind

———

March 31 [1980]

18.

Through my memory's uneven folds, I look back on a thousand vain and ludicrous details of my life; they delight and wound me. Though they came and went, they keep on beating. Outside the hospital windows[7] the day concludes with a concert of hues, violent pinks, secret beiges, and an orange that licks the purple stones. It's the tender touch of April's hands. All that was hidden under the lead weight of day, now lightens, uncovering its folds. I can see between the neighbourhood blocks two poplars launching their fragile veins, a few street lights contribute to this moving galaxy of the everyday, between the steel walls, a few Victorian roofs. Night is always a promise. Cars roll down Saint-Urbain toward Sherbrooke, it feels like one can almost guess at the gentle and difficult conversations taking place inside of them. These are the thousands pressing forward toward their destinies, clusters of grapes for future wine. Those who pass each other on street corners move up and down the circular splendour of this April evening. The hour advances, retouching all structures, inciting me to live. A skyscraper suddenly becomes a pure column of gold. I notice how it spontaneously shimmers. When the sky is nothing but a giant eyelid, lowered and filled with love, who are these people, where are they going, what do they want? Then solitude stops in its tracks and, with all its power, inhales every part of the city, lacking for nothing and marking everything with its desire to embrace it all. And you my love, you are among the hearts enlarging the city, one of the sources animating my hope. Evening gathers inside and around you. Love seeds the unlikely. If you don't love me still, what wound, what heartbreak has filled your voice with truths? When you noticed evening turning into frail night, did your incoherence make you regret having absented yourself, after being so keen to do so? You see life sit down to dinner, but someone has not heard the bell. Someone who will never break the bread of your memories and share their warmth.

————

April 1 [1980]
The very early morning light is still overrun by ghosts

————

19.
Apollinaire when your head was split open by a mortar shell
and your heart split open by an orange
today more sky and earth
stupor and fixed hope
my glances also roll in a basket of oranges
illusion is my fate a fountain and my blood
romance against the upright world
and for a love rolling in its branches
nothing by loves erupting on the funeral floor
we are together alone in the vague ethereal
the translucent shadow runs from us

[Poems at the Margin]

————

April 6 [1980]

20.

Poetry doesn't come easily, is never good enough, the work is slow and breathless, the meaning obscure and the love difficult and remote.

Let each poem, read and reread, fill me with premonitions and fragrances, rootedness and laughter. When the analogies settle into mirrors I always fear the worst, the famous femininity of the word, a myth forged out of alienation, a myth that weakens sentences, and against which I struggle. Preciosity and delicacy are nothing but qualifiers used to diminish the importance of the form, of the work. To use words like 'desire' and 'pleasure' without thinking them refined, because female eros is not death, enigma, elegance, and eternity, but a shredder of shadows, impetuous and revealing. Female strength is immediate, precarious, tangible, and concrete. Not to fear words and images of what is, at first glance, different, to flip the perspective, to create another place, from which to see, feel, understand. Consciousness is difficult, illusion tenacious, and to the educated consciousness, the body is remote. We murder the body, but the body always comes back from its ashes, from its mutilations. It loves infinitely. It is the body that loves, but we remain ignorant of this fact. We view the body as submissive on its path toward death, but it is something else entirely (which isn't a mystery), something inscribed in its genes and biological memory. The body loves and its creative possibilities surpass those of the mind. Its heart, in order to survive, is huge. It loves, to the point of never accepting the end, and even during the last convulsions, death is not in the body, but against it. The body is only flowering and fruit, wounds from which sap flows, deep tenderness. The body is the mind's root system, but the mind is not very good at listening to its roots. It imagines itself as ethereal, and by doing so becomes mediocre.

I am not afraid to use men's poetic techniques or words. I don't want to imitate them, but to help myself to them at my leisure. Let any line that screams banality create a feeling of déjà vu, but let all such lines, when gathered together, give the text new meaning. Sweep the metaphor clean of its baroque reign, and make the poem itself a metaphorical object. Unique, accessible, but slippery. Thin, naked as a blade, astonishingly obvious in a way that has never been seen before.

———

Now that we are alone, can't you hear worlds die out and unknown voices answer, aggrieved. Now that we are limited by immobility, the abysses blossom and drain. It's said that there are tender structures where brightness lies, rivers about which we know nothing. None will find us in our passionate desire. The trees have the sky, but we are alone.

[*Prose Poems*]

———

The brightness is more lively this morning
and the look that pays itself no never mind
before the dizzy spells are brought to an end

———

21.
Bottomless sadness once again, endless love, lost hope. Dead already. Then reborn. Dead again. To know, and then to understand nothing. So many underground things are readying themselves in the beautiful dark night of the heart. I am hardly any better than

those poor mindless children who keep searching for the same solitary truth. The same dissatisfaction, the same future dream, the same lack, the same search for the absolute. I would like to be so strong and love you without asking anything in return, but to do so would be false, for this is a totalizing passion, fully physical, like carrying a child, like a poem. And desires eat away at the body. Unsatisfied desires are birds with clipped wings filled with a nostalgia for open spaces.

Mozart speaks of resignation. The one who knows is sad. Who knows that neither willpower nor magic potion can offer any relief. Who knows that nothing will move, or change, and that everything will slide hopelessly, predictably, toward its end. And he is sad who knows and who loves without being loved in return, who is mired in a passion that is slowly destroying him in spite of himself. And sad is the one who feeds off a particular face. How long-suffering woman is, and her child is born and dies at the same time as she does; from her very first breath, woman is attentive to the world. How long-suffering woman is, what an endless and useless patience constricts women's throats, wrenching then immobilizing them. Destroy yourself, pointless insatiable pain, because the love of women is patient and lasts a long time, nobody can even imagine how long. Destroy yourself, world, in the confines of a woman's patience, because her love is perfection. By perfect I mean unchanging and without beginning or end. When you give in to this love, all will become yours: mountains and rivers and flowers and azure, deep roots and grains. Your fingers will search the earth over for unusual fruits, you'll return to me laughing, not believing your eyes, or hands, you will bring me the songs of birds, denizens of foliage so new and so fresh, you won't believe the source.

Death will arrive and will have your eyes.[8]

I haven't stopped thinking about this line for hours, crying, telling myself that I've nothing left, nothing but the desire to fall asleep forever fixated on this little image of your green-eyed look. A look with the perfect hint of tenderness, a touch overdone, a tad innocent. All I have left is this big secret, enormous, eating me from the inside out, this total lack of happiness, this utter solitude. I really want to die while I can still accurately remember your eyes. It's the only thing of value I have, and only time can rob me of it. I would like to die before being sucked into the open maw of oblivion. Let death have your green-eyed look. Why wake up to nothing but suffering, more mornings, more suffering, and more battles I can't fight? I'd rather be on a deathbed of ferns, your eyes. I don't want to wait around for the conclusion of this sad, hackneyed, emotionless story, when one day, in that parallel world (you ignore all signs of it) I'll hold you in my arms and nothing will tear you from me, not time, not willpower, not space. That's the sweet eternity of my death. (*Death will arrive and will have your eyes.*)

Sleep is a god abandoned on the bank
your voice looks for me in every gesture every smile
each pain gives birth to a look
that is the vanguard of tides
to draw inexhaustible embraces
poetry is tucked away in the nocturnal fragrance of armoires
beneath your hands loss has been lost

[*Poems at the Margin*]

15 April [1980]

22.

It hasn't stopped raining for several days, rain, sadness. Dead now from a strange death I also head out to rub shoulders with the foolish crowd. I am exactly like them. There is no longer anything different about me; I, too, keep secrets locked up in my heart, my impossible love, which eats away at me little by little on the way to its tranquil and ugly immutable night. I, too, have lost my soul. We go together as one, in a hurry, seemingly in a hurry to do something, to get worked up, pretending to understand, be happy, or be important. But they are the walking dead, and it's a done deal, I'm following them. From now on, I'll pretend to be alive. I've been snuffed out, I have no more illusions, no more hope. I'm pre-duped. I'm aware that supposedly time heals all things, that things go back to normal once we forget, that we pretend to love, to be happy, but that's false and pathetic, for out there somewhere is a person who has left, taking the essential part of me with him.

Someone has taken the seasons, the things, the days. Music is nothing but a distant echo of some ancient music, smothered at the root and made fruitless by lost love. One knows that memory will work everything out, the heart will recover and love again. But this love, which was the first, will also be the last. When death arrives, it will have those eyes. That alone I know. I sense this to be true, beyond all doubt.

———

The ghost dogs pick up the scent of your paralysis …

[Poems at the Margin]

———

23.

Not being understood, not understanding. Knowing that the game has already been played out, the cards drawn, the moves made, the days outlined in advance. Today, April 15, Jean-Paul Sartre died. (It is similar to when the Chilean regime fell and Allende died; I have the very distressing feeling that a close friend is gone, a visionary spirit snuffed out, that we are, and our world is, a little darker, and hoping won't help.) Sartre's death: a star gone out, we backslide into savagery, stupidity. Sartre's death: a giant chasm, silence. I write to keep from going insane, from falling into despair. I must breathe. I wish I were humble and rebellious, I wish I could go away without anyone being the wiser, to the place where my lover's eyes are fixed forever before me. Each page turned is frozen with fear, my mirror, my double. Nothing is going to change. Everything will keep trudging through this unavoidable sludge. Now, more often than not, I am reduced to these words: patient/sick person. I call my love: "Doctor." Things like exhaustion, struggle, oblivion, a lavish meal eaten in good company or throwing up in a dark little room, alone, have become almost laughable. Knowing ahead of time what life has in store for us. Moving as little as possible, not displacing the air, looking at this mutilated body, owning up to it. Dealing with suffering and boredom, grabbing onto the singular pleasure of a faint, vaguely famous, perfume. There's no one I can talk with about what's important to me, no one to lighten the weight of this desire. Even I am toeing the line. I'm not going to die; I'm just about dead. All that remains is physical pain, a knife pulled through a wound nonstop.

———

April 16 [1980]

I intuit you in this imaginary awakening ...

[*Poems at the Margin*]

———

24.

Little white page, you are without a doubt my only lifeline. I have no other resource but you in the face of this haunting madness. Today, April 17, 1980, the second day after my discharge from the hospital, my morale was slightly improved, when suddenly I felt that same wrenching of my head and body, the senselessness of things, the senselessness of these struggles. I had a revelation: we are not free, we decide nothing. All hope is superfluous, just a carrot dangled in front of an ass. Everything has been sketched out far in advance in some cartography of the body and of existence. Once again that feeling of absence caught in my throat. Immobilized in this bed, I watched the dimming light of morning, of midday, and now of two in the afternoon, knowing that I could huff and puff all I wanted and never move these hours. They fall like blades, they rip, they reduce. I thought of love, every movement of love carved into my memory with clinical precision. I thought about love's powerlessness, and of my flagrant selfishness. It's obvious that I love him for myself, just like his refusal to love me is selfish. Two adversaries trapped in the same labyrinth. I am reduced to silence. I must love him without wanting him, knowing that anything I do is destined to end, to be forgotten. To love from afar without making it real, without hope. And without hope, who am I, if not the shadow of his shadow, more shadow even than the shadow which will time and again be cast in his sunny life. My love for him is premised on having him; it's also wrong, and I should shut up.

———

25.

Calmly I regain my spirits, calmly I feed off my illusions again. Love calmly requisitions all its illegitimate rights. The way I love is disastrous for my body and my mind. Once again, I try to sustain myself with silence, with solitude, with dreams, with ignorant but thirsty and curious words. Night has also requisitioned its rights, pushing aside the clear thinking which says: he's never going to love you; all your time will be spent far away from him. And so my love for him is gratuitous. Endless energy no amount of despair can exhaust. Love, a bottomless well. Every kiss, every caress predates the source. A weird kind of time keeps watch in my head. I escape this miserable and rigid reality for exotic locales where my love has all the powers and all the rights. I am somewhere else, between other walls, walls eroded by sun. The future has the eyes of my love. Even, and above all, if the future is death. I now know what I want and I am going to invest everything in this line of thinking. I finally understand: I know what I want, or better yet, I feel what I want. I see myself very clearly. I estimate the amount of time I have left to live, assuming that the tumour is isolated like last time, and with the help of chemotherapy I may have a few years, assuming there's not another setback, a metastasis growing somewhere we don't know about. As with the enigma of the word, I must figure out poetry and this love affair. The central point all my drives depart from and return to. Understand. Seize. Confirm.

———

April 18 [1980]

26.

I must get over this illness and, from today forward, begin writing about my life. Give myself the illusion of living (when the heart beats). The illusion of living. This is supposed to be life. Doing things, living somewhere, passing faces, and feeling love. Trembling with love. Blowing on things that have gone out. There was an African filmmaker on the evening news. It was Mori, whom I slept with six or seven years ago. I was nineteen or twenty at the time. Already ... his handsome black face, his bushy romantic hair; he hadn't changed. I said to myself: how sad, I knew him and then I lost him. We made love. And then nothing. How stupid. How totally stupid. It's bullshit. It's life. I called him when I was in Paris, but I didn't even bother to leave my name on his answering machine. I told myself: there's no way he'll call back. Affairs, he must have had a ton of them. And now I'm so fucked. I wouldn't have the courage to connect with him. But I would like to make love with him again. As the body grows older, it's slower to forget. Am I forgetting Paul? No ... rarely a day goes by when I don't think about the shape of his body, the sweetness of his lips, the colour of his eyes, his bitter laugh or his tenderness. "I feel happy." — "Me too." Some echoes I'll never forget; some miseries will never relax their grip on my throat. I want to die, right now, here, from wanting to hold him in my arms. "Will you come back?" — "Yes." But he never came back. How bitter life is, how difficult love. All day long I am alone in this house with his ghost. I wish I could die right now. What good is it to pretend to live, to battle against my cancer, with no compensation at the end? This strange and omnipotent love. I came close, I came close to being happy. In September. I came close to living a waking dream, eyes open. It had, I remember, a blue brightness. I want to go back in time, to say what must be said, make the moves, or better yet, just be still and feel my joy. Don't tremble, demand anything, or quiver. I want to die in this old, rotted body today, because he doesn't need me, and yet I have such a terrible need for him. As I miss him so much and he misses me so little. The cancer is in my heart. My heart has a giant chasm into which worlds never stop disappearing. My heart has imprisoned me.

———

April 19 [1980]

27.

I write from ignorance, to ward off bad luck, to face myself, me who would rather run away from myself for the remainder of this day, afflicted by the darkness of my thought, its erratic nature, and the same intensely vivid dream that plays on continuous loop. Struggling against all inner fatalism. Passion's *diktat*. Exacerbated sexuality.

———

28.

I know that I am trying to take myself seriously. But it's not working. I write one good poem out of five. There are tons and tons of poets, misery holds us in its talons and mocks us. We stick together, hoping that somewhere out there in the public square we'll find a reader. The square is empty, and so are our hearts. Especially our lives, and our pale loves, exhausted in our dead arms; clusters of grapes for future wine. What intoxication? Will there be only one?

I neither add to nor subtract from the silence. My writing shouldn't consume my life, but expand and illuminate it, teach it how to transcend borders. Diminish that brutal contempt between the word and the world, between mediocre life and intense vision. And then there's the fraternity between poets. Everyone makes the mistake of thinking they know everyone else, of thinking they're better than they are and better than others. Each is shut up in solitude. Those who once sang no longer sing.

—

29.

It's better to have experienced something so brilliant, even if it's now gone. But in fact, not really gone, just out of reach, yet inscribed in memory, inscribed deep into the self. You can close your eyes and dive back into the joy you once felt, but it's painful. Because the memory is of something so happy and good, that even the feeling of remembering it, what was and is no more, causes a strange malaise to rise up in you. You hold yourself inexorably between two poles, two breaths, two places: the joy that was and the pain that is ...

Here, in this place, your lips have drowned what remains of my life. I am now very close to death. It's marching forward. I can see it moving toward me. In passing you give each other the same knowing look. Matching colours. My dalliance, my end. Without your desire I am alone. "You are beautiful, you are sweet." But at least I will have known this, this perfect tenderness. Two faces joined by something very distant and very deep within them, something in their desire which preceded them. An inner fecundity, they know neither its origin nor its end. It's just a pathway that has taken them from one eternity to another. From one silence to another. This love is the word in advance of the day. Let the veil preventing us from attaining this fullness be shredded, the fate of a gesture, of a word. Let them be fulfilled, before we face total oblivion, each apart, my life, your life.

—

April 24 [1980]

30.

I need to steady myself and face reality, without coercion, without hope, not some hoped-for reality but the kind that keeps still, an expanse oblivious to the passage of time, rooted in the immediate; without regret or sigh of relief. Love, useless, impossible, like a column of pure air positioned in the mind that promises nothing if not death. (Though we don't know the hour, the place, or the final vision we'll take from our lives.) The drowned get used to the light. Our shades shudder as one, the illusion is good. The winter is like a jacket thrown over this drama's shoulders. In the yellow passageway two people kiss. Like a train at a level crossing, things move rhythmically between light and dark. (Tomorrow daily tasks will wear their pleasures threadbare.) The system's meaninglessness is already closing in from all sides.

The earth is famished and exhausts us
a tree takes up the entire window
in the yellow winter passageway two people kiss
all things becoming clear and growing dark by turns
we are the enemies without fire or place
all bodies set against history

[*Poems at the Margin*]

———

April 25 [1980]

31.

Excerpt from a letter to Marie-Claude:
Following those first experiences of hopelessness, hope returns. I can't think of any plant more persistent than hope. The inevitable always seems like something that happens to others. They say that

you never accept the fact of your own death. I recently read an interview with Sartre, right before he died, during which he said: "I have no more than five, or perhaps ten years to live." Hope, always hope. I've listened to too many people destroyed by sickness who still believed that they would get better to not distrust myself, I know that the mind has no influence over the body. (The mind lies to the body.) We are so frightened by our powerlessness that we refuse to see it, and we comfort ourselves with the illusion that the mind can do something for the body, but it's not true. The most we can do is control our anxiety and live in the present, that's all the mind can do. Or learn how to be indifferent to what's happened to it. Things and people are easily replaced, what's important are the things that remain constant: the eternity of a tree, of the sky, of the seasons, and of the "other" (it doesn't matter if this other remains consistent.) What we learn from passion about the other is a marvellous breath that keeps on going. (In spite of us, and beyond us.)

———

April 28, 1980

32.

Letter to Yvette:

I have neglected to write, knowing that my letters would probably have a rather negative tone. Going out, seeing people, talking and laughing, I can manage, but in a letter I cannot lie. The very fact of writing ties me to the real. Today, after receiving your flowers and your friendly note, also after that beautiful letter, filled with March colours I felt so much tenderness and gratitude I'm making the effort to write.

How do you manage to be so calm? For my part, anxiety eats at my soul as the disease does my body. I'm not sure whether I'm dying from cancer or from too forcefully wanting my dreamlife to penetrate my reality. In September, the person I'm in love with returned, only to go away again, leaving me even more defenceless than before, more speechless, more stunned. I can't find relief from this pathetic story, this sentimental melodrama. Then I worked a lot, on my poetry, my university classes, I regained my energy, trying to forget about his absence. Physical absence: always the worst, I think. I have worked a lot this fall and winter, I began a new volume of poems in support of which I received a prestigious grant. Then, in February, I got the terrible news that my disease had returned, this time in my lung. I didn't have adequate moral fortitude, and the prospect of having to wage these new battles seemed impossible to face. The treatments, the operation, the physical depletion. Once again, I felt like I was suffocating. My illness put me in contact with him again, because, alas, the man who has such a hold on my heart is the same man who treats my illness. So, love and death are caught up in the same madness. My story is stupid. I make moves, but no longer believe in what I'm doing. Sometimes I think about what you wrote to me: let time take care of things. Meanwhile, the hours fall heavily in my memory like metal tears. Three years ago, I was care-free. In a single blow my life was destroyed. At the same time, I came to know two terrible things from which we probably can't recover: passion and death. On the one hand, my body experienced real joy, satisfaction, and also hunger for the first time, on the other, it learned about suffering, mutilation, weakness. For three years my life has felt unreal, too exhilarated to be tangible, concrete. As if placed on the edge of a cliff, what hope remains to keep me from slipping?

This relapse has me questioning everything. In order to fight you need a goal, and at least one good reason. If you only knew how I search for this one good reason, anything to give my life savour and meaning. Some hope that isn't just an illusion.

A giant silence has built itself inside of me. Each poem born is reduced to a minimum. I have never lived to write, but writing *should help me expand my existence, intensify it. Writing: a fecundity engendered by existence. I would gladly trade my poems for the sight of a certain face. I know I need to let myself go with the flow of things, that we are powerless against destiny. Now I just let things happen, my arms by my side, inconsolable. I have no power over love or life. Everything seems to have been decided in advance ...*

————

April 29 [1980]

33.

Rain, and another charmless and strange day that won't let up. I listen to Billie Holiday, the jazz and her scratchy voice take me away. I'm in a place still filled with possibilities, a place where suffering turns into sunlit images and fulsome rhythms. A large, generous countryside of endless sand and sea, or a city all lit up at night, a celestial gem, morning's mirror. People head out into the humid solitude of the streets. In this film, the lovers are reunited at the end; happy after so many days of hardship. But Billie's voice doesn't lie, suffering can't be erased, it accumulates like loveless nights so heavy at their end an even greater portion of happiness becomes possible. Racism or indifference, it's always the same with human beings, this intolerable solitude. I want to write poems that have the power of Holiday's voice, little tender and dramatic texts, continuous gravelly harmony. Once again, I resort to daydreams, immerse myself in a made-up life. I want him to love me. It feels good to imagine that there's still hope. When will I be cured of this irrational and ethereal love?

————

May 1 [1980]

34.

Letter to Monique (excerpt)

... Don't lose sight of the fact that the future isn't set in stone, but, just the contrary, at least when it comes to things not yet dreamt of and to our most secret projects. Does destiny exist? I wish with all my heart that it didn't and that we had a little bit of freedom to determine our tomorrows. I am recovering well from my operation, I come and go in the city, I move just to move, to persuade myself that I am really alive, that there's no time to waste. To see everything, to take advantage of spring, which pushes timidly through the ground. The form of my third book (you can read the first sequence of eleven poems in Estuaire)[9] *is becoming clearer and clearer in my head. I have written other things since these were published, winding my way toward a difficult, but open, form. The difficulty of existence, the openness of passion. I see myself in the shop windows. Anxiety brings me to my knees. I approach my reflection without shame. I know I have nothing to lose. Whatever I have left I must lose, until everything's gone and I find myself in the deep and uncultivated purity of solitude, of creation. Only death can stop desire's work. To cross the pre-existing modulations of existence, to attain this perfect silence. The extremely smooth water in which each word that floats to the surface creates a gentle ripple. The calligraphy of the heart and of consciousness. More and more I know exactly what I want, and since my two months of being sick I have had plenty of time to think things over, to confront my hopefulness. To know which direction to guide my steps, not over outside events, but over myself, which is the only thing I can control; to know what I want at last, and maybe even for the first time. Recognizing, admitting my joy, my suffering. Not compromising with the real ...*

I begin my weekly rounds of chemotherapy on May 26. Though I am very apprehensive about it, sometimes a vast feeling of indifference rises up in me, as if all of this was happening to somebody else. I so wish the future could match my will. I would make a beautiful "no man's land." It would be as sweet as a sea breeze or the texture of my lover's skin, or his lips.

All is not lost.

———

May 7, 1980

After a few euphoric days, wandering through the white labyrinths of my existence, gnawing on a few whispers, trying not to want to understand my life, I'm struggling once again against a despair too great to even name, or sustain. Monday, I read my star chart. As to what it said about the future, I'm not sure, but the descriptions of my childhood, my creative work, and my character were right on the money. I was led to believe that there were all these beautiful things predicted for my future (*pre-dict*: interesting word, "to say before," as if one said during). Twenty-five years old, year of toil, torn between obsessing over my powers of destruction (God knows they are ample) and my powers of creation; still, a year with the possibility of good luck. Golden years follow dark ones. A lively life, but sane and harmonious. A powerful love when I'm around twenty-six or twenty-seven years old, which will last forever (a curious stranger who will come from a group I'll find happiness in), participation in creativity. A strange powerless destiny; what hands will prevent me from reaching this stage of life, not yet my own?

Last night I dreamt about Paul with such clarity it upset me. "He is dead," I was told, but I could not bring myself to accept it. I was in distress, because the whole of my soul and life had died with

him. In contrast to my August dream, I couldn't respond to the
calm reserve of the one who told me he was dead. I couldn't say:
"No, I , and I alone, know that he *isn't* dead." In my dream I acted
like a madwoman. I wanted to see his face one more time, to have
a never-ending vision of that face. I felt so awful, because he really
was dead and I couldn't wake either of us up. Then suddenly, the
spectre of my own death rose up before me. The cancer spread, it
was in my throat and he was no longer alive to treat me. His death
was mine, and my love for him was my life. Where does such a
dream come from? Where do *we* come from? What archaeological
past rises within us without our knowledge? I have loved you from
the dawn of time, nothing can shake this force, not any passing
of the years, nor any other face. I don't want oblivion to take you
from me. You are my child and my father, because I feel as if you
have given me life, out of some eternal unspoken secret I am your
descendant, but I also carry you inside of me like a mysterious fruit.
You are my downfall and my splendour, my creation and the void
which annihilates me. The memory of you is the death of me and
my remedy. No destiny can remove you from my heart. I promise
you this. I will never renounce the person I become in your pres-
ence, in your absence. You are my caprice, my host, I gather you
in from everywhere through these natural insights, these breaths.
You still ignore your many sides, or run away from their power.
There will probably come a day when I'll be able to see you without
trembling, I will no longer be affected by your pained face hovering
beneath that mask of surety and egotism. How can we keep hold of
our most cherished desires, and keep them in such a way that they
stay with us, even though others arise? And how can our minds
combine sensation, passion, understanding, and giddiness, instead
of sacrificing one for the other? Shades that shall wander through
space for a day to rejoin night's terrifying necessity. Your body is a
torrent, your eyes a periwinkle horizon, a virile honey pours forth

from your voice, when your shoulders lean over me, the entire universe welcomes me, your lips are happiness and your hands a soil from which everything can serenely turn to gold. You are simultaneously pleasure and pain, beauty and disgrace, your maturity is a passionate lifeblood, an ocean that guides the movements of fragile stars. Your dreams are melancholy words and you're all alone in a past bloated with work and pride.

Me, I love you. I am the landscape all around you, watching. You're not coming back and I've stopped waiting. It's finally been said enough times that I've accepted it. In spite of myself. Everyone, even the star charts, see what I refuse to see: that it's over, that I will never hold you in my arms again. Yet, if I don't find a way to resolve my grief in this life, you will haunt me into the next. Unfulfilled desires are fault lines of indecency and misfortune. I can't give up. This festering wound will keep my eyes wide open, my skin alive, my thoughts obsessed, forever. It will enclose me in the paralysis of a tenderness lost, an infinite grief. I will never reach the bottom of this love, like an exhausted diver, I must resurface without having reached the object of my desire, without having finished my descent, without having touched the dark sand.

I did not touch the dark sand of your voice
capture the facing wall's pallor
the light of heat on the window

———

When I listen to certain kinds of music my heart breaks as if confronted by some appalling truth. I become transported by an immense, unexpected love, my tremors answered by nothing but silence and open space. We are alone and so inadequate, so lacking in wonder, so impotent in the face of life.

Death calmly climbs up the ramp toward us. I can feel it swarming around inside of me, victorious over my spirit, which watches, listens, and sniffs at death in an effort to continually convince itself that it's still alive, that it will go on, that one heartbeat will follow another. I have a thing for fierce and stubborn poems; I like wondrous poems that can steer my memory, understand my present, and fill the space with life.

———

May 14, 1980

More and more I aspire to describe the real as efficient and strong, devoid of metaphor — that poetic excrescence which dilutes sensation rather than maintaining, stimulating, and speaking to it.

———

In the study a flash of heat gleams ...

[*Poems at the Margin*]

———

Behind the hangar, high up, a bunch of fervent buds. The poplar cries out in love, certain neighbouring branches respond. Appreciating, once again, how any outpouring of tenderness brings your memory back to me. Dwelling in that time, its vitality. I want to tell you that, destiny be damned, with the full freedom of my mind I categorically chose you to be my eternity, beyond any quotidian constraints, beyond reason, beyond all hope of attaining my desires, of even having access to your body, in despair and gratitude I love you without understanding anything, and without trying to figure why I'm under the control of these drives, or whether this love is real, ethereal, phantasmagorical, or very old. It's funny. You exist, and I dream about you every day, and over the phone your voice was so full of tender feeling, the value and ache of which you don't even know. Out walking on the sidewalk, I crushed little buds, green kisses unaware that they are fruits, and their fragrance was so thick the world would have had to come to a complete stop, disappear, for me to inhale this pure miracle, let it penetrate and crush me with joy. All of these swoony moments, of which your body is the most profound, create my existence. I confess it, all I want is this love, to be alone on this beautiful day, for the sky to be like a naïve heaven on a church ceiling, and the wind cool, peppered with green fragrance, that Stéphan, my tirelessly tender confidante, return to me as he does every night, and that together we would talk about things and the people we know. When I open the door, the clouds and the flowers fill my eyes. The city makes room for them. We can see what we want of the real. For a moment of happiness.

Title: *Wrinkles*

Self-portrait[1]

My richest hours have come in those times when the environment seems to elevate everything we do, or better yet, seems to surround us, echoing our actions in apt and surprising ways. Moments when the intense music of being alive seems to resonate through us from the outside in. A word or conversation disappears into the ambient air, and if the night, filled with a thrilling clarity, fell, we could dip into its substance to finish our thoughts. Such moments necessitated slowing down, voyaging within one's own vision. I must still live slowly, collecting precious instants. Stopped on the side of the white road between two bare hills rising above the sea, summer had placed its sweet grasses all around. At Saint-Paul-de-Vence, under the heat-filtering pines, I approached the Giacometti sculptures, those strange telluric powers emerging from white walls and glassed-in bays. Summer has always fulfilled my hopes, it's a season that expands space. Stretched out under the trees, which seemed to fulfill all my needs just by existing, I had a premonition that you would come join me.

———

May 15 [1980]

May all that you dream of accomplishing come to pass. Just like spring, imperturbably bursting forth following the last frost. Your delight is boundless in its awakening. How could you doubt, for even a second, that the pollen-drenched wind would return along with the freshly opened buds releasing their playful perfume, and those white and blue skies, looking like an unconscious extension of the flooded winds. How, and through what sort of reasoned-out fate, could you doubt the full force of this conclusion? I'm the only one who knows what's in store for me, what I desire. The real, every side of which *does*, and should, shape my routine. I, too, am an earth moving through its cycles. Only you know what's up ahead, the shape of the now, what constitutes the power of this moment. If misery and joy are intimately intermixed, it's because you willed it so. I should try and be like a pure column. Myself, with an immediacy, without influence, without premise, without advice, or dialectical thinking. Those who told you what needed to be done were wrong, they know nothing of your mind's calculus, nor what paths unfurled themselves before you, nor to what kind of rest or vitality you aspire, nor its guises. (This kind of intimacy, hard to grasp or explain, should be part of your existence.) They know nothing of what is kindling so much feeling inside of you, and how much Paul is caught up in it. Your love, having shed its morbid bent, is now your life, pure and simple, and you live and choose it through your only power, that of being in love.

———

WRINKLES

Description of everyday reality.
Like photographs of my life.
Anecdotes I want to keep traces of.
Wrinkles of the heart and body, folds of the instant.

———

May 21 [1980]

A sad spring, yet beneath my sadness, even more determination. Live, I wrote it in blue on my soul. Bitter determination, don't give up. Yesterday, the referendum.[2] I knew we were going to lose, for

I know Québecois too well, yet I hoped for the improbable. Like how death is always stronger than life. Like children breaking the branches off a flowering tree for just a few sticks, retrograde and negative forces have stopped our momentum toward autonomy and progressivism. A stage which I thought sane, normal, and obvious. Yesterday's result showed me that my position was not shared. And now a lot of aggressiveness and determination is building in me. I believe that independence is inevitable, but I shed tears for those few older people who will never see their dream come to pass. Now we must expect a bludgeoning by order. Reactionary forces will drive René Lévesque out, under the pretext that he won't be able to negotiate a new constitution with Canada, given that he doesn't believe in it. We're in for a vast offensive, subtle, and demagogic rhetoric that will force out Lévesque and, by doing so, all progressive and liberal factions. The ruse triumphs at the expense of intelligence. Do not come back to this country; it's in mourning. Because of a public bludgeoning and terrorizing rumours, the majority has decided against itself, they have chosen the past instead of the future, prison instead of liberty, death instead of life.

———

May 26 [1980]

Maybe wrinkles can also be furrows, and every gash give birth to light, every fault to an idea, and you, you can follow me through the profundity of daily life. Every instant wears us out, we cannot forget the things that mark us, our bodies and our passions, our homes and our travels. I return to you as if returning to the beginning of a cycle. My illusions inscribe themselves on your face, your memory, and other signs with flavours I haven't yet come to know.

———

May 27, 1980

> *my love my event my white poem*
> — Francine Déry, *A Bulgarian Train*

I didn't know that you were going to come. Had I known, I would have closed my eyes, mopped up my thirsts, hidden away my ache, my fear, my vertigo. All of my landscapes would have calmed down had I known that another life guided these steps, these cries, these tremors. I didn't know the degree to which I could love your face, and that I could predict, invent, anticipate so many strange souvenirs, shivers, recognitions. Could you change to such a degree that you might let me in? You, offering me your hands, (this could be a believable novel). And your soft look. Our heads, as if pulled by gold threads, move close together as we talk, so close our words at times sound like the whispers of Cathars. We look at each other in a profane ritual, bent over our love as if over a precipitous sacrifice.

May 29, 1980

Wrinkles: signs of the body's tragic writing

I had nothing to do all day and so I just thought about things. The entire day was a beautiful empty space where I could imagine and feel you very palpably, and yet still so tentative. All day long I fed myself on this love without asking for any signs of hope, an event, or dénouement from him. Captured as I was by the iridescent expansion of my feelings, captivated to find them as fresh as before, as senseless, pathetic, and troubling. Seeing you on Monday was a festival, a sacrifice, a sweet destruction. I'm no longer struggling, but surviving in a state of deep intensity, carried away by the sleeping instant. Yes, my day was free, and while the sun shone with the heat of summer, big cool currents of air slipped down from the Arctic all the way to Montréal. The sky mixed the two currents, conditions that gave me a pleasant feeling of well-being. One part warm honey, one part icy wave, the air transformed into the skin of a rare miraculous fruit. Colours: a purple curtain hanging from a laundry line, the pure green of May grass, the asphalt and the grey hangar, the black bars of the balcony, a blue sky, a white balcony, and elsewhere a turquoise awning and an apple tree that looks silver at dusk. Familiar sounds stamp a watermark on your absence. This time of day is at once the most concrete and porous. The city's colours, contours, and scents are enhanced, its pulse relaxed; the overhanging tree holds its breath. I walked all day without looking for you nor meeting you, you were tucked inside of the past and the future, you were no longer alone, but smiling, as you sometimes do, as you did on Monday. What do they know of passion, other people, with their sage advice and studied excitements? What do they know, these Cassandras of death, of this love's overflowing life force, of its undreamed-of combative power? What do they know of desire's tremors, of its affirmativeness, of its thrilling certainty, its creative uselessness, its materialism, its pragmatism, its telluric power? What do they know of the whiteness of the poem that cannot be broken but by this one face, this one body, this one glance?

At night I swirl around in the vessel of your pleasure
you don't know if the light weighs down your dreams
if this quick cool breath
is another way of kissing and forgetting
I swirl around against clusters of other lives
inside as outside the sky wrinkles up
and the unheard-of river is frozen solid

[*Poems at the Margin*]

———

May 30 [1980]

Everything is coming back to me, surprising me; old rhythms, old dreams, old grievances. Once again, I journey through an exotic music in order not to face myself. Sometimes it's the only way to feel good when in the grips of the real. Thinking of Paul and our parallel paths I feel sad, and then the poem saves me from this heartbreak. The poem brings me satisfaction, the fulfillment that he has refused me. Love lives, breathes, and flowers in the poem. Through the text I am rescued from despair. The poem teaches me every possibility, proves every reality, makes manifest all desires. A helpful fiction.

———

here there are blinds with liquid slats ...

[*Self-portraits*]

———

June 1, 1980

My love story: kind of like Eurydice and Orpheus. Life and death, day and night, closely connected by one idea, one experience. But upside down: in the myth Orpheus is both Eurydice's life and her death. Because it is *he* who goes to hell to get her back, and it is *he* who, by looking back, sends her to her permanent death. What she sees in him, what draws her to him, is a two-sided mirror of herself, both her darkness and her light. Orpheus is her words, pulling her toward consciousness, toward the light, and at the same time, when viewed by the text, sending her back into oblivion and darkness. *What the writer is seeking is not the word, but the word's foundation,*

that which the word must exclude in order to speak, the abyss.
[Possibly a modification of a line from Maurice Blanchot's *Le part de feu.*]

———

June 1 [1980]

Is there anything more pure than this whiteness which, at the call of blackness, flows like water. *My love my event my white poem.* The mark of the black word on the white page. On a scroll that defies space and time, a white silk scroll with a few bamboo leaves like jittery writing. Everything breathes, but with a rhythm, like a pulse, like the tide. The secret source made visible. Promise kept. I feel like writing, if only to see the vibration of this all-encompassing light.

———

June 3–5 [1980]

In a world of conventions, the poem creates an unwavering light: an outline of your face. Describes otherness as a form of magic or magic itself. A blue magic, like the Blues, a kind of Edenic melancholy. Fleeing the past toward the future. This one has the exact proportions of a single body. The only help for the instant suspended between madness and confinement.

———

June 10, 1980

Again on the edge of despair. So, will I never pull myself out of this cycle? In the morning, hit with a terrible bout of nausea (I stayed in bed waiting for it to pass).[3] A long woozy day, a parade of nightmares in tight formation. Hope completely lost. Love's absence, a lump in my throat. My eyes riveted on the chasm of my existence, agape at the extent of the futility, the many letdowns, the frustrated love. Paralyzed I watched, day after day, my own death taking place. The silence of these lands. There's no place where I'm okay. In my body least of all. I despair of all food, all fucks, all realities. Once again shut up in this house as in a deep sleep. Waking into a natural clarity, simple and lucid, a consciousness of the world. But the schizophrenic breath filling up my head is making me blind and deaf, stupid, prostrate before my existence, unable to grasp the most meagre sign, the slightest meaning. A terrible solitude.

How can I avoid such ennui, such meaninglessness? Wandering through the city looking for friends with whom, alas, I have nothing in common; exchanging a few opinions, a few words, to what end? The workings of my creativity are found elsewhere: where desire vibrates. What man, except for him, can move me? And he is so remote, renouncing his feelings, he has completely banished me from his thoughts, from his daily life, from his body. I am overwhelmed by this heartache and nausea, and I may as well go out guns blazing, for I don't know how to fight this powerful and abominable suffering. *Delight in destruction. Destroying is delicious.* If only it were possible, leaving nothing of my past or his but smoking ruins. Seeing him again, his face stripped bare. Our twenty-year age difference scattered like futile, vanishing dreams. Principles too, and social values, mocked, reduced to being innocuous impotent shadows. Me, left with my share of this unconstrained love. Abolish time but create space. Just a bath of pure air to intoxicate the body. And him uncovering the meaning of appearances and elements. Nothing but calculations entombed like cadavers, and above, pushing with quasi-divine ramifications, landscapes of never-ending words. Life's abundance. The fecundity of shared love. A hand is sufficient to reinvent all of life. I know this, I who no longer speak to you. Death quickly approaches. I know this too, I felt it in your absence and in the child I don't have, will never have, and in the regret you don't feel, that you will never feel. Tell me, with your fine scientific objectivity, that destiny doesn't exist, that all hope is never totally lost, that we are capable of changing, to meet each other, to stay the same, to die by grace or gently come back to life. That, on the strength of our will and divine passion a commiserating god watches over us with his choir of ancient benevolent angels. Give me faith. Tell me that he won't relentlessly crush us, but rather show us the road, and that there will always be time to return, to head out, or to change direction. You still smile when you see or hear me. I love hearing your wise laugh, I love your hands, your eyes, your silhouette, and your voice. I love everything about you with a wounded and adolescent intensity. Seeing you without finding you is like having to face your death. I go deep into myself searching for your face, like remembering someone who has died, knowing that I can no longer touch him, speak with him, share time with him, know his thoughts. The most divine knowledge man possesses is a consciousness of his own death. That is the source irrigating the entirety of his struggle, his creativity, his hope. He fights against death because he knows it. Animals can't remember the death of the other, or know the fact of their own. Man tries his entire life not to give in to himself or to others, but death forcefully drags him down with its captivating, frightening, ugliness. Nothing escapes it. He may as well hate it, for no amount of willpower can stop or reach death as it advances toward him. But you my love, death cannot take you from me until it takes me from myself.

June 11, 1980

Lost, totally disoriented, with no reality to call my own, as a woman, as a Québecoise; disoriented, rejected every day, socially, as a poet. Dead, continually dead to myself, sick, neurotic, tirelessly in quest of a reality I can grasp, something that moves me, something to believe in, a reassurance, some form of understanding, consciousness, peace. Mutilated body, mutilated mind, mutilated love. Heart doesn't fit into this reality. But accepts this immobility, suffering, silence, and emptiness. No attempt to break the flow of despair, of the real: *all things becoming clear and growing dark by turns.*[4] I should not hurry my life, nor give up on going out or doing things: I should not give up on the hope of the white poem. To close your eyes upon your lover, without moving a muscle, or upsetting your inner harmony, without wishing for day to come, keeping still through a singular night, a stone night, a mineral night, open to any eventuality. When I close my eyes, the summer that's taking place outside my window returns in an album of images. Green eyes fixed on the strange golden hollow in a neck, on a shoulder. Sleeping. Days go by. Each without any meaning. The minute I do anything, go somewhere, talk to someone, I get this bad feeling that I'm doing things just to pass the time without actually taking any interest in them, that I'm just deluding myself by telling myself that if I move, and speak, I will feel like I am living, so I don't become totally numbed through inactivity. Anything that isn't about my health or my writing is completely without interest to me, or meaning. I watch myself do things as if I were watching someone else. What a strange and painful feeling to lose track of my life ... I have only to close my eyes and, contrary to all logic, I am free, all landscapes, seasons, and faces are available to me, the secrets of the most violent affections. There were instants, just below the surface, when I could detect the taste and the music of such passions, impossible to describe.

Make your own misfortune, yes, but do so, in all cases, not out of weakness but by will, like a composition, an artistic work; don't undergo your fate, even if it's happy. Have but one love, because how would it be possible to share such an incredible shudder of the skin? And seek it among distorted shapes and streets ablaze, opulent salons and chrome-filled restaurants, parks tangled with autumn, rooms upholstered with flowers or frost; let yourself die under a lamp and be reborn on account of a single shade pulled down over a harmony of stones.

———

June 12, 1980

Have just seen the gem: *Solzhenitsyn's Children.*[5] Time in Paris, delighted, bowled over.

———

June 17, 1980

I've begun a long poem about possession.[6] Love and death eat at the same table. I have decided to call my third book of poems *Self-portraits.*

Happy, happy to be writing. One single little green notebook that sings in my hands, it doesn't take itself too seriously and has promised me lots of space to stretch out. I feel drunk on words waiting to be realized, a pent-up energy at the heart of this dream. Each syllable inscribed by love. A man in infinity bends over, his laugh is a child prodigy, he can't control his hands, he has fallen in love but is so gently oblivious that he fears he has lost himself.

This poem is about common things, if it upsets a reader, it won't be because it's formally difficult, but rather because it unleashes the convulsive powers of the unconscious. It moves in two ways: a surface breathing (description of a concrete reality) and a dive to the watery depths (monologue in two voices). The unconscious is the Other that speaks inside the self, of the other, or to the other.

Love is the motor, the conducting wire, with its dual signs of death and fecundity, its blinding satisfaction, the mutilation caused by its long absence. The masculine side either surrenders or attacks, the feminine side either plummets into self-annihilation or builds herself a kingdom. She seeks both light and darkness, irrational in her instinct to either destroy or be destroyed. Unbeknownst to him, she anticipates his movements. This poem is about the endless solitude of warring factions. He is a master of barriers, she wants to annihilate concepts and conduct codes with everything in her power. Even so, beneath the velvet blows of their struggle, a trace of complicity insinuates itself, the game almost draws to a close. While on hold, passion risks tears and laughter, an authentic tenderness depletes the drama. When we have finished growing old we shall discover the world.

I have so loved the secret splendour of the cold

A sort of tentacular eroticism has linked the thought of the one to the other. He goes out of his way to flee, not from her exactly, but from himself, at least the part of himself that houses the mystery of intelligence, there where the vital drives shred the norm and the laborious everyday is smashed to bits. A strange passion damages him, because he refuses and rejects it, even when he's deeply asleep she monopolizes his thought. When he returns to her, he does so to confront the remnants maintained by his hatred and desire, and she, snared by his brief return, lets herself lean into the pleasure. It breaks her. He monopolizes her thoughts and she keeps watch for any crumb connected to him: actions, situations, forms. She falls asleep in her own lie, blowing up all out of proportion the body of the other, regrets, reminiscences, abandonments, and the diehard confrontation of her will against his.

———

June 27, 1980

I felt so sad and weary looking at the ocean this evening.[7] I didn't feel as moved as I have in the past, even though this place approaches my ideal. Yet all love dies. No other discovery has matched my first few visions of the ocean, a splendid revelation, for there's no place on earth that can compare. I felt excited, filled with its illusion. I was only nineteen or twenty years old, and so moved that I trembled. But now, haven't I become practically dead, incapable of feeling enthusiastic, unfit to love, the kind of person who talks too much about herself but knows less and less about who she is, where she is going, and what might be worth the bother of experiencing? How difficult I find it to be present to the moment, always questing after a moveable eternity, somewhere out there or in memory. The sea vibrates wave after wave, nothing can distract it from its task and its song. I stand before it, waiting to learn a lesson in permanence. We are so alone, how is it possible not to suffer with worry, how can we be our true selves, others are such terrible judges. A seagull takes flight and disappears into the blue. Each instant, composed of so many regrets and hopes, feels like an anvil.

I just finished a poem I feel good about. I'm not sure if the feeling will last, but for now, this poem pleases me. It blends the anecdotal with the deeply thoughtful, the "self" and the other. Really, it is centred on the unsayable. Its vexatious nature, its breathlessness. It attempts to penetrate the interior of desire, not to meet it on the surface. It shows how desire challenges norms, and as a form is unreal, unrealizable, is "elemental," like thirst or hunger, like fire, water, air, and earth. When I began, I put it into a more theatrical form, where the "she" and "he" were distinct entities, but in tightening the form they became blended, united in increasingly disparate scenes and, by that fact, more intimately symptomatic. "He" and "you" are the same person when seen through her. She, stretched out in a sort of shifting tension, takes the place of the self-portrait.

The eye sketches her pain ...

[*Self-portraits*]
June 17 to 27, 1980

———

June 28, 1980

MEMORIES
COINCIDENCES

1. *Sign and rumour*, 18–21 years old (1973–76)
Description of childhood and adolescence. The quest for totality and the absolute, imagination, solitude. Pierre.

2. *The Life Beyond*, 21–24 years old (1976–1979)
Stéphan, Magdalen Islands, *Sign and rumour* comes out, the Bon-enfants,[8] the dreamed-of life (ocean). Illness, hospitalization, Paul. Rehabilitation, time in Paris, Paul again, despair, hope.

3. *Self-portrait*, 24–27 years old (1979–1982)
The Life Beyond comes out, life as a Montréaler, more Paul, sickness, the present, the future. (*Self-portrait*, 1982).

———

July 11, 1980
I have thought a long time about this life, mine, and I define myself not by my character traits, tastes, faults, and preferences, but by my actions and feelings. A terrible deficiency: the archaeological present.

Not managing to be here. I invent crazy futures out of fear of not having *any* future. It's an ontological weakness. I wander dreadfully. A diffuse, yet pointed boredom preoccupies me without actually keeping me busy, like when a person talks without really saying anything. A stubborn solitude haunted by lost faces and mythic characters. A body exacerbated through hatred of itself. I am on the edge of a precipice, I know it, but I have no idea how to back off or cross over. Where is it, then, this so-called life filled with moving friends, stimulating discussions, landscapes undiscovered, a face … that is really a country? I was somewhere and I saw nothing, I was spoken to and I understood nothing, I didn't read, I fled, I didn't write, I screamed, yet I felt and I still feel my feelings swarming deep down inside of me, a soliloquy spoken by the words themselves, a life-giving form, which projects a new light onto the real. Who can distinguish! 'Distinguish,' there's a word that remains in ignorant whiteness. If only I could belong to myself, alone, I would finally be myself, always present. No longer would I nourish stubborn hopes, or lost moments, captivated as I would be by the newness of the imme-diate. The written immediate. Embraced with an intensity. Iconoclast of its own liturgies. Passionately on its path, each step monolithic, desiring, but satisfied, facing reality without any fraudulence.

above the roughness a great expanse
where insightful leaves sway
Sunday roams

———

Sentences should be born, rhythm should be established, but the timbre of the words should remain approximate, unfocused, and fugitive. The impossibility of writing takes up more of my time than writing does.

———

I would have liked to keep turning around ...

[*Poems at the Margin*]

———

July 18 [1980]

I used to adore opening my arms, giving and receiving. I used to be so confident and spontaneous in my sensuality, I would love to get that back. I now live in a corporeal prison, a prison of the imagination, I neither love nor dare anything. Paul cut off my arms, my hands, my lips. Paul reduced me to the bone. And a strange fear dogs my slightest impulse, as if the slightest imprecision could make all societal prescriptions come tumbling down. I no longer know where my desire is heading, nor what I want from all the strangers I'm haunted by. I have a taste for you, if only you knew. I would give anything to have you near me, here in the company of earth's astonishing abundance. You're leaving today on a family vacation. All well and good. I'm nothing, I've a double life. Marie at her friends' place in the country, sitting by the lake she'd like to spend the rest of her life at, not making any wrong moves, nor speaking against the other, the one secreted inside her relentless madness. Deeply submerged, her stars fixed, without issue or miracles, already dead, almost incurably dead. I want so much to silently slip inside of you, take over for your smile, your laugh. Here is where solitude ends, when you give yourself to me, strangle me.

I made up my mind that I want to settle down one day here, at Lac Mégantic. To write and think. I know this lake so well I can't help but love it. On some afternoons the landscape looks almost Japanese and, what's more, the nights here are perfect, without question, nor echoes. I've got nothing to report except for following the rules and living the anonymity of my daily life. But who lies waiting and watching behind this silent and boring facade? Who knows why she can't stop believing, despite herself and against all logic, like survival, like surrender? Who no longer counts the days but knows their weight? Who keeps watch over herself and the world without making sense of either, making things up?

———

July 23, 1980

Sick, the days go by in such a way as I barely notice them, stuck in this little apartment. I barely notice what time of day it is. Without a daily routine, there's only disorder. How I wish I could wake up in a cool room, with windows opening onto nature. Have pleasant meals, a silent, felt-lined study, a balcony on which to sit and dream, to do me good. But here, crammed between the noisy street and the hangars out back, the galley kitchen, the cluttered living room, lacking brightness or sweetness, I suffocate. Love lost, poetry out of reach. Difficult to keep my spirits up.

———

July 25, 1980

I'm going completely nuts! I constantly bemoan my state, I'm wasting time, life is there and I don't see him.

to S. K.
The lake is consumed on the curve of blue
the floor cools down at the countryside's cue

little magnanimous streets where your albums are
(but summer was a shadow where we pitched tents)
now we pass by the distances

[*Poems at the Margin*]

I hear the cry of a crow (or a seagull), why am I suddenly unsure about the sound? Anyway, the cry is coming from a long way off, from the depths of the country. How beautiful life is now!

———

I love it when a little corner of the window reflects in the glass of my writing desk (sending my thoughts and boredom far away). It makes a corner of beautiful raw blue that reminds me of the sea and conceals, in its uppermost part, the exoticism of a bamboo blind, one third drawn, and underneath this part of resounding sky there's a rooftop with a white border that looks like the prow of a ship, below, a glimpse of brown stones that cannot help but give the impression of an old French castle.

But I will never be able to express the honesty of this light, its delicateness, the way it lends itself to dreaming of places that live in the depths of memory, places that rush into it, augmenting its power.

———

Today, August 7, 1980

Death again, haunting me with lethargy and fear. I feel it inside of me, a vile beast, hostile, an alien inhabiting every inch of my body. Me, who, with every fibre of my being wants to live. So, I dream, I dream about love and about beautiful landscapes. I try so hard to meet life's sweetness, with all my heart I look for it, with all my body aspire to it. I want endless, miraculous love, but I won't ever have it. In order to better survive, I must not hope or wait for anything from existence, otherwise I tear myself to bits from this senselessness, this boredom, this interminable city in the heart of summer, when what I dream of is greenery, waters, tender luminous breezes, the pure scents of an early morning when you open your window onto a rebellious clearing. I feel called by an entire landscape, spacious mountains, cold lakes, soft pines, where time no longer controls things, diluted by infinite space. And me, my eyes surveying the supple brightness, it will be as if I had been washed of my illness from the inside, calmed by the comforting words of the wind. But I shouldn't hope for anything, I must live without asking for anything other than just being here, death is beside me. I still have hope, despite everything, pointlessly, for something which won't happen. A very sweet event, crazy too, revealing a part of existence I'm unaware of, which won't happen. No coincidence lies in wait for me, my path is smooth and scorched. The days are heavy, the nights vast and beautiful. Death is gaining, little by little, its silent terrain. It's the stronger of us. I brace myself, but it can do anything and I am nothing. I can feel it ravaging my breath and my throat. My heart, also, is alone and closed off, even friendship fails to make it believe I've a future. Even poetry ... no sign will be arriving to transfigure my existence, to calm my nausea, or to make me say: yes, it's possible, there *is* a creative feverishness through which we can know and realize ourselves.

Self-portraits[1]

Wide-necked bays nestled in the land ...

[*Poems at the Margin*]

———

Little yellow chairs ...

[*Poems at the Margins*]

———

August 8, 1980

A brighter sky this morning, an intensive perusal of my plans. I think over my relationship to language, to writing. About my great love, the way it transforms the gloom of daily life. The only passion that's grown. There's plenty of blue sky to make me happy, cool, copiously translucent blue filled with needful chatter. I have only one conviction left, toward which I bound with great strides: the self. This incurable language that sticks to our skin. Which we go in search of. Which enlarges and explodes its own limits. I am shamelessly devoted to and respectful of the French tongue. I feel an urgency, an investment in its presence, to let it speak what exceeds me, what is more me than me: language itself. To work with the language, in it and through it. The practice of my vocation and the practice of my selfhood are intimately connected, written with the same happiness, the same effort to know, the same desire to follow my hungers until they are sated. (May this day never come.)

———

POETRY

Writing in action, so that when poetry strives for simplicity it can be critiqued for playing it safe. Which narrows its field of action (song). Prose (it's very costly) won't give in to the possible: whether formal license or "reading habits," because its goal is to make the text efficient, to project its discharge of energy into the reader's head.

The current view is that poetry must inhabit the rupture and interrogate the metaphorical ground. No rules, under the contrarian zeal of a single rule: avant-gardism at any cost. This register must be adhered to from the first word.

Is this why, for the last several years, the most thought-provoking books of poetry have come from abroad (the writing of certain feminists, for example), and that the forsaken poem looks so pathetic to some readers?

But every poem draws life from the theory behind it. Let's take on the fad for writing "anything at all," but use *all* the means available, including lyricism or traditional syntax. Because, when read, the word's astonishing power operates on so many levels that we might want to use a so-called ordinary turn of phrase, as we would poetic sound patterning, while still being open to grammatical license, or audacious rhythm.

———

August 10, 1980

Many days to come and poems to keep (as promises are kept). I want my life to be uplifted by eloquent encounters. Meanwhile, to keep writing, practicing my vocation, working on myself. I think of autumn, of my love of autumn, intense like red and blue quartz,

of long work-filled autumn days, dispensers of adorable melan-
choly. Then winter, which I no longer fear, I have so many poems to
articulate, so many moods to identify, so many feelings to acquaint
myself with.

Perplexing space
now the wind lifts up
the setting sun appears
a few grasses in the foreground
under the heights of mauve
dreams darken against the light
on the bark and in the stone
and farther on without limits
existence

[Poems at the Margin]

———

[Québec, August 12 to 14, 1980]

MAINTAINING A SENSE OF ABUNDANCE

Tasting everything, the sun sinking, the wind lifting, the vacant
heights above the Laurentides and this deep warmth of feeling.

———

To have lived indigo in empty places ...

[Poems at the Margins]

———

Alone, my time taken up by this endless sadness, this lack. Lack, dissolving me, stomping on and pressing me into stone until I'm fossilized, othered, a sad memory. Loving humbly, out of sight, as if nothing must displace the old splendid feelings. Why light a sacred fire only to put it out? Oh, fight against it, did you say? I didn't delude myself, I knew hope's hidden side, those old unedited days. Each has his place, fists tight, palms hidden, eyes down. Who will speak the beautiful name of my love, the landscape of my tenderness, the music that kept watch over my childhood, and which has never left me? O music, my last and only refuge, my only religion, gather me into your sweet limbo so that I may sleep inside of you forever. Beloved grandfather, help me, during what little time I have left, to account for the thousands of poems, the thousands of dreams I've had, equivalent to so many lives, harmonies, and beautiful things that I have not yet achieved and which I haven't the creative energy nor strength to capture. My body, which I've hated so, return it to me as a token of love, show me the beautiful path of well-being, take me through memory's paths to that beautiful island where I knew, so rare in my life, happiness, close up this engulfing wound into which my entire being is disappearing and dying. Cure me of my distress, my solitude, my sadness, me, at the bottom of this endless well, guide me toward the light with a motion of your hand, speak to me of the primitive harmonies haunting our roots. Forgive me for not having loved you enough, wherever you are, extend to me what I failed to give you. Save me from death for a little while longer, stave off dishonour, make summer's wonders and the flowering apple tree come back to me. Show me the return of good things, abolish my suffering, show me those tranquil winter salons where cellos play, improving the universe, O you who are buried in the wretched earth of that place I have loved so much. Each day is so hard, if you only knew about my love, if you only knew about all the love I have inside of me, caged, shaking, unable to get out. And all of it joyless and enervated, with no possible outlet, ingrained in an inheritance of silence and refusal. Give me the life that I was never given.

——

I love you so much, you can't even imagine. Any moment now you'll forget me, for in your life I'm nothing but an isolated, unbelievable act. You are what I'm made of, my only emotion. Though it's all over, you can't imagine the infinite, intense, unspeakable solitude which your presence keeps always before me. You can't know the degree to which what's left of my world is populated yet empty. I want to devour, to explore my existence, I'm not tempted by death, not even for a moment (even though that thing can so easily come to pass, despite me). But without you, there will always be this little lack, a feeling of insignificance, lost years during which I loved you, catastrophically, while here I am plunged into formlessness. I was thrown in front of two indistinguishable deaths: the dissolution of my body and that of my mind. Aridly suspended before this irreducible, unavoidable fact, my will and my hope crumble. There's nothing left but to run away, to try and survive, to confront the obstacle mercilessly killing us. To secure some more time, there's only one solution: run away. Don't focus on the ever-expanding negative or the pain, but vanquish them with the thousand pleasant details of daily life.

You can't imagine how much I love you. You are a rock, a fixed point. You don't know me. You are indifference. Death is indifferent. Life is also indifferent. Whether it decides to crush us or save us is a crapshoot, there's no justice, no destiny, no love. I love you so intensely, you can't even imagine. What terrestrial wave will appease me, what oblivion bring me back to life? When I'm reborn between these horrors, what pleasure will shed light on my surfaces and my depths, make of me what I am and what awaits me? Me alone, with neither eyes nor hands. When will I see, and touch, and live?

———

CARNIVAL IN VENICE

This once colourful city overrun by the crowd in its last flickers of light. Venerable city of love, dying and denying death, with its mythic lunar carnivals where Pierrot and Columbine ...

The landscapes and harbours of Claude Le Lorrain. The spectacular twilight, entering into night as though diving into an ocean where everything seems possible, and even likely. The sudden snow, just as quickly melted. Mercurial light. What does the body say? Who or what can comfort it? What illusion will annex it?

———

The importance of music. Certain baroque composers. Vivaldi, delight of my childhood, eases my illness, makes me envision strange eternal landscapes. Lengths of poplars through which a golden light plays, bathing the leaves, the grasses, in a perfect, immortal, ever renewed splendour.

———

Coming face to face with facts and events in the poem. Photographic facts, evidence: this thing is, it's like this, this thing was. Distancing metaphor and symbol, meaning is still created, but it's open, offered up. The real appears for itself alone, for the writing, which is a connective movement. Ever-present lived experience shows and sounds through movement; the drives and the meaning move aside, love arrives. He is there, him.

———

April in Paris. Door ajar, light, air, smells, especially alert. I had the feeling there was a place where consciousness could experience life as tactile and illuminating. Not here, in fear, having returned to closures, cloistering, waiting. To live, to crawl out of these wells, these crevasses, toward the universe, the world opening its arms, me opening my arms to the world. To encounter spring's brilliance and rebirth at last, my body emerging from parsimonious poetry toward an inalienable prose, which could encompass all possible futures. Leave the prison of my illness in order to breathe in every possible experience. Seductive encounters, sceneries, seashores, white mountains. Write *Carnival in Venice*, a text that looks outward-facing in comparison with my too-inward-facing poetry. A multi-faceted story in multi-faceted sentences, musical. Analogies, bursts of energy, the resonance of black on white. Adorable masque play (carnival), death/love, looming conflict (Venice).

———

August 22, 1980

I look at the outline of these mountains, above which there's a big sky and drifting clouds, all subtly shaped by their movements. Already, here in the middle of summer, I can't help but sense that these midsummer clouds are heading toward fall; I can see them further still, changed by the harshness of winter. Stark at noon, splendid at sunset, the mountains stand elegantly mute. I have a fleeting vision of colourful, golden places where the furtive step of dawn or dusk approaches. A change of scenery, city [?][2] but almost dead, and yet, a revival of my spirits, the look, becoming an imaginary city, with glazed porticos, cathedral rooms, with long vertical gardens enclosed by age-old poplars. Kitsch decor, purified, arriving at the essence of a city, in an enigmatic street, dying, arriving at love.

———

Fatal error. I must write about the here and now, at home, these unchanging states, these wood homes, smelling of pine, of cedar, these muddy yet soft waters. To piece the magnificent present back together. Everywhere we look, things and moments scatter, disintegrate, but here the word comes back together.

———

August 24, 1980

I know of only one way to grow more receptive to the unyielding real, to sound, to the present, serious and simple: the moment you open a book and read. Each page turned is distinct from the others and you know when a moment has ended, another begun. Even a written poem stays unsettled, though I go over and over it, reflect upon it, it fights me in fits, its full meaning escapes. I'm always on the forbidden threshold of the text. Poetry irritates me more and more. I wish I could feel that last measure of certainty now that I've begun, with *Self-portraits*, writing my latest book. (Afterwards, the move to another form.) My path moves more and more in the direction of meaning. Not symbols, but description (short and efficient), and reflection. What does it mean to reflect? A mirror reflects. The crucial thing is to push subjectivity to its limit, to reflect, to reflect the heart and through it everything around it.

For in the haiku, it is not only the event proper which predominates,

> *(I saw the first snow.*
> *that morning I forgot*
> *to wash my face.)*

but ... becomes or is only a kind of absolute accent (as in given to each thing, trivial or not, in Zen), a gentle fold which nimbly creases the page of life, the silk of language.

Haiku ..., the articulation of a metaphysic without subject or God, corresponds to the Buddhist Mu, to the Zen satori, which is not at all the illuminative descent of God, but "awakens to the fact," apprehension of the thing as event, not as substance, reaching the anterior shore of language, contiguous to the matte quality (altogether retrospective, reconstituted) of the adventure (what happens to language, rather than to the subject).

— Roland Barthes, *The Empire of Signs*[3]

This is what I aspire to with all my being: to bring across a moment of brief, non-mystical illumination, the act, the event in writing; our minds, our consciousness, can only experience the event. The event is the instant, a non-continuity that provokes thought. But of what? Nothing! Simply the event of being here, an act that, through its very presence (said, written), defies death. What I call meaning is alive in every part. The instant that powerfully signifies one thing only: itself. Coincidences which create form. A refusal to read into things moral or symbolic meanings, avoidance of all impressionistic muddles.

*... acting on the very root of meaning, so that this meaning
will not melt, run, internalize, become implicit, disconnect,
or divagate in the infinity of metaphors, or the spheres of
symbol. The brevity of the haiku is not formal; neither is the
haiku a complex thought reduced to a brief form, but a brief
event which immediately finds its proper form.*

*... this precision obviously has something musical about it (a
music of meaning, and not necessarily of sound): the haiku
has a purity, the sphericity and even the emptiness of a musi-
cal note ...*

— Roland Barthes, *The Empire of Signs*

*We say "to develop a photo"; but what the chemical pro-
cess develops is undevelopable, an essence (of a wound), that
which cannot be transformed, but only repeated under the
instances of insistence (of the insistent gaze). This makes
Photography (certain photographs) similar to Haiku.
Because the writing of a haiku is also undevelopable: all is
given, without provoking the wish for or even the possibility
of a rhetorical expansion. In both cases, one can, one should,
speak of an* intense immobility: *connected to a detail (to a
detonator), an explosion forms a little star in the pane of the
text or the photograph: neither the Haiku nor the Photo-
graph makes us "dream."*

— Roland Barthes, *Camera Lucida*

———

[September 1, 1980][4]

*The wild geese take flight from the bulrushes
the icy bank the matte horizon*

each flying goose leers with haste and fear
already late the opal wind waters
furrows in the intense decay
the outline of a profile grabs hold of the mountain
its envelope thickens and bristles
and it's the cold

[Poems at the Margin]

——

evening rain …

[Self-portraits]

——

TA-I ALBUM
(numerous drawings and poems)

To express the Ta-i, the "great principle," the fundamental soul of the subject. To see things from a new angle.

A sense of space.

Taoism: the way of not following any way is the ultimate way.

——

Every book I write is an adventure. I despair of finding its meaning. I move forward with the writing: I live, and breathe through its unpremeditated form.

Every book lacks meaning (a justification for existing, therefore). As the writing advances, the book's meaning decreases, but its presence comes forth (is brought up to date). I am searching for a book that is nude, immobile, yet where everything is in continual motion.

It's a task that makes me want to write. We trace a few lines onto the vacant present, a few wrinkles on the surface of lived existence.

———

September 3, 1980

a tremble betrays the sunlight roof
the back of its leaves shine
everything unveils the river's place
an audible mass swirling toward its emptiness
constant and blued
the wood burns
the wind carries its thrilling scent
to the needled and rocky cliffs

[*Self-portraits*]

I love this country (mine!), so little has yet been said or done about it, happily. What a novel pleasure, inaugurating one's own space. At every turn I discover something new. I feel exalted by the honesty of its colours and shapes. Rough, Nordic, at times "Japanish" (mountains, birch, pines in mist); wrathful, tremendous river. There's so much here I've still to discover, a lifetime would barely suffice. It's waiting for a language. No one has invented it yet. A space empty of imagination, with a passionate geography of forms, textures, colours, moods, sounds, scents, harmonies, asymmetries.

———

September 4, 1980

To live in a little village like this, and not budge one's solitude too much. A little house between trees overhanging the blue gulf, the blue mountains. The sun rises on the riverside, the banks of which remain wild, and yet the village is so old, so French. The light moving over the white porches, the corrugated roofs and the dormers, makes the houses stand out against the grass, already yellowed (just barely yellow, a very blond and fine yellow, like a child's hair or crumpled velour). And there, pain and pleasure keep as still as possible in this stillness of given things, in the plenitude of fragrances: cedar, spruce, poplar, wood burning in the foyer, iodine from the river, and kelp; the fragrance of flowers, the last of the season, so copious, how could I even begin to count them? These, the sweetest and most penetrating fragrances, friends that replenish and calm the mind.

Notebook, I want you to keep all of this for me, so that all I have to do is open you to find myself back among all the things I've been enchanted by during this brief trip. Now, from where I sit in the perfect light of 10:00 a.m., the river is a furrow of stars and azure, the far bank like a frozen wave in their path. A scent wafts, then retreats, then returns, corresponding to this vision. How can literature be made adequate to this, be made to coincide with the real so as to sufficiently conjure it, not losing even one small trace? If writing could achieve that first movement that sets everything in motion, could reveal and relay presence, quiet and indivisible. It's an impossibility, and yet the attempt, the projection, articulates and communicates the real. This is so continuous that stillness (sometimes called 'the instant') perpetuates certainty. How can we grasp it all, and what of reality to grasp?

River: rhythm of ice and azure
infinite violet shoreline
                    by way of a pure afternoon in September

———

READING ON OCTOBER 16, 1980[5]

Poems without lyricism, written using a photographic technique, thus, according to a quiet kind of evidence showing that the real is not elsewhere, deferred until a later time, but pointed to here, now.

———

September 6, 1980

This evening I write for your solitude ...

[*Poems at the margin*]

———

all that which will survive ...

[*Self-portraits*]

———

the face's blond oval ...

[*Self-portraits*]

———

Field of night
immensely tenable
nothing moves nor rustles
the lamp is lit
or the campfire wakes up
traces the ocean's wave
which will carry to our banks
the void that will occupy us

delicately deliciously
with its night

[Poems at the Margin]

———

The music tonight makes my childhood, as I wrote about it in *Sign and Rumour*, feel so close. Classical music, the order of things, the order of the world. Eternity. The night, an immense curtain billowing like clear water, water it's easy to move through, seamlessly, silently, without touching or disrupting a thing. Infinite space.

———

October 23, 1980

Five days of terrible anguish.[6] How is a person supposed to live through such moments? Create, get through this so you can return to the poetic line's good feeling, meaning's musicality, the space written against death. Don't admit that you are beaten by, enclosed in, restrained by, and bound to anguish.

———

October 26, 1980

When I awoke, I was overcome with the intuition of a poem (not an idea, but a series of fugitive "visions" of images, a flood of sensations). This sudden abundance moved me. I wanted to seize it, but it went by so quickly. I recognized things from my past as they fled by, particular acts of tenderness beginning to form and then melting into darkness. These visions comfort me in the face of death. Even though I am fragile and powerless the repetition and presence of these moments feels solid and gives my life a feeling of immutability.

An energy discharge, an expansive dream, a fixed movement, a long exhalation of the material world. The poem, brief and made new with each reading, is the form most suited to these kinds of sensations. Seizing them, and their immense pleasure. Living. They reassure me in the face of death's ever-growing empire. A way of feeling warm as winter approaches. This year I do not fear it, strangely, for the first time I'm not apprehensive about it. That vast deserted stretch no longer frightens me like a vault. Now I take my warmth outside for a walk. I don't know if they are going to be able to cure me. Yet, after a month of being shut in, panicked, during which everything lost its meaning and savour, I'm waking up once again from this long nightmare. I keep watch and everything moves me. We drove the Bonenfants to the airport. Watching people board the planes roused my fighting spirit; to fight this illness, its cruel disenchantment. The misery of waiting for that hour when I can fly off to other worlds, other places, to those thousands of striking colours. Life has so many different aspects, contradictory, complementary, I want to make an inventory of the whole of it. Poetry is my food, my vine shoot, my life preserver. I can still use writing as a defence against silent panic. People who find words stale have simply lost their ability to feel wonder.

———

who went down the road
under an embryo of sun
and knew in turning
through the braid of still heat
that it is neither too soon nor too late
happy bodies that begin to awaken
say the same thing
the arc of the hill unfurls

toward the marsh and the upright clouds
the shore silts up and greys
its large trunks its underbrush
a windblown blind on a veranda clacks

[*Self-portraits*]

———

November 2, 1980

To write, and what else? See, feel, taste, touch, be like a door opened onto the world. And listen, until borders vanish. Become one with this icy and melancholy fall. Radiance itself, grey like a precious stone cut into the flesh. The city, last night, shooting high up through the transparency of indigo. It was an amazing show made of fake ice, fake frost, fake stars, and the mountain was an ocean with tiny lights scattered over its waves. Farther off, visible from the highway, the promise of the city's edge and then the fields, woods, and water. Space encircling. The suburb, timid under its trees, like a cornered animal. Montréal consumes space, its arteries so wide they let in the sky, it has no cover. The highways run along Westmount and let you see through windows into private homes: the lustre of a hallway, a library of leather-bound books, and the leather lamp of a studio, the neon of a tiny kitchen, the psychedelic purple of a teenager's room … lives aligned, absurd, bewitching … The poor neighbourhoods, with golden kitchens where families gather to play cards, living rooms replete with old-fashioned knick-knacks.

Winter will not get inside me. Winter is a world waiting to be written. To heal. Get through the worst moment, until the fresh air blows again through parks and rooms. Love, feel moved, head outside. Like the end of a terrible night, or showing up to a party at a friend's house where everybody is waiting for you. The bright hallway fills you with happiness, to be so ensconced after the bitter outdoor cold. You shake the snow off your boots, coat, and wool scarf, and you see from the threshold a succession of rooms filled with a joyful crowd, mingling, talking, laughing. Once you go inside, your name echoes from room to room, and the friends you love best come up to you, wearing sympathetic or radiant smiles, holding a glass in their hands, or their arms open, and you grow even warmer from their hugs, kisses, the rustle of intermingling fabric and hair, the slip of one hand into another, happy ... I see so many kind faces. May friendship build a fence around me to keep out my suffering and fear.

———

What is my life like? Between my treatments it's good. The seasons, this cozy little apartment, the few poems that manage to escape my mouth and that I sometimes read in a small café, or somewhere else. Evenings at the movies (the smell of popcorn, of dust), the crowds in the adjacent cinemas, sometimes dinner at a small restaurant, the few friends who comfort me during suppers and parties. Someone you pick up from or drive to the airport. I talk about travelling, but don't leave. I feel good here. Maybe during a week in the heart of winter. Just for a dream of palm trees, sand, and ocean.

I am happy, I hope this life never ends. To me, Montréal is like a gorgeous "all-purpose mess." I love every part of it, at all times, during every hour (even in English). I can't leave this land, this feeling of ease, the sloppiness of this sky, these wastelands. Whether you get up early or late makes no difference. Going to the movies is my high mass. I love the ritual of it. My poems are flashing, furtive, fixed films.

My happiness knows no bounds: there are books to read, films to see, people to discuss things with, good dinners to treat myself to, junkets to the North amidst the beautiful white snow, the pleasure of the cold.

I feel happy, there are lips to kiss, letters to write, poems to write and read aloud. I feel happy, I have already lived such a full life, loved so much, learned a thing or two. I feel happy, planes come and go, and I can write all that I want to write, I needn't choose.

Night wandered everywhere at once
and now and without wellness things deferred
acts that will not be accomplished
weary gestures that will mark the path
up to the depth of night
shop windows filled with pale underwater silhouettes
hasty circulars splitting apart blindness
and wonderment
here is the piece of clothing placed on the chair
and the masked expression
of the hands' lengthy decision
the night will have a spectacular end
under the horizon's frosted mirror
pulled from its wound passed out from its glow
its bleachy smell drifting one last time
through the emergency rooms
the ice-cold counters
we hear only the pointes of a dancer's feet
over the black floor of a theatre
a rustle of her angel costume
then nothing

[*Poems at the Margin*]

Self-portraits
1979–1981

Wrinkles
Surfaces

It's winter, it gets dark early. The park is empty, grey, lit by a few mauve street lights, the grey sky stretches out behind the mountain's silhouette, with a touch of bluish-pink at the horizon. Sad gradations of darkening clouds, swarming cars, a lone pedestrian or two. Inside each car, the lives of individuals caught up in their own stories, preoccupations, hopes, loves, pains. The richness of many lives, even the sad ones are rich; an accumulation of things said, gestures, scenarios, insights. Words of suffering, words of love, conversations held in the chilly shadows of dusk, in the pale light of dawn. Gestures filled with desire, hasty and trembling. O gentle touch, a tad bashful, extremely flattering. Then, what an expansion of twilight, playful, pale, a cold dirty blue, what a welcoming foyer, doors open, what a gentle face, what lips. To live lightly, delicately, without overly disrupting either persons or things, mulling over the seasons, their basket filled with smells, colours, veiled dreams, sounds.

———

Here's the plan: write for long stretches, constantly, note my feelings, perennial pleasures, atmospheres, thoughts, leaving nothing to chance, let the pen's passion steal it all. Build a book out of sweeping aromas, the real in its entirety ... On hospitals: aquarium walls, neon halls, old men in doorways, naked beneath their open gowns, with flabby, purplish skin, the sadness that is suffocating the sinister end of this century, and more. I sit up in bed and dream, I look back on things, I reconstruct in an attempt to recover my old feeling of wonder at life's abundance. Beautiful landscapes, warm houses, relaxed conversations, a face comes, then departs, sometimes

I remember how I felt, but that business is no longer important or essential. I am living, I'm no longer bored, every moment is so precious, so delicate, I must fulfill the poem's promise.

———

Here ...

[*Poems at the Margin*]

———

[*December 1980*]

I'm slowly reborn, and live, feel moved by a different body, become familiar with another way of being, another crazy arrangement, undo the positioning of places, create an existence and objects, do as I please, find another heart. A time of the first shared secrets, first kisses. Come to know a richer destiny, a sweetness more ample. Tell myself: speak of universes roaming through infinity and never reaching their end, evermore in pursuit of image and name. The real happily flees, what latitude for investigations and conjectures, for crazy ideas, dwellings, and escapes. Powerful dreams delight and taunt me. I feel the weight of my loneliness, but what a feeling of well-being. Desire a book of poems put together as the arc of an entire life. This music is transporting me to the back of an exotic bar, it's sultry, I feel at ease in all my limbs and in my clothes. An American evening, glasses, lamps. The sea nearby. It rocks back and forth, creates eternity. The sea is the only witness. The path still burns with the day's splendour. All night long, by other means, I will find myself anywhere else.

———

it's white outside ...

[Self-portraits]

———

My memory is haunted by Venetian festivals, that cult of light and ocean. I will go where the image awaits me. There, the only place where the poem can fulfill its promise, its beat resound, and its rhythm scan the blood of arteries. What gold falls between the trees in the gentle heat of an unchanging April. And I know that the old civilizations, their splendours, their pains, their appearances and natures shall come to me. The white stone expands the sky, there's a path of passionate dust, foliage that gurgles like a spring, all the way to the unruly wheat approached by the sea. The Mediterranean (Adriatic) sea, weak wave, you are the endangered mirror of our minds and bodies. You whisper your marvels without the help of tides, you have no anger, you are placid and sober as a great lake. The pines lay their baskets over your banks, protecting you from wrinkles. Venice, you have seen the epochs go by, tasted all the fruits, you have been urbanized since then, but your light still shines with pomp, its bursting rooms, its Doric columns. All civilizations, all of modernity, press against your flanks. How have I managed to live even a single day without you, how have I forgotten your perfume, the outgrowth of your streets, your colourful crowds, your music, your calls to the sea, those nights when an African wind wafts over your rooftops. I carry you as a talisman for my poetry. I will follow this path toward you with conviction, and without detour, if my life will allow it.

———

Have we spoken enough about the intense spirituality of our senses? We will never be able to fully account for all the things we see, touch, taste, feel, hear. We are but bodies continually shocked by waves of perception. We move through a world of signs, numerous and moving.

———

for the flimsy door
which opens onto the balcony
steered like a boat in the sun
for having gone out into the street
the face carried like a palm
on the surface of the river
and gently placed over the intense dilapidation
eyes larger than hunger
arms more open
that everywhere the heat decreases along the horizon
opening the galleries of ice
the train stations the waiting rooms
and going down very narrow alleyways
tiny places with awnings
or more muffled crypts
to welcome the motionless
the body and its vertigo
and love stripped bare moves forward

[Self-portraits]

———

Montréal, December 31, 1980

I still love you. And if my body is slowly entering into the legend of its own death,[1] my mind is not yet affected, except in its capacity to communicate (because that's done with the body), but inside my thoughts a cycle of images and numbers goes by, is lost, multiplies. A poem haunts the wings, but doesn't show itself. Tears, my onto-logical weakness, keep holding it back. I see my suffering increase through the suffering of others. The poem that would calm this intolerable vision of their faces and bodies wants to appear, but is hung up by my overwhelming confusion. These pale words lack the needed degree of goodness, strength, solicitude. As with desire, they stay on the sidelines of my suffering. What I feel when you come near is unspeakable and fragile. I will never be able to name it. I explore the entire area, passionately. The words on the periphery approximate the meaning, but when I try to move into the centre, its powerful presence blinds and enchants me. All poems resist, and once written die of inexactitude.

The body weakens, but the mind keeps on going. I feel assailed by my dreams, amazed by their precision. I can clearly see your body, your eyes, your laugh, all in exact locations, I can identify the light by its complexion, texture, density. I'm somewhere I've already been, or where I might go, in this life or another, but in either case, I've no doubt it's a real place. A grab bag of memo-ries, things I've read, places I've been? And always that light which haunts me, its every nuance serving the text. But, right now that text escapes me. I'm so weak and so orphaned by pain. So little stimulated from all sides, I'm reduced to an outline, to this illness rut, where all signs diminish and become self-referential, where suf-fering shrinks the universe.

I want to say it's a blue door, or a colourless one immersed in the blue shadow of a late afternoon, which, in a little while, you will open (maybe, I can hope), to discover a strange sea vista. And you will find yourself alone in a cavernous room, bumping into things, dimming the light from the window, then taking ownership, just as heat takes ownership of air. You, laughing, discovering your thirst and your hunger, reaching the end of your years. Each wrinkle working on the heart of things. The lightness of being, almost undetectable, flowing like sand in sleep, one final very delicious embrace. The roundness and density of every instant, having taken its assigned place in the whole, could be pulled out and examined. The lifespan would become a sequence of perfect and clear moments, a sequence of profound poems that could, in talking to you, say everything.

———

January 2, 1981
Healing dreams and dreams of this moment only manage to get as far as your succulent fullness. The ripe fruit of dreams. Brazilian music, easing me into lengthy dreams about the ocean, filled with your green eyes, so that even here masterful music responds to the harmony of the immersive and clear light (a transparent blondness that sparkles and moves thin shadows). Every few minutes the snow beats against the window, while inside there's a fire, calm and protecting. Somewhere else he, too, leans toward it, and in the silky flame, like an exotic sunset gathering strength, his patience, his passion, knowing now what light shall cover the world. Summer, previously unknown, heavy foliage muffled with flowers, abstract skies filled with a constant ringing. A trembling horizon, and above the incessant crash of waves, so forceful that their enormous good heart can be heard in every street, comforting, protecting, perpetual. Summer fills the windows, temperate with the ceaseless rustle of leaves and birds, retreating waves. Infinite idyll. Forms stripped

bare. The sea winds fill your breast. You are no longer ill or alone. And if you suffer at all, it's because you are in proximity to such perfection, to being so moved, astonished almost to the point of tears. Everything is still. A handsome male body walks by, smooth, slightly thick in the middle, his hips and legs still svelte, every wrinkle a story, each sign of fatigue another reason to love him, to be generous. I no longer laugh. I never laugh, me, who knows how to. Already, I no longer laugh. But your laugh is my obsession.

———

And yet I'm so alone, poetry has fled, the poem hardened. I look for it, long for it terribly, but what a failure of imagination and existence. Nothing happens. I am nothing. I write so little. And yet there's a poem always waiting that could give me meaning, energy, and resolve this waiting. Will something show up some day to bring me back to life, delight me in my misery, me, who is increasingly nothing more than a shade, nothing more through and through than a shade? So few faces, so little soul. I cultivate a memory of fucking, like one last fire in the terrible surrounding cold. Imagination is eating me up. I no longer live anywhere but in my dreams.

———

a defoliated tree
where the harsh sun moans
the hangar shimmers
beneath the absent expanse of white
above no bird glides
no breeze moves a tress
nor caresses the cheeks
the lips barely stir

in the disintegrated white of the shadow
the nightlight forgotten in midday
the heart now moves only in dreams

[*Self-portraits*]

———

January 20, 1981

He is handsome like a straw-coloured morning. I would give worlds
to be able to see him daily. His eyes of green are an endless ocean,
his skin the fantastic fruit of the most overpowering summer night.
I speak to him and hug him in my dreams. His eyes are fabulous,
his shoulders cast a powerful spell, create a sacred happiness. I will
never stop loving him, he fills my silence. Why aren't you here, and
why do I love you? And if you came back for me, I would go with
you without regret or fear. Just to look at you brings me joy. I love
you for no reason, I admire you for secret reasons which you don't
even suspect. I love you for being so strict and sure of the real, for
being so mercurial and so terribly contradictory, both sensible and
egotistical. So vulnerable. My clear water. Your memory is as sweet
as an orange. Each time you bat your eyes, your lips swoon over
mine. I was made to look upon you and I will never stop writing
about you. What a pleasure. To see you going, to speak of you;
landscapes multiply inside of you, they are made new, they darken
and lighten. Deep down, you are so solitary, so completely different
from me, so deaf to my words, to my world, to my joy's dark fruit.
My love for you, though it has no reality, is completely free. Real-
istically, I no longer hope for anything, I have been released from
all hope, all desire. I live in a dream, in my dream of you, vivid and
fecund, ethereal. My imagination. My clumsy departure. My regret.
I talk about you all the time. I continue to betray myself. I have to

rid myself of you on a daily basis, nevertheless, I am getting close to a place where I will no longer think about you. I must.

I've just gone on a delirious jag about Paul. Keep saying it. Keep saying it's over. A contradiction. Useless suffering. A feeling that won't die, yet is already dead. There's been someone else, who's brought me a lot of happiness, but has now left. Maybe he'll do that often. I'll become attached to him and then he'll pull a Paul and go back to his peaceful existence. I'm a little afraid. We pay dearly for any happiness we manage to wrest from this life. Yet I should let things and people be. Not rock the boat. Ask for nothing. Be simple, immediate, attentive. Listen to the richness of others, their worlds, their stories, their compromises, their courage, their deceptions. I think I love him. I have loved every man differently.

———

January 23, 1981

My solitude is boundless. Its magnitude frightens me, fills me with fear. Giant, desolate places. Yet some part of me is happy, because my health has improved and I want to hurry up and live. But I'm afraid. I no longer feel any love. I cry out for love, and would do everything, anything, to be loved. But what do I have to offer? Nothing, if not an endless burning memory of Paul. Why is it that the only person that I really truly and deeply love doesn't love me? But if he came back to me, enchanting and saddening with his gentle voice, what could he give me besides endless despair? So, love me, love me, me, the one who has lost her ability to love. Love me, make me. I am transparent. I'm not playing games. I love you. But never as much, that's for sure. I'm wary. He took my soul. Only the poem, at times, can give Paul back to me, his body and his mind. Sometimes I am inside of him, in the silent kingdom of his fear. He always drives me back into an extreme form of solitude. He consigned me to be forever alone, even when I'm surrounded by people. He has left me to my death. He is very far away. I don't even really know where he is. A single kiss like the one from two days ago overwhelms him, and he runs away, fearful and worried. *Mia via*. To kiss is such a little thing. It's really nothing at all. There's almost no consequence to a kiss. The words I speak to you out of the confusion of my memory are far heavier and more serious. They take you nowhere, and yet that's the only thing you enjoy. I am so alone. I have so much need for love and tenderness. The whole world couldn't satisfy my hunger. Yet I give nothing. I don't listen to anyone. I think only of myself.

———

January 24, 1981

O living. It's so hard. Recently I've seen tons of people. I've gotten a lot of love and affirmation for my poetry. Praise from Gaston Miron, Jean Royer, and many others. Attention, words, warmth. Celine and René Bonenfant. Fondness for being protected, for being both a free agent and protected. Fondness for meeting with people, talking, being accepted, and laughing.

That's why there is no poem.

———

identical villas ...

[*Self-portraits*]

———

What good is keeping my chin up if the neck doesn't hold, if my head shatters like an ice shelf breaking apart and the tumour will have won over my lung and my heart, and I'll be laid in earth with Grandfather; I know that the apple trees will still flower wherever our bodies are buried.

———

Genuine fiction is written almost without erasures. It's barely edited, defined by that moment when the word or image takes over. A continual flow of the self without correction is also the creation of a fiction. Kerouac at his typewriter reinvents his journey across America; what is the real connection between lived experience and autobiographical form? The only real is the roll of paper inserted into the machine capturing the imagination, the outline of letters. American images, where is Kerouac, in the text or on the road?

———

To write or not to write, surpassing limits and traditional forms, a way to permeate the real, pure fiction. A cold, clear, almost clinical precision, yet "poetic images" (clichés). An image that is clear and reflective of the idea. Speech of the unconscious. To multiply my desires, take control of this solitude, this confusion. I want to be completely present when it matters most. I am mercurial in form, my existence says nothing about me. I am the fictions I tell myself, the tumultuous instant during which I dissect my percep- tions, the story I tell myself. I am not a fixed entity; my thinking isn't personal. I experience my existence as unstable, mine only by virtue of my believing in it. Every memory, every expectation forms me.

A poem doesn't repeat itself, it's immediate. This is the fiction I live by. Or maybe the poem, wanting to near objective reality, represents it and by doing so eliminates it. I can't speak about my own death, nor about my illness or my love. In my efforts to corral them they escape, herded to the periphery. When I circle around you, I take on a face, a body. "You" bring me into the world. Everything you do obliges me to respond. The way I respond reveals who I am, my tastes, my anxieties, my alienations, and a mountain of other things. I could write the script of my life, the life I imagine I'm living. Not the lie, the real thing, the life that moves me, that motivates me. The one that steers my actions, brings on my metamorphosis, nails me down, demands something from me. Reality is not direct, immediate, or stable, rather, it exists in my elaboration and projection of it.

From now on I have to write every day, mould the poem, force it into being, force the ideas, subjugate my perceptions, own them, revise it all, the forms and ideas, all my ways of working, isolating them, destroying them, resolving them in a new way. I need to invent connections and motivations, destabilize, abolish fears and misgivings. Nothing has changed about the way we think about poetry, about our notions of this thing we call poetry, for over a century. The garb, the surface, changes a little, but the ideological tawdriness remains the same. Between the textual biases of the two different sorts of readers: those who beg to be told a story, and those who read to discover the infinite, there is no significant difference. Mysticism of speech, mystification of the word. The power to say is equal to prayer.

———

but only the lamp …

[*Self-portraits*]

———

Night as far as the eye can see
like the sea steering this difficult sleepiness
the return of things

——

February 15, 1981

We have already said why creativity flows, in our view, from an unconscious desire to run away from death. On the other hand, perhaps this would not be the case if we knew the exact date of our death. But given that escape is impossible, anxiety must reach its peak and lead to behavioural inhibitions. In addition, illness slowly transforms our biological equilibrium, and that of our psychology, such that our resistance to death is progressively weakened.
— Henri Laborit, *Éloge de la fuite*[2]

——

February 17, 1981

SELF-PORTRAITS

Journey across a variety of landscapes and places gradually opening onto a "no man's land."
The self-portraitist builds directly from the materials, the common spaces.
By taking a leisurely stroll through places from his own past and that of his culture, the self-portraitist should "invent himself," in other words, figure out who he is.
His writings are tombs where his "real" body is buried.

> *Inevitably, from Montaigne to Malraux and Barthes, self-por-*
> *traiture centres on the experience of death. The text of the*
> *self-portraitist therefore becomes a glorious body, revived,*
> *a corpus offered to the community of readers: "this is my*
> *body."³*

———

February 17, 1981

I should be overjoyed, given that each day is a victory over death.
But are they really a win, these lost days, supposedly mine, without
creativity, passion, or brightness? Nothing to do. Dismal stupor. All
my energies band together, attempting to convince me that my life
is good. But I feel bitter and pessimistic. My desire to be loved is
overwhelming, and I have nothing more to say or do. Not a single
idea about the film or a poem.⁴ Emptiness. I'm neither curious nor
hopeful. I should create a fiction out of my life, but which one? It's
as if all my imagination has been drained. My personality shattered,
disintegrated. I don't know what I think nor what I want. With
the exception of love. But I think about it less and less. For love's
green eyes are both so hard and so gentle. Why did he turn me into
such a bitter, cautious, and at root, small-minded person? I need
to get what I've given, to be nourished with the energy I've lost.
I want someone to need me, to fret over me, to worry about me.
I want them to be jealous and possessive. I want to be shaken up,
freed from myself. I want to be constantly reassured that I am alive
because I am loved. My heart has stopped freaking out. Resisting
death is first and foremost an internal struggle, and my inner life
has grown weak, caved in. I put as much fire under it as I can,
but my days are so vast and empty, they are tasteless, odourless,
colourless. I should be welcoming them like gifts of light, prom-
ises of poems. Yet I am ungrateful. Fate or God has made sure I

have a lot of attention and kindness, at least around me. There are people who are alone, really alone ... And yet I wander without attachment, home, well-being, or light. Without understanding or accepting whatever it is, with an old-fashioned romantic ennui against which, the more I fight, the deeper I sink. I wander through my own texts without even really recognizing them. Every poem I have written falls apart upon rereading. My invented universe is too tenuous as to be the kind of realistic fiction you can hide in. Deep within I am cowardly, craven, dependent, and mediocre.

Yet somewhere there must be someone or something, or a moment in which everything could change. I do have a chance. I want so much not to miss it. Where is it? How many years will I have to wait, or will death beat me to it? Will I be denied the time to live, or to understand my life, to be fully present for it? The oppression never lets up. I no longer have the strength to use my creativity as a weapon against death. Words without value or power come to me, their inanity, their vacancy frightens me, like a knife against my throat.

Stéphan said that I wanted to be sick. Maybe it's true.

At least when I feel sick, I know I'm still among the living, that I'm still putting up a fight, that I'm still breathing. That it's not over yet, because I'm suffering and I'm scared. I so want for life to be beautiful, but my life has no more flesh and blood. I'm useless. There's nothing, or practically nothing, I hope for. Things are so vague and dreary. I could take a thousand photos of myself in an effort to convince myself that I have a face, a body. I have no meaning and no reality in this world. I exist for nothing and no one. I have no place that's mine, neither kingdom nor secret. I am a shade, the shadow of a woman who loved a certain set of green eyes in the winter of 1978 and was not loved in return, was extinguished by derision, pain, insignificance, solitude. The return of stupidity and stupor.

———

February 18, 1981

Grandfather, how did you manage to stop being French so quickly, and what a shame for me. But unbeknownst to you, some of your feelings from abroad were passed down to me: a nostalgia for a certain kind of light, for summer, for the ocean, for your birthplace. That place where your first memories, no doubt amidst anxiety and poverty, were forged. Were you born in a house overlooking the port, or with a view of the glimmering Mediterranean, or in a dark humid alley reeking of rot? What use are these stupid thoughts? Maybe it's simply that, near the end of your life, when you went back to Marseille, and then told us about your trip, I realized, for the first time, that there was a "somewhere else" (and not just in books), and that through you, through that deep connection that brought us together, this place was also a part of me. My roots were there too. I think that you secretly suffered from being here and not there. Yes, secretly, and because I felt connected to you in an intuitive and feral way, I was infected by your heartbreaking nostalgia. There's an elsewhere. My nostalgic longing for the good life is not for *Mon oncle d'Amérique*, but for my "Mediterranean mother." No wonder it took you so long to go back and see for yourself. No wonder you feigned an indifference that surprised and fooled us all. But, as a child, I picked up on so many things, as I was linked to you in such a deep and visceral way. And if, as people believe, a child's brain is like pristine wax, your imprint was direct, it made me who I am today. It's from you I got this dream of finding a love that would fulfill me because I would be everything to him. I wanted, since I was very young, for you to believe in me and see in me your hopes, your continuation. I wanted to be what you were proud of, and I only write for you. I wish you could have seen my name in the newspapers, and known that people were already talking about me when I was only twenty-five years old, more than you were spoken of during your entire lifetime. And it was *your* name that appeared in all of these trifles taken for important because of ego-flattering. Grandfather, a lie reigned over our house. You deserved to be there, given where you were, but you only got so far. Even when very little I could already tell that you wanted more, but that you were prevented by fear, weakness, helplessness, insecurity, or, I don't know what. You only became a professor when you would have liked to have been a magnificent conductor or composer. Everyone feigned boundless admiration, and you gave your daughters the deferred hope that they would make something of themselves in music, become stars in some way. In the face of your disillusionment I, when a child, told you I would go far. I took on the responsibility of becoming you. Your name became mine. For always. Truthfully, I didn't choose it of my own free will. I was you. I am still you. I dream of finding your reincarnation in a man, a man who would steer my success and support me. And through his love I could find the acceptance you denied me, because of my desire to replace you. Because you loved me a lot, but you didn't believe in me. I was a girl. To take a little girl who wants to be a writer seriously and believe that she could go far? To ever believe such a thing? Her words are listened to the way one listens to dreams or games that will fade with age. (A concert musician can be rigorous, but never a writer). It's this dualism that tears me apart. Even at twenty-five years of age I still see myself through your eyes. Your view of me is still inside of me. I write to prove that you're not dead, that your name will resonate in the future I'm hoping to forge, in the work I want to hand down. I write in order to show you that I shall surpass you, I'll get to that place you couldn't get to, the place I promised myself, and in the name of my blessed love for you, I would reach. And that I asked you to believe in, but was met by your indifference, your silence. You were focused on something else. Like Paul, you don't want to know me and you don't love me. As with Paul, I boast about my successes in the hopes you'll focus on me (and Paul did, every time, he applauded), but also like him, afterwards you turn away, you find me tedious, and then I am left alone with my unresolved love for you.

Trapped by love and my ridiculous pride in this endless cycle I will join you in the kingdom of the dead. It hasn't even been five years since you died, but now, still, you're not here to change your views, to tell me that I can achieve even more if I want to. And I want to. But I'll never achieve enough, nor can I be sufficiently reassured that my name will live on. I'm perfectly aware that my motives are petty, such permanence illusory. Because the work and the name that will remain (if they remain) will never be mine or yours. And this glory, should it arrive, will never be yours, even if it has your name, because you died in complete anonymity. I'm blessed by so many memories. You, improvising on the violin, me saying: please keep going, which made you immediately stop. It was as if you feared falling from the taut string of my conviction. That would have never happened. And the time when you showed me a concert program from Paris listing a short composition with your name beside it. You were so proud it was painful. This is why I'm so fixated on the idea of publishing in France, and going there, so my name might be known on a far greater scale. This is why I feel this burden of responsibility. No one forced it on me, I took it on out of some crazy desire to please you.

But I have no other reality than this vacancy I signed up for, than this attachment to a name I wear like a flag. Neruda had the Chilean people, I have you. This is why I wanted some man to completely believe in me, to free me from myself. Or at the very least from my oppressive superego. I've built my entire being on that slim foundation, though my reason knew better. I can't go back: Uguay is my name. In my little-girl mind I've never had any other. Just the opposite, I will dig myself deeper and deeper into this identity.

————

February 21, 1981

Loneliness. Intolerable and difficult loneliness. Yet I'm surrounded, listened to, protected. I create this loneliness. In spite of myself. With the enormity of my aspirations, my insatiable desire, my restless passion. Kingdoms, days, faces will pass. I travel extensively through the same, the only city. A particular idea of God has taken seed inside of me. When the Absolute gives us the slip, ideas about God show up. And about love. Total. Unique. Which asks for nothing and gives all. Because we can't help but plumb the depths of our selves, of our feeling. But we can't ask the other (nor any person) to feel the same thing, to have the strength. And so, we come to wander through the blank ruin of our hearts, hoping for the improbable, leaving behind the end of torments. "Ask and you shall receive." You who have suffered in words and acts, remember us. To wait less and less, but still be available. Door open. Eyes forward. Obstinately holding on to being. BEING. Through all the gestures that emerge, the feelings that flow in, through all the memories we keep in our dense, fake core. What I want is to forget, to erupt, to stop being careful, to love without judgement or pettiness, to break the laws of genre and style.

Let the tyrannical ocean resound in me once more, its great seafront of dark pockets and gleaming surfaces. Because being alone shouldn't frighten me. My internal music is my greatest strength, my ability to come back to life, to transform the other's absence into an intensification of the self in the world. From those who show up, who will show up, into the places I will be standing, in recognition and transformation. I like to know a place, a person, and then to see them under different circumstances, at different times, as more or less accessible. In different spiritual states. But life surges up in me. And I love it. How large and free of consequence the world is. The paths proliferate. Suddenly, the words are his. Having dispersed, they return, gathered together under the image of the father. He who makes everything happen. Knowing full well that I am making this up. The pretext: this love without a future, without a solution. This long enigma that I drag behind me (it's never up ahead). It's an archetypal quest insofar as God abandons me, turns his face away, ignores me. And I implore him. To guide my acts, grant my hopes, comfort me, respond to my bursting vitality. But my desire is surrounded by nothing but desert.

In the desert of life, I design and forge mirages. Who will come to numb my pain?

———

Life wells up in me. I love. It erases itself: I die. Moving from one extreme to another, I entertain strange dreams, lengthy mad desires, agonizing illnesses. I dream of home and water. Lots of water: vast lakes, hidden pools, rivers that have the echo of the ocean in them. I also dream of death, which is the opposite of water symbolism. Nothing can ease the despair I feel because I am not loved as I love. I become attached so quickly. I have so little hope. I should attempt only to think about one day at a time. Each day is a desire to solve, a thought to absolve, pulling me toward the non-presence of the world and of things. I live too much in dreams. I should try and force myself to be present. Invest the real with the informative capacities of my being, learn how to breathe.

My inability to compromise, my totalizing passion, my "absolute thirst" haunt me so much that all things seem mediocre. I ask for too much meaning, given that our lives, so small and fragile, get bored of and are forgotten by history, and even their own stories.

I need love to make up for what is missing inside of me. I'm so afraid of feeling dead that this obsessive inner vitality drives me to love, to want to love, to make things happen, to satisfy my inner need to be present to the other. I am mired in the absurdity of my ways. I have neither abundance nor peace. I will no longer allow myself to be destroyed by love. By a single love.

[FINAL NOTEBOOKS]¹

This morning I was brushing my teeth when I had a vision of happiness. This fleeting, feverish, and ridiculous moment happened in the sordid hospital. I would like to know where, in what sedimentary layer of our being, do such feelings live? So that I might finally, definitively, have access to them. Rifling through memory only gets you so far. Those dreamlike memories we form when we let the mind drift, travelling, walking, or sleeping, come a bit closer. Sometimes I see this long, rectangular facade, which extends away from an indeterminate and vague space. It's a house, out of which comes a triangle of golden-pink light. A light, like the light of dawn or dusk, pours through the panes of the house's large windows into its vast blond-wood rooms, which are furnished in an indistinct, if understated, style, vaguely old fashioned. There is always this very gentle, yet extremely penetrating hallowed light. The scent of damp grass seeps through the windows.

Maybe these visions are a result of the dreadful "gruel" that they serve in this hospital, which brings up memories of the breakfast ritual on Perrot Island. Grandfather. Grandmother. The little yellow and white kitchen, the smell, the feel, the sound of summer mornings, of leaves lightly rustling as a background music to these rituals. Grandfather ate "gruel" every morning. He is the only person I've ever known to eat it ... Wouldn't it be nice if I could return, even for an instant, to the perfection of my childhood, into that particular time and place? Childhood is not just one uniform or distinct thing, mine was made up of both bad times and good, contentment and worry.

Reading was my great comfort. A safe love. I remember waking up with everything in its place, sweet and present. The same routine, creating a sense of order, as well as delight. And no negative feelings, just a feeling of the fullness of being alive. I would sit on our veranda and open my book. I could hear the waves hitting the pebbled banks, the whisper of the leaves, the sound of a falling apple, its perfume-releasing bruise. There was an intensity to each present moment, no anticipation, no regret. I *was* the cozy home, the hours passing, the country walks. I was the very affection that surrounded me. I wish I could recreate that atmosphere now. Seasons were my eternity. Death didn't exist. Each season was proof that all things return. There were so many beautiful and good things, so many moments free of searching, memory, or suffering. Some strange incapacity prevents me from living like this now. I am always waiting for something, filled with anxiety, dogged by a quest, in a constant state of need. And yet, maybe if I could get back to a child's state of non-hoping, it would be enough. But it was really my trust in being loved that satisfied and calmed me, freeing me to pay attention to a thousand different things in the world, to learn, and not just to be self-centred, questing after some reassuring presence. To find my home, my density, my pleasure. To discover my creativity, because I was free. To see the seasons once again, their intense and dependable continuity.

———

Same day, two in the afternoon
Paul made me read the radiology report: *Total disappearance of the metastasis.* His eyes gleamed, his face shone like never before. He was happy. He said to me: "I didn't expect such a positive response, so fast." He looked to-die-for handsome. Handsome from his happiness and, though he didn't know it, his sudden return to love. "You will be able to write and to make your film now. Everything's fine."

Walking next to him, overwhelmed for a first and a last time, by the eternity that's been on repeat these last three years, I say yet again: "You are handsome." And the mind flashes with new life, with love, resuscitated from a deep life force, a deep love source. And he says back to me: "You, too, are beautiful." An emotional outpouring from him who never utters an excess word. I am still in love with him, until all worlds end. All the poems in my *Self-portraits* resemble him, and address him in the vast clarity of his remoteness, his care. I am joined to him by strange bonds that have nothing to do with stereotypes about love, though they borrow from that language. I am bound to him by forces both tenuous and wild. A swelling of the heart and veins. A profusion of images. A fantasy of blue sky and green sea, and grey too, the grey of dewy mornings filled with potential. His eyes, those dark, secret fruits of my joy, are so beautiful. To have lived only to know such eyes. In them I see myself, I find myself, they enchant me. He drains me into the world of poetry. O Paul and Stéphan. Lights that dispel my ennui and fill me with energy, instilling a fight in me I wasn't aware of. With unheard of powers, divine endearments, ready to carry the weight of dreams and fairy tales. Of words. Would that I had only known this one moment of insane happiness. "You, too, are beautiful." It reminds me of winter, 1979, when two beings grabbed each other in a yellow hallway, drowning in pleasure, and gave themselves over completely to a kiss. So happy to be together. Looking at each other in disbelief, but not doubt. And yet.

Yet my love, if only you were still stretched out beside me.
If I could have your body again, that fulfillment and beauty, that maritime light, I'd be an entirely different person,
as would you.
What a long path of torment and loneliness we have travelled,
we are so distant because of our differences, yet so close because
we're both fighting the same battle.
The twofold gift of finding out I'm cured, followed by your

confession: "You, too, are beautiful," has filled me with a crazy lyricism as you leave, and the cool and fertile fragrance of the woods welcomes and protects you.
I die and am born of the same love,
the same love has made me both crazy and clear-headed,
through it I have conquered and lost inner kingdoms,
and your face has made me mistrustful, combative, resounding, and receptive.
You forgot me.
I forgot you.
Every man reminds me of you,
I neglect and resurrect you with every step I take
I see you as a god, a father, and a child,
I'm not expecting anything provable or realistic, neither suffering nor real joy.
Only this conviction, that I love you and your faults, I love your weaknesses, and your tremendous strengths.
You are my magic,
the white page on which I write the sign.
Your sincere enthusiasm increased my immense pleasure in this good news tenfold.
It wasn't you who helped me live this last time around, it was someone else.
But you are folded inside all others like an enjoyable and difficult dream.
All poems begin and end with you.
With you like an oracle. But not the cold oracle of fate.
But the feeling of love (or friendship, which is the same thing).
The gentle listening, the rare leafy rustling of a tender confession.

———

February 25, 1981

The span of a seduction.

I want so much to be seductive. Even, and above all, in the midst of lack.

To be seduced by everything around me that seems beautiful and good.

To channel it all into my body.

To be seduced in order to be more seductive.

Source aspects of existence so that I myself become a source, and seductive.

To seduce in order to be comforted, to comfort myself, and not die.

To seduce in order to make myself more attractive. Not a particularly noble motive.

To make myself into no one. But a continuous scattering of pains and joys.

To be loved, so as to feel special.

———

February 25 [1981]

A snowstorm this morning, very early. Back from the hospital. Hopeful. Fairly calm. Not just from the good news. But from a tender word. From coming close to joy. From sharing something furtive and silly, but real and amazing, from the particular joy of having gotten better. Not being on my own in the fight against this misery.

Now, empty days.

Put the shattered pieces of the mirror back together.

Refashion a space of seduction.

The self-portrait.

Make a path between and through people and things.

Draw from there the power of both renewal and continuation.

Forget you, completely. Never again be negative about you, or
anything else.
No longer wait. Act.
Because acting sets the mind to going.
Push anxiety away. Discover. Travel.
Establish a vital space,
because you're not it, despite what I think.
By building it, I invent it.
By inventing it, it defines me.
It's not sleep's invention.
It's action upon waking.
It's through actions and acts that spaces are made.
We should define limits and limitlessness.
We should push back the borders and make them flourish.
The body is the only proof of existence (of its existence in the
world). Through it alone the space of being is born, the place of
seduction, desire, its resolutions, its metamorphoses.

———

It's like a Chopin prelude, this opal light, this rain of constant snow.
The grey furniture in the cold brightness of morning.
In the difficulty of coming to be, everything has its place.
My childhood and adolescence, bathed in the rhythm and sadness
of Chopin's preludes.
The infinite solitude of our position on earth.
Already this dust weighs heavy in our hearts.
Already feeling old. Already lacking passion, laughter, daring.
Reading Nelligan's first poems[2]
Things as they are, boredom, the body and the mind already con-
sumed by it.
We are absent from both ourselves and the world and figure in a

strange dream, wintry, sclerotic, filled with old perfumes, obsolete forms.

An incessant nostalgia.

A conventional landscape of anticipation.

To be born into the rigid mark of images.

Other eras. Old feelings.

To be born under a prism that embellishes what was and is blind to what is.

Such that one burns down the desire of what could be, what one wants it to be.

The unfortunate idleness of a childhood closed in on itself.

Now I walk inside myself
I am alone inundated with a slightly tawny pale light
a wealth of landscapes are hitched to my sides
in the richness of April or July
noble trees are capable of rearing up
birds criss-cross
cutting the air with their sharp eyes
with their familiar and calming cries
there is the sea or the city
the same crowd
the multiplying of cries
the pleading faces
disappearances and appearances
now I am alone forever

[*Poems at the Margin*]

———

You abandoned me in the deepest depths,
a place from where I can see death

and have become so irreversibly conscious of it
there's no place I can now be without it.
You abandoned me to suspicion, isolation, fear.
When I had need of you, you withdrew behind a shadow of
expertise.
When I got better, you loved me a little bit ...
You abandoned me to the control of objects in a universe of soul-
less surfaces,
where having become no one I understand nothing. I have not
returned.
I'm so scared,
I am alone and there's so little love.
So little contentment, so little certainty.

———

February 26, 1981

ENVIRONMENT OF SEDUCTION
SELF-PORTRAITS

A mix of genres. The heavy burden of the self is absolved through
lyricism.
Pick the locales. But first the name.
Seduction. The desire to.
Perceptions, like acts of constraint or discovery.
Where can the text be made possible?

Prepare the film,[3] project yourself into it, project your writing into it.
Act in it. Create a drama. The drama of where the text lives.
Because I don't have any relationship to the making of the text.
My practice reveals nothing about how it's made.

The film must be created like a poem.
Images should be chosen like words, so that the image doesn't serve just to channel the script, or to support a passage from a poem.
The poem should not be projected onto the screen nor illustrated.
The screen (the film) should be the poem.
The fiction speak of me.

———

I slept where there was no more room ...

[Poems at the Margin]

———

March 5, 1981

So alone.
So little and so poorly loved.
So sad I want to die. Devastated. Rejected. Alone.
So little passion. So little enthusiasm. So much insignificance. Vertigo. Indifference.
I fill time just to fill time.
Live to live.
I am not loved. It's so obvious.
So sad I want to die. Love is my only lifeline. There's no love.
Nothing. Complete emptiness. The insignificance of doing anything, of taking action.
I'm a dupe. Duped. Rejected.
The hard life. Things as they are. The absence of desires.
O Paul. Why? How? Why?
This bitterness inside of me.
This suffering. This open wound in my head. These eyes torn out.
This constant lack.

———

now we are sitting on the large terrace ...

[*Self-portraits*]

———

March 16, 1981

Letter to Franciska

This coming Spring will be strange. I was so sick, I really had to fight to keep hopeful in spite of the anxiety that was killing me, so that now, with everything going so well, I want to act with the calm of a visitor who has come from afar. But I am still looking for someone or something unknown. My time is vast and empty. Even though I go out quite a bit, see lots of friends, people ..., but I do things without conviction and talk without really feeling it. Happily, I've returned to my writing, which has taken a funny turn, so I'm not sure where it's leading me. I would love it if some day you would read my work. Especially if you come to Montréal, which would make me so happy. Incidentally, you would risk showing up right in the middle of filming, because, as I already told you, they're going to make a movie about me. I'm not sure when they are going to begin filming, but it might be in April.⁴ I wonder how successful I will be in getting involved, in order to ensure that the experience is enriching, because I'm not even involved in my own life anymore. Such that I am sad when I should be happy, I am dead when I should be alive. Everything around me should be giving me a feeling of contentment (if not happiness), but nothing does. There's something inside of me that suffers without relief or reason, unspeakable, unjustified. My life sucks and I don't know how to get past all of this and move on. Inside it's all degradation and darkness. I'm aware that complaining changes nothing, I almost feel ashamed, but, almost against my will, I am dragged down. There are so many obstacles, such alienation, preventing me from thinking about things and acting on them. Deep down, I'm still a teenager. I've become aware of the fact that, even though I'm about to turn twenty-six, I have yet to conquer all my demons. Quite the opposite. I dream of getting away, of fleeing. Taking off, confronting other places, other people. Of getting caught up in some all-consuming, demanding work the rhythm and restless activity of which would allow me to forget myself. Because it weighs on me, I want to change my entire existence overnight. It weighs on me, but I do nothing ... When you have battled for years just to stay alive, you can't help but interrogate the meaning of your life, becoming aware of the preciousness of every moment and the importance of living in the present. But every moment seems empty to me, and confronting this void fills me with terror. Accepting it ...

———

March 22, 1981

A month before my twenty-sixth birthday. I'm sick of being unhappy. Mired, imprisoned, suffocated. God! How do I pull myself out of this, where can I find a bit of brightness inside and around me, where can I find that sense of abundance that I so abominably lack? I want to flee, to start my life over. To find support and strength. Live passionately. Confess the un-confessable without suffering for it. Stop fighting with my demons, about demons and horrible nightmares. Paul, my dear love, I no longer desire you except in dreams. You surreptitiously return to me in sleep, and your indifference toward me is the rejection of the child by the father. I feel stripped of all reality. I am so fearful of dying before having experienced happiness. Yes, I think that is my worst fear: dying before having been happy even once in my life. This is why I'm so on edge lately. Because I fear death, because its constant presence frightens me, I am determined to find happiness, it's as if I feel I must act fast to find where the treasure is hidden because the game is almost over.

This morning the sun showed up along with a few little fairy clouds, they looked so light and soft, floating in front of the brick facades. They chopped down the only tree I could see from my window. An elm. Like all the elms in Montréal, it was suffering from an incurable disease. Yet, when they came to cut it down, it still had a few surviving branches with buds on them. Like me, it kept up the fight in its own way, still hoping to flower (even just a little). But they cut it down before this could happen.

And me, what is going to happen to me?

I feel as if my life has no meaning, since I've never felt, even once, a certain kind of happiness. A particular idea of happiness that would justify this endless waiting and this useless existence. My oeuvre is so mediocre it couldn't justify anybody's existence on earth. It will perish in the cavernous silence of my arteries. An insignificant and stupid body of work. The pursuit of the true poem, conscious and musical, while I'm blind and deaf.

Now the sun is hidden behind a mass of clouds, but it's still nice out and I dream I'm in a plane, flying away like the clouds. Then the sun comes back, shy, partial, ready to flee. I'm at the theatre. The street, the city, the real often seems to me like a stage where the sun controls the lighting. We play characters, we cue each other's lines. We are nothing but apparitions of the interior life. The text is mediocre. It has nothing of the great lyric tragedies, or farcical romantic comedies, but is constructed sequentially in fragments, shot through with inanity and futility. Our director is a master craftsman without genius and our little destinies are crushed by stereotypes and fashions. Ideology is omnipresent. Desires are remote-controlled, slotted into the catalogue of possible desires. Our little biological orgasms are on a level with our little programmed fantasies. They reek of tedium, bungalow life, travel tours. They reek of kitchens and Sunday strolls. The habitual, waiting for death. They reek of work done just to "pass the time." To "pass the time" for what? To get to death as quickly as possible? They stink of the rich man's wine and the poor man's beer. They stink of the enormous mauve loneliness of the marshes on the Magdalen Islands, and the wind that drives people mad, while a gull cries and its cry rips through the grey of the sea and sky. Solitude is easy.

What costs effort is being together. All happiness costs a fortune's worth of energy, willpower, and prayers.

I don't want to die yet because I am going through such utter distress, because I am deeply unhappy, if not entirely without hope. I still believe that, despite everything, I can one day find some form of happiness, some kind of reason why I'm here. Some well-being in being here. Some proximity to what's real.

O Paul, why didn't you love me?

———

March 30, 1981
I dreamt of that house again last night. It was beautiful, if incredibly hard to describe. But still luminous. My dreams of happiness are always dreams of this house. I ask myself, what could it mean?

———

the cry of a seagull deepens the air
divides the streets into uncertain spaces
there's no warmth in the grey wind
and we are sitting at the table
where fruit and cups of coffee have been placed

we've fallen silent
attracted by the coolness of the grass and the clouds
and everything that passes
darkening our faces with shadows
the room smells of cut wood and water
we know that outside everything is getting ready
to slowly appear

[Self-portraits]

———

[June 1981]⁵

This morning upon waking I walked into the living room to find it filled with a powerful light resembling molten metal, I entered into it as if into deep soft water, without harming or burning myself, abruptly absorbing a delicious sense of well-being that I wanted to hold onto for as long as possible. Fearing that this perfection, this improbable colour, this immediate challenge to death might slip away I walked quickly out of the living room. I didn't want to deplete this happiness, I wanted this light to enter through my eyes, flow through my head and my veins, so my body, breathing through this incandescence, would remember it, and never use it up, in its arteries, nerves, and muscles, and know that the beauty of early dawn exists in the fragmentation of dreams. And then I went into the semi-dark kitchen where calm and ordinary night, filled and sustained by birdsong, still hovered over the humid floorboards.

———

So long as it's night ...

[Poems at the Margin]

———

the heat forms a circle around us
settled in the back of a room
under a trellis of sparse foliage
or a freshly painted corner
your face standing out against the dawn's empty blue
next to the tender meaning of everyday objects
the honey drawn from its ochre bowl
the milk clouding into the coffee's blackness
the curtain pulled up that won't come back down
all your muscles and thoughts will have completely relaxed
I will be sleeping in the middle of a smooth metamorphosis
having slid under the cold palm of a stone sky
so empty I can see the trajectory of your words
and the world will be an initial gong
whose vibration's protracted rings we could sense
in our walls of sand

[Self-portraits]

———

Sometimes when I watch you walking I want to be you and, holding myself back a little, I suddenly divide and slip into your gait, experience from the inside why it's sometimes slow, its alluring agility, feel the verdict of your bent shoulders: depression, exhaustion, or just that habit of staying on your feet too long. And then there's the power of your breathing, and your heavy hand, shaking, lifted in anger, or plunging into water as if washing your face. And when I make my way up to your voice, I reach the place that suits my steadfast desire, know what controls its slow inflections, *its breezy pauses; those long stretches of silence where everything seems endlessly menacing, hesitant words knotting the throat. I want to experience your morning body, stretched-out long and relaxed. Your straight hips, hard, brown, the slight expansion of your muscles as you make an effort to sit up, the expanse of your back a harmonious, knotted river stilled for a moment in the cold cone of dawn, your neck bent, your body under the sway of morning's gentle deafness. Could I but be inside your body such tender feelings would be mine.*

[*Prose Poems*]

———

Outside, a great white light, neither chilly nor warm, without nuance, inside an obsession over words, to make them live and articulate my overflowing desire.

But desire: a hopeless direction, departure and brief insights, and all the silence of the future. I no longer move. Neither music. Nor form. Nor energy. A great solitude, like a long expanse of arid, desolate land, burned or iced over. Nothing but silence. Only the expansion of desire to speak of.

———

night butterflies clinging to lamps ...

[*Self-portraits*]

———

There's no amount of sleep that could erase these long walls imprinted with distressed and screaming faces, no amount that could recover (my love) the corridor of trees relaxing in the April light, stretching out like happy creatures heading out into a morning in full bloom, no amount of sleep to trace all the lines and surfaces of your body, to satisfy my thirst for its contrasts. Time moves slowly in the insomnia of great years that never let up. There's no amount of sleep that could erase the essentials of life, keeping only its delicious surroundings. The landscape and its hidden source, the face and its effortless ease upon waking and the sequence of the sun's position on charmless familiar objects.

[*Prose Poems*]

————

the days follow the contrasts drawn across the wall ...

[*Self-portraits*]

————

[*Lac Mégantic, August 1981*][7]

What would we be without beauty, what part of our humanity would remain? Without Schubert, without Renoir's *Bathers*, without Apollinaire's poetry, what would the world be? Without these magnificent mountains and this splendid lake, like a Japanese landscape, what would we be and how would we live, what would we retain? Without the beloved's face from which all beauty seems to emanate, how could we continue to live?

————

Today is September 18, 1981. I no longer keep track of the calendar, as if my life is no longer but an endless flow without importance or reference point, I will let my memory try to reconstruct things, if that's even possible or needed. My connection to reality is all but lost and I feel like I'm being dragged toward death. The treatments are increasingly unbearable, unacceptable. Paul is no longer in my life, and what light was left went out with him. It's funny, that place I was stuck in for so long has no more room for hope. God, even God himself as left me. Now things are going a little better. Yet, how much longer can I hold on? Do I want to? And what poem? What book will come of it? What event? Since there's only one face left. This inner silence which increasingly goes hand in hand with my taste for words, for poems. Writing saves me from despair. Hoping for that happiness that comes with finishing a poem, of not failing. If just once harmony, rhythm, and meaning weren't *next* to the poem, but integrated, held together in a perfect joy of expression. The vividness of the poem, its fragile beauty, its inexhaustible goodness, its boundless generosity. Concentration. My concentration and my capacity for work and reflection have been undermined so terribly by this disease. I've become nothing but a groggy body, waiting and suffering. May God help me. Without him I can do nothing anymore. Nothing.

———

Sometimes it was necessary
for the sun to show a bit of rosiness at the windows
so that we would feel less alone
from whence arose a few false memories of how beautiful things are
and then everything settled in the raw whiteness of the real
forcing us to close our eyes
yet we were on the watch for our amazement
hoping for a humble and gentle night without end
where we might sink into the waking dream of our bodies
                                                    [*Self-portraits*]

———

he no longer looks past this light going out ...

[Poems at the Margin]

———

Dear Monique,
I haven't written because I was sick, so very sick. I really thought
that this time around I wouldn't get better. I've lost so much weight
and cried so much. I even changed doctors, which in the end doesn't
change anything, but I have a woman now and she is very devoted
and maternal. But there it is, I am still alive, at least for a little while
more. Enough time to make the film, to write a few poems, at least
I hope so, because I received a grant from the Arts Council, which
is a stroke of luck. I don't know what's become of you or what you
think of me. My loneliness is vast. Not that I'm not surrounded
by kindness, but everything lacks meaning and I am completely
devoid of energy. Sometimes I can barely lift myself up in bed. I
only have one metastasis left, it seems, but my system has grown
so weak from the treatments, and from a heart operation I had to
have because of them. I wanted to give up. But I can't quite do it,
because it's not easy to lose all hope.

———

So long as you can still write about your misery, you can recognize
it. It has not yet managed to transform the entire world, only to
make it terrifying and difficult. This disease has taken me to such
extremes of misery that I have become completely alienated from
the world. I've moved beyond the very limits of terror into a space

of total meaninglessness. No word has a hold on reality, the reality that rejects me. I can no longer write, I am doubly unhappy, doubly anguished, still and even more alone. It's an indestructible solitude that even writing cannot break.

Notes

FIRST NOTEBOOK

1. *The Life Beyond* is also the title of a manuscript of poems Uguay wrote between the summer of 1976 and the fall of 1978. It was published in September 1979.

2. Written in the hospital, two months after being admitted and three days before being discharged. While hospitalized, Uguay wrote several poems that would be included in *The Life Beyond*: "O the straight splendour of wheat ..."; "Now the wind is blowing and my dreams are hard work ..."; "The day unwinds with an inner rustle of silk"; "Every tendon of my body is connected to the weapons of earth ..."; "He pulls sombre curtains over my pain ..."; "I would like to splash my legs in all weathers ..."; "Precipice of night ..."; "And yet apples and oranges do exist ..."; "I will go everywhere else ..."

3. Translator's note: Lyric from Jacques Brel's 1977 song "La ville s'endormait" ("The City Falls Asleep")

4. Uguay's older sister, who died at the age of ten months.

5. Uguay's maternal grandfather, César Uguay, was a violinist and Professor of Music at the Collège Jean-de-Brébeuf in Montréal. Marie Uguay (born Lalonde) had a great admiration for him, which is why she took his name as her own when she began publishing.

6. Perrot Island, close to Montréal, where her maternal grandparents owned a summer home on the banks of the Saint Lawrence River. Uguay spent her childhood vacations there.

7. A childhood friend of Uguay's, who lived in New Brunswick. (This letter, as well as all the other letters reproduced in the *Journal*, were copied into the original notebooks.)

8. A professor Uguay fell in love with while studying with him during her first year of college.

9. Lines from Uguay's poem "He pulls sombre curtains over my pain ..." from *The Life Beyond*.

10. Translator's note: A riff on a line by Gustave Flaubert that Uguay quotes at the start of the second notebook.

11. Photographs that Stéphan Kovacs took to illustrate Uguay's book *The Life Beyond*.

SECOND NOTEBOOK

1. This notebook was originally titled *A Love unheard of*. That title was crossed out and replaced.

2. Number 7, March 1978. Six poems from *The Life Beyond*.

3. The poets Jean Charlebois and Alexis Lefrançois.

4. Translator's note: Marguerite Duras, *The Ravishing of Lol Stein*, perhaps as quoted in Marcelle Marini's *Territoires du féminin avec Marguerite Duras* (1977).

5. A line from the poem "A plant placed on the anvil ..." from *The Life Beyond*.

6. Uguay and Stéphan Kovacs were planning a long trip to France at summer's end. This would be her first to a country that had long captured her imagination. Uguay and Kovacs would travel around France for a little over a month and then settle in Paris during October and November of 1978.

7. Uguay's maternal grandfather was born in the south of France. His mother was from Piedmont, his father from Marseille.

8. Adèle Hugo, a daughter of French writer Victor Hugo.

THIRD NOTEBOOK

1. This notebook includes Uguay's trip to Paris in October and November of 1978 and her return to Montréal in December of that same year. The first part, written in Paris, has been omitted because it did not contain any autobiographical writing, only drafts of poems as well as the last poem in *The Life Beyond:* "A sleepless night of statues ..."

2. A novel by Anaïs Nin.

FOURTH NOTEBOOK

1. In addition to these titles, two others were crossed out: *Descriptions* and *Secrets*.

2. From the introduction to *The Life Beyond*.

3. Author unknown.

4. A slightly modified line from Uguay's poem "He's unaware of being looked at ..." from *The Life Beyond*.

5. All following quotations are from Gaston Bachelard's *Intuition of the Instant*, translation by Eileen Rizo-Patron [modified]. Northwestern University Press, 2013; 3, 6, 14, 21

6. At first, the texts gathered under this title were a series of drafts of long prose poems, never finished, but the impulse behind them evolved to become the poems that would go into *Self-Portraits*.

7. A friend of Uguay's living in British Columbia.

8. A friend of Uguay's living in Québec.

9. Addressed to a French friend, Franciska, living in Paris.

10. A reference to Marguerite Duras's *Hiroshima, My Love*.

11. Uguay had sent the manuscript of *The Life Beyond* to Gallimard and had received a favourable response. Gallimard had arranged to publish a selection from it in their journal *Cahier de poésie 3*. Yet, when her book came out with Éditions du Noroît in September of 1979, her contribution was redacted.

FIFTH NOTEBOOK

1. A notebook with a ripped binding and pages missing at the end (no doubt the reason for a gap of more than two months before the next notebook).

2. Translator's note: A working-class neighbourhood of Montréal.

SIXTH NOTEBOOK

1. Though begun in June, the first half of this notebook has not been reproduced because it contains no autobiographical prose, only drafts of poems or of short narratives that sometimes morph into the first poems of Uguay's *Self-Portraits*, including: "the branches shattering themselves against the sky ..."; "don't leave me here ..."; "and this face has come here for so long and so often ..."; "to write to you of memory ..."; "July *Lac Mégantic* entrenched in fruit ..."; "my whim my host ..."; as well as the poem "You teach me how to age ..." from *Poems at the Margin*.

2. Gaston Miron, *The March toward Love*.

3. Rainer Maria Rilke, *Duino Elegies*.

4. Translator's note: The French text has a play on *connaître* ['to know'] and *co-naître* ['co,' meaning 'shared,' in front of *naître* 'to be born'] that was not possible to reproduce in English.

5. Poem not in the notebook, but dating from the same period.

SEVENTH NOTEBOOK

1. Originally titled *Romances*. The working titles *Nightly Rate, Whim, Incest(s)*, and *Incestuous Poems* were also tried out, but were eventually crossed out in favour of *Wrinkles*.

2. Epigraph crossed out.

3. A writing project Uguay was working on and the initial title of this notebook.

4. Translator's note: "the sea having fled with the sun" is a riff on a line of Arthur Rimbaud's (*"C'est la mer allée / Avec le soleil"*) from his poem "Eternity."

5. The first recurrence of her illness since her operation in November of 1977, despite the preventative treatments she had sporadically received in the interim. In the coming weeks, her treatments would be more intensive and take place almost daily.

6. Translator's note: "'Seven-league boots' originally arose as a translation from the French *Bottes de sept lieues*, popularized by Charles Perrault's fairy tales" [Wikipedia]. The boots are magical and allow a character to take very long strides.

7. Uguay was hospitalized for tests, and then again for an operation on her lung. Her stay would last until mid-April.

8. Title of a 1951 book of poems [*Verrà la morte e avrà i tuoi occhi*] by Italian writer Cesare Pavese.

9. Number 15, spring 1980. Unpublished poems from *Self-portraits*, titled here as *Poems*, with six drawings by François Vincent.

EIGHTH NOTEBOOK

1. The original title *Wrinkles* was crossed out and replaced with *Self-portrait*.

2. The 1980 Québec independence referendum on whether the province should pursue secession from Canada and become a sovereign nation.

3. Uguay was having to undergo new cancer treatments, at times very difficult. They would continue sporadically until the beginning of October.

4. Line from the poem "The earth is famished and exhausts us ..." from *Poems at the Margin*. Translator's note: the full text of the poem can be found in the seventh notebook.

5. An ONF documentary about the Parisian intellectual left, directed by Michael Rubbo.

6. A poem titled "the eye outlines her pain ..." from *Self-portraits*.

7. Uguay was vacationing on the coast of Maine for a week (June 23–30, 1980).

8. Céline (Fortin) and René Bonenfant, the founders of Éditions du Noroît.

NINTH NOTEBOOK

1. Uguay had added: *or Portraits light and dark*, but then crossed it out.
2. Word indecipherable.
3. Translator's note: for the following quotations I consulted Richard Howard's translations of Roland Barthes *The Empire of Signs* [77–78; 75–76] and *Camera Lucida* [49]. Translations slightly modified.
4. The beginning of a short trip to the region of Charlevoix (Saint-Joseph-de-la-Rive, L'Isle-aux-Coudres, Pointe-au-Pic).
5. Uguay was preparing to give a reading at Montréal's café-theatre Xodo.
6. At the beginning of October Uguay's cancer had metastasized. She began intensive weekly treatments at the hospital which lasted until the end of November.

TENTH NOTEBOOK

1. With the return of a metastasis in mid-December, Uguay was put on a more difficult and exhausting treatment regimen.
2. Translator's note: Henri Laborit, *Éloge de la fuite*. Gallimard, 1976, 88.
3. Translator's note: Matthew 26:26
4. The idea for a film about Marie Uguay, directed by Jean-Claude Labrecque and produced by ONF, had been in the works for some time.

FINAL NOTEBOOKS

1. Comprised of two notebooks, both untitled, in which Uguay wrote only intermittently. Her health was deteriorating quickly, and the intensification of her cancer treatments depleted her energy.
2. Translator's note: Émile Nelligan was a renowned Canadian poet (1879–1941).
3. Jean-Claude Labrecque's film about Marie Uguay was in preparation and Marie was supposed to work with the director on the development of a script.

4. Uguay worked with the director in developing the script for the film during March and April, but she had to stop everything at the end of April with the return of a new metastasis. They finally went ahead with the filming in September of 1981, during a brief remission of her illness, though it was limited to a two-day interview with Jean Royer.

5. Even though Uguay underwent numerous cancer treatments during the months of May and June, she remained active. The follow text was one of the few things she wrote during this period (outside of the notebooks).

6. At the beginning of July, after returning from a week's vacation in Maine, Uguay was scheduled to begin more intense and grueling treatments, which would require complete bedrest.

7. Though Uguay had gone to a friend's house in the country to rest, in mid-August medical complications forced her to return to Montréal. She was readmitted to the hospital, where she would remain until her death on October 26, 1981.

Chronology

1955

Marie Uguay (née Lalonde) is born in Montréal on April 22 to accountant Jacques Lalonde and his wife Denise Uguay. She is their second daughter. Their first, Hélène, was born in 1953 but lived for only ten months. A third daughter, Cécile, would be born in 1959.

1961–1968

Attends primary school at Coeur-Immaculé-de-Marie (*The Immaculate Heart of Mary*) in Montréal. Many of Uguay's summers during this period were spent with her maternal grandparents at their summer cottage on Perrot Island, not far from Montréal.

1968–1972

Attends secondary school at Esther-Blondin, located in Montréal's Saint-Henri neighbourhood. Develops an interest in the dramatic arts, which leads her to participate in several extracurricular theatrical activities.

1972–1974

Studies literature at Marguerite-Bourgeoys college in Westmount. Writes first poems of *Sign and Rumour* (winter 1973). After finishing up her studies, Uguay makes her first trips to the seaside and to New York.

1974–1975

Begins studying communications at the Université of Québec in Montréal, but withdraws at the end of her second year. Meets Stéphan Kovacs in November* of 1975. They will stay together until the end. Death of her maternal grandfather César Uguay. He was a violinist and professor of music at Collège Jean-de-Brébeuf in Montréal. Uguay held him in great esteem.

*Translator's note: there's a discrepancy here as Kovacs' introduction says they met in September.

1976

Spends May through July on Magdalen Island, where she writes the first poems of *The Life Beyond*. In October, her first book *Sign and Rumour* is published by Noroît Editions. Publishes a series of poems alongside of photographs by Stéphan Kovacs in the magazine *Vie des arts* (*The Life of the Arts*).

1977

After suffering from a pain in her right leg all summer, Uguay enters the hospital in September and is diagnosed with bone cancer. Starts her *Journal*. To slow the progress of the disease, the doctors amputate her right leg. At the end of November Uguay is released from the hospital, but will return intermittently to receive cancer treatments.

1978

In March, publishes poems from her manuscript-in-progress *The Life Beyond* in the magazine *Estuaire* (*Estuary.*) In July, she participates in a poetry reading at the Théâtre de l'île d'Orleans. Sojourn in France from August to November.

1979

In June, Uguay gives a poetry reading at the Galerie Motivation V. Writes first poems of *Self-portraits*. Vacations at Lac Mégantic in July. Second book of poems, *The Life Beyond*, published in September by Noroît Editions. Reading of her poems on Radio-Canada. In November she gives readings at the Salon du livre de Rimouski and the University of Québec at Montréal. Publishes a short text on poetry in the magazine *Possibles*.

1980

In February, the cancer returns as a tumor in her lung. Begins more intensive treatments. In March, poems from the working manuscript *Self-portraits*, alongside drawings by François Vincent, published in the magazine *Estuaire*. On March 28, Uguay participates in the Night of Poetry at the University of Québec at Montréal. Her reading is included in *La Nuit de la poésie 1980* (*A Night of Poetry 1980*), a film directed by Jean-Pierre Masse and Jean-Claude Labrecque for ONF (National Film Board of Canada).

After the cancer treatments fail, Uguay undergoes a lung operation at the beginning of April. Takes part in a poetry reading at the College of Rosemont at the end of that same month. Vacation on the coast of Maine and Lac Mégantic. Short trip in September to the Charlevoix region. Relapse at the start of October and more treatments. Readings at the Theatre-Café Xodo in October, and the Dramatic Arts Conservatory in November. Meets Jean-Claude Labrecque, who decides to make a film about Uguay. Another relapse in December, followed by more intensive treatments.

1981

Uguay's cancer goes into remission at the end of January. In March, she begins collaborating with Jean-Claude Labrecque on the film about her. Publishes poems from *Self-portraits* in *Estuaire*. In April, takes part in a poetry reading at the University of Montréal, as well as one at the Salon du livre de Québec. Recurrence of her disease at the end of April, return to treatments until June. Receives the Air Canada Literary Award. In June, vacations on the coast of Maine and at Lac Mégantic. In July, another relapse and more intensive treatments. At the beginning of August, Uguay's stay at Lac Mégantic is cut short and she returns to Montréal to undergo more surgery and treatments. On September 28 and 29, Jean-Claude Labrecque films Uguay being interviewed by Jean Royer. The following day she is readmitted to the hospital. Publishes poems from *Self-portraits* in *Possibles*. From October 18 until November 29 her poems are read and sung by actors in a show titled *It's more beautiful than ever* at the National Library of Québec. On October 26, at the age of twenty-six, Marie dies. She is buried on Perrot Island, next to her grandfather.

1982

Release of the film *Marie Uguay*, directed by Jean-Claude Labrecque and produced by ONF. In June, a cultural centre named after her is inaugurated in the Ville-Émard neighbourhood in Montréal. Noroît Editions brings out her third book of poems, *Self-portraits*. Uguay is posthumously awarded the Émile Nelligan Foundation Medal for poetry.

Afterword

THE AGONY OF TIME:
ON TRANSLATING MARIE UGUAY'S *JOURNAL*

> "The Journal is not really a confession, the story of oneself.
> It's a Memorial."
> — Maurice Blanchot, *The Space of Literature*

This is a book about desire. A piercing *cri du cœur;* but also, paradoxically, the cool-headed self-examination of a woman simultaneously under the influence of an intoxicating desire and the threat of an unthinkable loss. The desire is for a man twice her age, the loss is of her life. How does this story, age-old in its pathos and fatality, begin?

In September of 1977, less than a year after publishing her first book of poems, twenty-two-year-old Marie Uguay checks into a Montréal hospital complaining of a persistent pain in her right leg. She learns that she has bone cancer. One of her oncologists "saves" her by amputating her leg. At November's end, an utterly changed Uguay is released from the hospital. Her body is, as she would describe it, "mutilated"; her heart, soul, and mind are, by contrast, illuminated by a "sudden burst of love" for her fifty-year-old oncologist, Paul. This is the moment the published version of Uguay's journal begins.

"That which is known, attained, possessed, cannot be an object of desire," wrote Ann Carson in her essay on Eros and the

Ancients (65). Desire in the Classical tradition is always connected to lack, with love as a form of madness. There is no middle ground. For what remained of Uguay's life — approximately four years — her devastating emotional lows oscillated with beautiful, imaginative highs. Anguish and anxiety, elation and creative ecstasy. Her illness and her pursuit of an "object of desire" that insisted on remaining unknown, unattainable, and unpossessed pushed Uguay's poetic temperament to the very edge. But this is only one side of the story. As Stéphan Kovacs, Uguay's live-in boyfriend, artistic comrade, and the eventual editor of her *Journal* reminds us, private journals "tend to express conflict and pain, while leaving out all the other parts of life." Indeed, Uguay's *Journal* does not satisfy us with much in terms of her day-to-day existence. We learn almost nothing about mundanities: food, chores, family obligations. Instead, what Uguay invites us to read is a detailed examination of desire's brutal effects, a case study of its destructive power, and an investigation into its complex nature.

I write that Uguay "invites us" to read her. This is speculation. Kovacs claims that Uguay kept her journal without any thought of publishing it. But I wonder. The writer behind this journal, though young and at times guileless, nevertheless had a sophisticated understanding of her vocation and of her talent. It must have crossed her mind that *any* writing she left behind, however clandestine its contents, could or would be of public interest. That her journal is raw, and seemingly unedited, strikes me as another kind of poetic experiment, in keeping with her goal to clear away all the detritus of social norms and self-censorship to find the truth of love, of life, of language. Before reading it, I had thought Walter Pater's over-quoted claim that success in life is "to burn always with this hard, gemlike flame," and "maintain ... ecstasy," a tad exaggerated. But if anyone ever so burned, it was Marie Uguay. Pater further hazards that, "it might even be said that our failure is to form habits:

for, after all, habit is relative to a stereotyped world" (Pater 1913, 236–237). Uguay would agree. Indeed, this very conviction provides the theoretical fuel that fires her intensity. As she urges: "you must go past preconceived notions, prejudices, fears, and habits, move beyond obtuse reality to a reality both more painful and more pleasurable: the unknown, the hidden, the contradictory. Open the senses up, learn from them. Move through the opacity of silence to a place where nothing is predictable or fated, a place where we can really invent our lives and our loves."

Desire was for Uguay both relentlessly destructive and marvellously inspiring. It was also gendered. Not essentially, but structurally. Uguay knew that the patriarchy warped love. She knew this, and it infuriated her. A key word throughout her journal is 'alienation.' It has many valences: Marxist, Freudian, colonial, cultural, feminist. "A two-thousand-year-old alienation," she writes when examining the obstacles facing artistic women, "doesn't retract its morbid, horrifying claws overnight." Uguay also understood that her desire for the love of a powerful man was a form of alienation. At times written in stone: "nothing about my desire or the way I love can change"; at others a puzzle her poetry might unravel: "Nothing will stop me from getting to the root of these various alienations, because, for me, that's the best way to get over them, to break them, and to bring about, on the other side, the reunification of the woman and the individual through the creative act." Uguay understood that gender oppression made what Simone de Beauvoir called the "mutual recognition of free beings who confirm one another's freedom" almost impossible (de Beauvoir 1974, 286). Yet this was the kind of love she (ideally, unrealistically) wanted: a love freely chosen and honest. Desire, or love? What was happening to her? On this point she wavered. "The object of desire is always an object," she writes, "because desire's drive exists only in the self, not in the other." This position is echoed by Marguerite Yourcenar:

"The two emotions [passion and love] are close to being opposites. In passion there is a desire to satisfy oneself, to slake one's thirst, in some cases coupled with a desire to control, to dominate another person. By contrast, in love there is abnegation" (Yourcenar 1980, 71). Uguay's was a hungry soul, often in the grip of a seemingly bottomless appetite for sex, knowledge, poetry, meaning; other times pummelling herself with lacerating promises of abstinence: "I must not hope or wait for anything from existence, otherwise I tear myself to bits ..." To further understand her desire, she turns to women writers and artists: Marguerite Duras, Liliana Cavani. She is especially bowled over by Max and Lucia, the shockingly unorthodox couple who "embrace their pleasure without guilt or regret" at the heart of Cavani's 1974 film *The Night Porter*. Her fascination with this film illustrates Uguay's attraction to locating social resistance and critique in a rethinking of sexuality and intimacy. This position is reflective of her historical moment — the late 1970s and early 1980s — when some poets in Québec, in contrast to the politically engaged (*engagé*) writers of the 1960s, were turning their gaze inward. This inward turn was not necessarily a rejection of the social sphere or progressivist agendas, however. As Uguay writes: "you won't necessarily find the source of your life, the foundation of the breath, by turning inward. You must allow your life to spring forth, to shine through." She believed that a poetry that could channel the true experience of our sensual existence in the living world could potentially be more revolutionary than the literary rule-breaking of the historical avant-garde: "desire beats with the material heart of the world, it is the powerful instant, all possible and impossible signifiers."

"[P]oetry, desire, and life ... were synonymous for Uguay," Kovacs tells us. Alongside Uguay's vivisection of her desire, we see her working assiduously to refine her poetic theory and technique, seeking a form in language to match the somatic and seasonal rhythms of her embodied and emotional experience, which were complex. Uguay's accounts of her sensorium lead me to wonder if she was a synesthete. She is constantly seduced by "colours," and the vision of a stranger's face can open myriad narrative portals. Despite her frequent protests against mystification, which she associated with alienation, many of her poetic apprehensions are emphatically in the realm of the visionary. She experiences insights suddenly, like an onrush of water or a burst of light. She reads metaphysics and literary critics: Gaston Bachelard's *The Intuition of the Instant* is especially important to her thinking, but also Roland Barthes's *Empire of Signs* and *Camera Lucida*; she also turns to the poets, both from her native Québec and abroad, Gaston Miron to Pablo Neruda.

My encounter with Marie Uguay began in 2016. She was on a list of Québec poets given to me by my colleague, Frédéric Rondeau, a scholar of Québécois poetry. Reading the Boréal edition of her *Journal*, I fell completely in love with her. Her writing, her intelligence, her passion, her courage. In some ways the encounter felt fated. When I was in my twenties, a dear friend of mine, a brilliant poet, died of a rare cancer. I had just wrapped up a book about this old loss when I began reading Uguay. I inhaled her *Journal*, and when I was finished I missed her so much I knew I had to translate this book. Translation is a way of prolonging and savouring an encounter. In my enthusiasm for the project, I thought little of how painful it would be. That realization would come later.

For a variety of reasons, I wasn't able to begin the day-to-day work of translating the *Journal* until I had a sabbatical leave in spring of 2021. It was about year into the COVID-19 pandemic, and I sheltered in place with Uguay. Notebook by notebook, page by page, I moved her beautiful French into English. At times this felt like a betrayal. Though Uguay had a love for certain aspects of American culture, and certain places in the U.S., notably New York

City and the coast of Maine, she did *not* have any lost love for the English language. At one point she declares that her love for Montréal is so strong that she feels it, "even in English." At another, while surrounded by Anglophones at Concordia University, she writes: "I can't help but feeling that I am in a city other than Montréal." Uguay was "shamelessly devoted" to the French language. As a poet, French is her *patrie*, her homeland and her home. If you *can* read her in French, you should. This book is a bridge for those who do not have direct access to those shores.

While translating the *Journal* posed linguistic and literary challenges, they were small hurdles next to the emotional strain. Many were the times when I was overwhelmed by Uguay's sadness or circumstances and would collapse into a flood of tears. As I moved the final words of her final notebooks into English, part of me felt that I was laying her in the earth all over again.

"When I'm realistic with myself, I can see that [Québec], with its yawning gaps and colonized mentality, eats away at me," wrote Uguay. While fiercely devoted to the French language, to Montréal, and to Québec, Uguay also struggled with what she perceived as the smallness sometimes present in her community. As a poet, while she wanted to capture the very particular experience of Québec, as both a place and a state of mind, she was also cognizant of, and desired to be read by, an international community. For her work to be known in France and elsewhere. She deserves as much. Marie Uguay's *Journal* should be read alongside such brilliant examinations of female desire and heterosexual love as Marcelle Sauvageot's *Commentary* (1933) and Elizabeth Smart's *By Grand Central Station I Sat Down and Wept* (1966).

I titled this preface "The Agony of Time," a translation of *l'angoisse du temps*, a phrase Uguay uses in her journal. And yet is it not quite satisfactory, for there is no perfect English equivalent to the French word *angoisse*. It sits somewhere in between our *agony* and our *anxiety*. Because she was dying of cancer, Uguay was sometimes in physical agony, but she also suffered from anxiety. She was painfully aware of the fact that writing is a "métier that takes time," as she put it in Jean-Claude Labrecque's documentary film about her, *Marie Uguay*. "I constantly have this strange feeling that my days are numbered," she tells the interviewer Jean Royer, and that "my writing will never attain the maturity I aspire to."

"I once looked on [time] as a friend," she goes on, "but now I'm terrorized by [it.]" When she shared this fear with us, she had only a month left to live.

If the journal form is a "memorial," as Maurice Blanchot claims, and the purpose of a memorial is to restore a person to memory and to life, Marie Uguay's *Journal* succeeds. It is a work that once read, will not be easily put away.

— Jennifer Moxley, Maine, USA 2022

WORKS CITED

Bachelard, Gaston. *Intuition of the Instant*. Translated by Eileen Rizo-Patron. Evanston, IL: Northwestern University Press, 2013.

Barthes, Roland. *Camera Lucida*. Translated by Richard Howard. New York: Farrar, Straus and Geroux, 1981.

Barthes, Roland. *Empire of Signs*. Translated by Richard Howard. New York: Farrar, Straus and Giroux, 1982.

Carson, Ann. *Eros the Bittersweet*. Chicago: Normal, IL: Dalkey Archive Press, 1986.

De Beauvoir, Simone. *The Second Sex*. Translated by H. M. Parshley. New York: Vintage Books, 1974.

Pater, Walter. *The Renaissance*. London: Macmillan & Co, 1913.

Sauvageot, Marcelle. *Commentary*. Translated by Christine Schwartz Hartley and Anna Moschovakis. New York: Ugly Duckling Press, 2013.

Smart, Elizabeth. *By Grand Central Station I Sat Down and Wept.* New York: Vintage International, 1992.

Yourcenar, Marguerite. *With Open Eyes: Conversations with Matthieu Galey.* Translated by Arthur Goldhammer. New York: Beacon, 1980.

Acknowledgements

I would like to thank Ken Norris for bringing this project to the attention of Marc Côté at Cormorant. Thanks are also due to Marc, for believing in this "labour of love" and sticking by it and me. Knowing that he had committed to publishing Uguay's *Journal* in English kept me going. I feel lucky to have had the privilege of both his editorial eye and that of Sarah Jensen.

My colleague Frédéric Rondeau introduced me to the work of Marie Uguay and co-organized a celebration of Uguay with me at the University of Maine on the fortieth anniversary of her death (October 2021). I am eternally grateful to him for introducing me to this amazing poet, and for answering my questions about Québecois usage along the way.

Thank you also to my husband, Steve Evans, for proofing the entire manuscript and providing helpful feedback.

— Jennifer Moxley

Born in Montréal in 1955, MARIE UGUAY died of cancer in 1981. Her brief, dazzling career ensured her a special place in the Québécois literary landscape. Between her first poems, published in the early 1970s, and her death in 1981, she published three collections: *Signe et rumeur*, *L'outre-vie*, and *Autoportraits*. Uguay was posthumously awarded the Émile Nelligan Prize for her body of work, and the Maison de la culture of the Ville-Émard district in Montréal was named after her.

Poet, essayist, and translator JENNIFER MOXLEY is the author of seven books of poetry, most recently *Druthers*. Her book *The Open Secret* was awarded the Poetry Society of America's William Carlos Williams Award and was a finalist for the Kingsley Tufts Poetry Award. Moxley has translated several books from French, including Jacqueline Risset's *Sleep's Powers* and *The Translation Begins*, as well as Anne Portugal's *absolute bob*. She has served as a panelist for the National Endowment for the Arts Translation Fellowships (U.S.) and teaches creative writing, poetics, and translation at the University of Maine in Orono, Maine, United States.

We acknowledge the sacred land on which Cormorant Books operates. It has been a site of human activity for 15,000 years. This land is the territory of the Huron-Wendat and Petun First Nations, the Seneca, and most recently, the Mississaugas of the Credit River. The territory was the subject of the Dish With One Spoon Wampum Belt Covenant, an agreement between the Iroquois Confederacy and Confederacy of the Ojibway and allied nations to peaceably share and steward the resources around the Great Lakes. Today, the meeting place of Toronto is still home to many Indigenous people from across Turtle Island. We are grateful to have the opportunity to work in the community, on this territory.

We are also mindful of broken covenants and the need to strive to make right with all our relations.